IMPLEMENT
— *with* —
IMPACT

A STRATEGIC FRAMEWORK *for*
LEADING SCHOOL *and* DISTRICT INITIATIVES

Jenice **PIZZUTO** | Steven **CARNEY**

Solution Tree | Press
a division of
Solution Tree

555 North Morton Street
Bloomington, IN 47404
800.733.6786 (toll free) / 812.336.7700
FAX: 812.336.7790

email: info@SolutionTree.com
SolutionTree.com

Visit **go.SolutionTree.com/schoolimprovement** to download the free reproducibles in this book.

Printed in the United States of America

Library of Congress Cataloging-in-Publication Data

Names: Pizzuto, Jenice, author. | Carney, Steven, author.
Title: Implement with IMPACT : a strategic framework for leading school and
    district initiatives / Jenice Pizzuto, Steven Carney.
Description: Bloomington, IN : Solution Tree Press, [2024] | Includes
    bibliographical references and index.
Identifiers: LCCN 2023044741 (print) | LCCN 2023044742 (ebook) | ISBN
    9781954631571 (paperback) | ISBN 9781954631588 (ebook)
Subjects: LCSH: Educational leadership. | Educational innovations. |
    Educational change.
Classification: LCC LB2806 .P58 2024 (print) | LCC LB2806 (ebook) | DDC
    371.2/011--dc23/eng/20240102
LC record available at https://lccn.loc.gov/2023044741
LC ebook record available at https://lccn.loc.gov/2023044742

Solution Tree
Jeffrey C. Jones, CEO
Edmund M. Ackerman, President

Solution Tree Press
President and Publisher: Douglas M. Rife
Associate Publishers: Todd Brakke and Kendra Slayton
Editorial Director: Laurel Hecker
Art Director: Rian Anderson
Copy Chief: Jessi Finn
Production Editor: Paige Duke
Proofreader: Elijah Oates
Acquisitions Editors: Carol Collins and Hilary Goff
Assistant Acquisitions Editor: Elijah Oates
Content Development Specialist: Amy Rubenstein
Associate Editor: Sarah Ludwig
Editorial Assistant: Anne Marie Watkins

Acknowledgments

Change equals learning. This is a recurring theme throughout our book, and wow, writing this book, we have been through changes! Thus, we have learned a great deal along the way. A couple of essential things we have learned: learning together is better, and having a team and champions can be the difference between success and failure. Much like raising a child or teaching a student, writing a book is not a solo adventure, and there are several foundational influencers, mentors, and advisers who help a book come to life.

We did not write this book in isolation; we had support and encouragement from our foundational influencers. Without them and their focus on treating us with a human- and learning-centered mindset, this book could still be ideas on pages waiting to be brought to life.

First and foremost, we thank our guiding coalition of champions, our families. Dan Pizzuto and Chris Carney believed in us from the very beginning. They sacrificed weekends, evenings, and outings together; encouraged us to push on when it became difficult; fed us when we were hungry; and dragged us out of the house when they saw we needed a fresh perspective. Chris and Dan, we thank you for being our biggest cheerleaders and champions! Your patience and constant support helped bring this book to life. We are forever grateful.

Additionally, we would like to thank our children for their encouragement and support throughout the process. They never complained when we had to sacrifice time with them to research, write, and collaborate. As a matter of fact, our children were terrific sounding boards, advocates, and enthusiastic cheerleaders. Thank you, Michael Pizzuto, Angela Combs, Tesia Carney, Madison Carney, and Nick Carney. We appreciate you and are now free for some crazy adventures!

Coalescing ideas, research, and years of experience into coherent, compelling writing, while exciting, is also very challenging. Seeing your own errors or determining when to rethink a section becomes difficult. Fortunately, we had an amazing and talented team to champion and help us. We have tremendous gratitude for Kylene Hashimoto and Terry McCarthy, who read, reread, and provided feedback to us to improve the book for our readers. You are absolutely the best! Our children were important in this journey, and so were our parents. We thank Susan Smith and Jim Carney for believing in us, loving us, and modeling for us how to be forever learners. We love you.

Thinking together is better, and we want to thank our friends Stefani Hite and Jonathan Sharples. These two brilliant leaders were fantastic thinking partners, allowing us to discuss the book's development during our monthly learning collaboratives. Thank you, Jonathan and Stef, for sharing your insight, conversation, and wisdom. Jenice wishes to thank the Oregon Response to Instruction and Intervention team: David Putnam, Jon Potter, Lisa Bates, Beth Ferguson, Dean Richards, and Tammy Rasmussen. Your influence as early incubators, thought partners, and cheerleaders for bringing implementation science to educators was invaluable.

This book was born out of a moral obligation on our part. We aim to build implementation literacy globally and see implementation science make its way to the education sector because we know that when we know better, we do better. We want to acknowledge and thank the Global Implementation Society for sharing this vision with us and supporting implementation across all sectors, including education. We owe a deep debt to the researchers, implementation scientists, and leaders in the implementation science field. As you read, you will encounter many outstanding individuals and organizations that have contributed to the implementation science field. We thank them all.

We each have had the great fortune to encounter mentors and leaders in our lives who saw things in us that we did not see in ourselves. These leaders lifted, coached, and encouraged us to be more than we thought possible. Thank you, Keith Myatt, Brian Horne, Janet Locascio, Betty Flad, Angela Peery, and Zelinda Zingaro, for seeing, pushing, and inspiring us.

From the very first conversation we had with Claudia Wheatley and Douglas Rife, we knew Solution Tree was the publisher for our work. Solution Tree's philosophy and their attention to developing books and materials that improve educational outcomes align perfectly with our focus on making implementation science clear, concise, and comprehensible. We are grateful to Claudia Wheatley, Douglas Rife, Amy

Rubenstein, Paige Duke, and the entire Solution Tree team for their pivotal role in bringing *Implement With IMPACT* to life.

Solution Tree Press would like to thank the following reviewers:

Caitlin Fox
Instructor and Practicum Facilitator
Red Deer Polytechnic
Red Deer, Alberta, Canada

Ian Landy
Regional Principal of PIE
School District 47
Powell River, British Columbia, Canada

Nathalie Fournier
French Immersion Teacher
Prairie South School Division
Moose Jaw, Saskatchewan, Canada

Janet Nuzzie
District Intervention Specialist,
  K–12 Mathematics
Pasadena Independent School District
Pasadena, Texas

Visit **go.SolutionTree.com/schoolimprovement**
to download the free reproducibles in this book.

Table of Contents

Reproducibles are in italics.

About the Authors . . . . **xi**

Introduction **1**

Shifting the Culture 2

Growing the Implementers 3

Taking a Strategic Approach to Empower Implementation Teams 5

Calling for Deliberately Developmental Implementation 6

Using the IMPACT Implementation Framework 7

Mapping Out Your Learning Journey in This Book 8

PART 1   15

chapter 1
Implementation Is a Science **17**

Caring About Implementation Science 21

Defining Implementation Science 23

Getting Strategic About Implementation 23

Understanding the IMPACT Implementation Framework 25

Bringing Human- and Learning-Centered Design to Implementation 27

Conclusion 35

Define Implementation Science With Your Team *36*

Assess and Align the IMPACT Framework With Your Organizational Strengths *38*

"Implementation Is a Science" Learning Journey Map *39*

chapter 2

Implementation Means Change for All **41**

Embracing the Need for Change. 45

Navigating the Difficulty of Change 47

Supporting People Through Change 51

Conclusion. 56

Evaluate a Change Theory 57

"Implementation Means Change for All" Learning Journey Map 58

chapter 3

You Can't Do This Work Alone **59**

Gathering Your Guiding Coalition of Champions 63

Defining Implementation Teams 64

Identifying Team Characteristics and Behaviors 67

Building Teams and Configurations 68

Recognizing How Implementation Teams Are Unique 83

Conclusion. 84

Reflect on Building Effective Implementation Teams 86

Map Essential Team Behaviors and Characteristics 87

Assess Individual Characteristics and Behaviors. 88

"You Can't Do This Work Alone" Learning Journey Map. 90

PART 2   91

chapter 4

The *Decide* Stage **93**

Gearing Up for Success. 94

Assembling Your Implementation Team 102

Naming the Problem and the Need for Change (the Why). 104

Developing the Goal 109

Identifying the Evidence-Based Solutions. 110

Assessing Organizational Readiness. 113

Conclusion. 116

Decide *Stage IMPACT Implementation Planning Template* 117

The Decide *Stage Learning Journey Map.* 118

chapter 5

The *Plan and Prepare* Stage **119**

Building the Foundation 120

Identifying the Active Ingredients 124

Selecting Implementation Strategies 126

Developing a Plan to Monitor the Implementation 135

Conclusion 147

Plan and Prepare *Stage IMPACT Implementation Planning Template* *148*

The Plan and Prepare *Stage Learning Journey Map* *149*

chapter 6

The *Implement* Stage **151**

Growing the Implementers 153

Building Supportive Structures 155

Cultivating a Learning Culture and Using Improvement Cycles 160

Gathering Implementation Data 172

Harnessing Data for Strategic Action 180

Conclusion 181

Implement *Stage IMPACT Implementation Planning Template* *185*

The Implement *Stage Learning Journey Map* *186*

chapter 7

The *Spread and Sustain* Stage **187**

Sustaining Success 188

Starting at the Beginning 190

Navigating the Implementation to Sustainment 193

Cultivating Partnerships for Spread and Sustainment 203

Celebrating and Rewarding Implementation Success 204

Conclusion 206

Spread and Sustain *Stage IMPACT Implementation Planning Template* *208*

The Spread and Sustain *Learning Journey Map* *209*

Epilogue **211**

References and Resources **213**

Index **221**

About the Authors

Jenice Pizzuto is a systems, change, and implementation expert. She is the founder and CEO of IMPACT Lead Succeed. Jenice is a passionate advocate and ally for educators focused on bringing human- and learning-centered design elements to the forefront of all change efforts. Her vast experiences nationally and internationally as a consultant, administrator, Oregon Response to Instruction and Intervention implementation facilitator, Learning Forward Learning School Alliance facilitator, literacy coach, mentor, systems-level support specialist, and teacher have contributed to her commitment to a learning and improvement mindset. She has successfully supported large and small school districts to improve outcomes systemwide. Jenice uses her experience and expertise as she consults with all interested in performance improvement in an educational setting to achieve their goals more effectively. People she has supported sum up the learning experience in these words: *intentional, comprehensive, productive, empowering,* and *collaborative.*

Jenice currently serves on the board of directors of the Global Implementation Society (GIS). She was a founding member of GIS and served as the Professional Learning and Resources Committee chair. Jenice visits and supports schools in Bali, Indonesia; leads a global Science of Reading Collective; and collaborates with other leaders in the field of implementation to help make socially significant outcomes in human services. Her volunteer commitment also includes serving Learning Forward, where she helped form the Learning Forward Oregon affiliate and served as president and vice president of the Oregon affiliate. Jenice received the award of Lead Mentor while serving as a mentor teacher and has been recognized as Woman of the Week by Women Supporting Women, Kastl Law, PC.

Jenice received her master of education administration from Lewis and Clark Graduate School of Education and Counseling in Portland, Oregon. She received her teacher licensure from Portland State University. Jenice enjoys presenting to, training, and supporting schools and districts nationally and internationally.

To learn more about Jenice's work, visit the IMPACT Lead Succeed website (www .impactleadsucceed.com).

 **Steven Carney, MS,** is a visionary leader in the educational sector, renowned for his foundational role in opening two innovative high schools aimed at fostering upward mobility. Beyond his achievements in founding educational institutions, he is the CEO of the IMPACT Learning and Leadership Group. Here, he champions the advancement of implementation literacy on a global scale, assisting schools and districts in materializing educational innovations with profound efficacy. Since embarking on his educational journey, Steven has had roles spanning from elementary educator to district administrator, each position underscoring his expertise in mobilizing organizations, regardless of their size, to bring about meaningful educational breakthroughs.

As a prominent member of the Global Implementation Society (GIS) and a pivotal contributor to the Implementation Standards Committee, Steven played a key role in crafting the GIS Competencies for Implementation Facilitators. This work exemplifies his dedication to enhancing professional learning and nurturing effective collaborative cultures centered on impactful implementation and outcomes. His leadership within Learning Forward Washington State and Learning Forward California further highlights his commitment to excellence in professional development, driving forward the mission to bridge the gap between innovative educational strategies and their practical application.

Steven's relentless pursuit to end the implementation gap mirrors his broader commitment to the educational landscape. His strategic support of both large and small organizations in implementing educational innovations has led to significant improvements across a variety of school settings. A seasoned presenter, Steven has shared his expertise on a wide array of topics, from the cultivation of collaborative cultures to the integration of evidence-based practices. His distinguished career includes pivotal leadership roles, such as elementary, middle, and high school principal; assistant superintendent of instruction; and coordinator for the California County Offices of Education.

Steven's educational background is as diverse as his professional experience. He obtained a bachelor's degree in liberal studies with a concentration in communicative disorders from San Diego State University and a master's degree in educational leadership from National University in San Diego. This solid academic foundation has propelled Steven's career, allowing him to make lasting contributions to the field of education and establish himself as a leader committed to fostering innovation and excellence.

To book Jenice Pizzuto or Steven Carney for professional development, contact pd@SolutionTree.com.

Introduction

When you have a sudden realization, one that you didn't see coming, and one that you know viscerally is right, you've tripped over the truth. It's a defining moment that in an instant can change the way you see the world.

—Chip Heath and Dan Heath

Have you ever been involved in the rollout of a new reading curriculum; a professional learning community; a new behavior program, such as positive behavioral interventions and supports (PBIS); a multitiered system of supports (MTSS); or another program, practice, or strategy? Have you seen the new program, practice, or strategy take hold and improve outcomes in over 80 percent of the schools or classrooms it was rolled out in? Well, we have.

Yet, unfortunately, we know that getting a new program, practice, or strategy solidly in place enough that the recipients of the innovation actually gain results is rare. Why is this so? The implementation gap is a significant issue that prevents our most effective strategies and resources from reaching students and being utilized in a way that leads to lasting enhancements in education. The madness of the adopt-and-abandon cycle persists, and it is costly. In an article titled "What Does It Really Cost When We Don't Pay Attention to Implementation?" Gerald R. Williams (2015) brings the reader the shocking cost of non-implementation:

> Without focusing on skill-building to improve fidelity to EBPs [evidence-based practices]/EIIs [evidence-informed innovations], an average district may spend $300,000 on training for 600 staff and only achieve a Return on Investment of 30 teachers actually using the EBP/EII in their classrooms as intended. Therefore, most students will not benefit. (p. 4)

Our goal as authors is audacious and, we hope, compelling. We want to build implementation literacy globally. We want to stop the madness of the adopt-and-abandon cycle and get what we know works to the staff and students who deserve, and are waiting for, our very best practices. There are a sufficient number of valid, reliable, evidence-based options for educators to select from to solve problems they face. And there are talented educators selecting robust solutions. But what staff do not have is the implementation literacy to take a solution to full and effective implementation. Education lacks the implementation-literate systems needed to build and support the structures, policies, and practices for implementing the solutions well enough to gain results. The haphazard attempts waste human resources, capital resources, and, perhaps most importantly, precious time.

Building implementation literacy in the field of education supports getting what works to those who need it in an expedited manner. To do so is a moral imperative; it is our call to action. This book aims to create a movement in education that focuses on how well educators implement a new program, practice, strategy, or policy. Schools can no longer sustain the practice of leaping from initiative to initiative and getting haphazard or limited results.

In the remainder of this introduction, we'll discuss shifting school culture around adopting and implementing new initiatives, providing ongoing training to support the growth of implementers, ensuring that implementation efforts are guided by an implementation team, prioritizing deliberately developmental implementation, using frameworks to guide implementation efforts, and mapping out your journey through this book.

Shifting the Culture

We begin this journey with you by diving straight into culture. Schools urgently need to shift the culture of how they adopt and implement new practices, programs, and strategies. Many educators are familiar with this famous quote: "Culture eats strategy for breakfast." Most of the time, the quote is credited to legendary management consultant and writer Peter Drucker, although the author is debated. Whoever authored the quote, the concept is rock solid, especially in schools. No matter what strategies you have put in place, if the culture isn't right, you won't achieve your goal.

Schools around the world lack a culture that focuses on getting change done right and well, a culture that ensures the change actually gets into practice and makes a socially significant impact. This challenge is echoed in the work of educational researchers Stephanie Levin and Kathryn Bradley (2019), who note that without a strong culture of change, educational initiatives often fail to move beyond the planning stages, resulting in minimal impact on actual teaching and learning practices. Furthermore, implementation science researcher Aaron R. Lyon and colleagues (2022) highlight the disconnect between the adoption of new practices and their sustainable implementation, pointing out that without embedding effective implementation practices into the school culture, lasting change is unlikely. These perspectives underscore the necessity for a systemic approach to change that goes beyond mere adoption. Establishing a supportive culture is an essential part of making a meaningful and lasting difference in educational outcomes.

School cultures must shift away from adopting and abandoning, blaming and shaming, and chasing the latest fad or shiny object in the education field and toward effectively implementing evidence-based practices.

Our purpose is to build in educators the knowledge, skills, attitudes, and competence they need to get change done right and well, and to build a culture centered on:

- Effective implementation
- Human elements of change
- Adult learning
- Growth and improvement

In short, the culture centers on implementation through deliberate growth.

Growing the Implementers

We have devoted our educational careers to the study of ongoing job-embedded professional learning, adult learning (andragogy), and change theory, which collectively stress the importance of professional learning systems and designs to foster effective and sustainable change. Educational leaders and staff developers know the importance of providing training and support to school staff. We see this support play out in the days and weeks leading up to the start of each school year in educational systems across the globe. However, schools give little attention to the ongoing growth opportunities required to sustain implementation and produce outcomes throughout the year.

Episodic learning events or occasional flyby trainings aren't the practice and extended learning opportunities teachers need to implement most evidence-based innovations. Such learning opportunities generate knowledge and minor skill development around the innovations and innovation components, but they fail to produce deep, long-lasting change. Hence, most implementation efforts result in an implementation gap, the *knowing-doing gap*—the gap between knowing what to do and knowing how to do it (Pfeffer & Sutton, 2008). It takes three to five years of frequent and ongoing practice, development, and growth to produce the deep understanding, knowledge, skills, attitudes, and contextual adaptations needed to yield the intended results and sustain high implementation integrity (Fixsen, Blase, & Van Dyke, 2019). We must develop deliberate systems of learning that constantly grow the implementers and improve implementation.

From the beginning of our research on ways to close the knowing-doing gap, we were struck by three things.

1. **Overwhelming evidence points to the importance of building innovation- and implementation-specific competencies as a pathway to individual, team, and organizational improvement (Hord, 2009; Kegan & Lahey, 2016; Lencioni, 2016).** Successful organizations spend quality time and appropriate resources identifying the specific knowledge, skills, and attitudes needed to implement the change initiative right and well. These organizations tend to understand the investment required up front to foster organizational readiness and a deliberately developmental system designed to accelerate implementer and organizational growth.

2. **Organizations that close the knowing-doing gap commit to a set of conditions for an "everyone culture," where colearning is expected and everyone has the opportunity to grow professionally (Higgins, Weiner, & Young, 2012; Hite & Donohoo, 2021; Kegan & Lahey, 2016; Khan & Moore, 2021).** These conditions include using the voices and experiences of implementers to help design, support, and monitor implementation strategies and activities, including ongoing job-embedded development and growth opportunities. When educators engage in a learning community structured to solicit reflection, evaluation, and integration of innovation-specific competencies and learning, implementation challenges are resolved, and implementation is sustained. In the pages ahead, you will hear about organizations that have used these principles in their implementation design, and you will learn how to use an implementation team to build, support, and monitor a culture of deliberately developmental implementation. You will see the practices that implementation teams commonly utilize to help everyone move from knowing to doing and to develop lasting organizational growth that leads to significant outcomes.

3. **Effective implementation requires deliberate leadership that puts time, resources, structures, and mechanisms in place to enable development and growth (Kegan & Lahey, 2016; Lyon, 2017; Powell, Waltz, Chinman, Damschroder, Smith, & Matthieu, et al., 2015).** Organizations that build the context and constructs to ensure learning for everyone every day accelerate their implementation timeline, increase implementation fidelity, achieve results sooner, and meet goals faster. When learning for all implementers is front and center, improvement is inevitable.

As we recognize the critical role of ongoing development and the need for a culture of continuous learning, we must also acknowledge the strategic nature of such endeavors. Taking a strategic approach to implementation ensures that the efforts invested in developing implementers align with the broader goals of the organization, thereby maximizing the impact.

Taking a Strategic Approach to Empower Implementation Teams

Building an implementation culture begins with an implementation team. Our mantra is, "Together, we are better." Together, we can build effective and efficient change that manifests in day-to-day classroom practice.

While building and utilizing an implementation team may seem like an obvious thought, we have found while consulting with educational organizations across the globe that it is not at all a common practice. We commonly see schools adopting a high-quality evidence-based practice; focusing on basic training, limited coaching, and support; and then moving on to adopt another program, practice, or strategy. What we don't see are schools putting a team in place to support full implementation of the evidence-based practice.

School leaders work hard to enhance the quality of their schools and improve the effectiveness of their teachers. They understand the need to identify suitable approaches to school improvement and then use those approaches. Most school leaders recognize the importance of effective implementation and understand it would be ideal that they support their staff to implement well. And yet, leaders find they have capacity challenges and lack the right strategies to facilitate teacher buy-in or provide the support needed to increase sustainable implementation. Having an implementation team is a strategic way to radically increase your organization's implementation capacity.

Although similar in size and function to many leadership and school-improvement teams, implementation teams (as described in this book) have unique characteristics needed for building high organizational and individual implementation capacities. They create a culture of practice and increase the organization's capacity to foster professional vulnerability, growth, and collective efficacy, all while providing the right kinds of learning and support to facilitate rapid and sustainable change. They generate what we call *deliberately developmental implementation*. Different from leading change experts Robert Kegan and Lisa Laskow Lahey's (2016) concept of a *deliberately developmental organization*—"an organizational culture where employees engage in deliberate and intentional growth as part of their daily work" (p. 3)—deliberately developmental implementation is the process an implementation team uses to make ongoing job-embedded learning and implementation improvement deliberate and absolutely central to any change initiative. Implementation teams create implementation-ready cultures that value implementation integrity and fidelity. Like deliberately developmental organization, deliberately developmental implementation results in ongoing and strategic professional growth and human development.

Calling for Deliberately Developmental Implementation

The world is changing, and schools are changing. We often hear the refrain; education is changing, and change is hard. Change is not new to education; however, what is new are the speed, complexity, immediacy, and increase in factors associated with the change required to navigate and meet the needs of students, families, and staff. The urgency for schools to get better at getting better is palpable. The stakes are just so high. In the education sector, it seems common practice to normalize failed implementation efforts, blame the implementers, and argue about the validity and quality of the selected evidence-based practice without ever implementing the practice fully and with fidelity.

For decades, we (the authors) have both been concerned about implementation in schools. Year after year, we witness district and school leaders who adopt innovations designed to have a lasting impact on teaching and learning outcomes, and who later abandon or minimally implement those innovations. The importance of implementation is beginning to make its way to the improvement-planning table, and it could not come soon enough. Education professionals understand the need to adopt evidence-based practices to help meet the needs of their learning communities. School decision makers commonly ask program developers to prove their programs' efficacy. However, the act of adopting an evidence-based practice (EBP) is one thing; implementing that practice is another thing altogether (Fixsen, Blase, Horner, & Sugai, 2009). Identifying EBPs alone will not create significant outcomes in schools—getting the promised results requires deliberately developmental implementation. And deliberately developmental implementation requires leaders, systems, and teams focused on intentional efforts to shift the culture and change practices. Effective change requires leaders, systems, and teams to deliberately develop the culture and the people in the organization by using human- and learning-centered design elements in the change efforts.

Utilizing deliberately developmental implementation with your implementation team increases your learning organization's ability to navigate the most critical variables impacting sustainable change and realized outcomes; that is implementation. Given the continuous shifts that impact staffing, students, and funding, we believe the field of education is poised to recognize and adopt the practice of deliberately developmental implementation and implementation teams. To do EBPs right and well, educators must build deliberately developmental implementation teams.

Using the IMPACT Implementation Framework

Frameworks help organizations *learn to learn*; they provide a road map to success and a route to solve problems, adjust, adapt, and rework *before* the road is closed. Frameworks support adapting to the realities of implementation while maintaining the integrity of an innovation. An implementation framework provides the implementation team with a guide to monitor and support the implementation effort from inception to sustainability. In this book, you will utilize the IMPACT implementation framework.

The IMPACT implementation framework is your tool and guide as you implement your new program, practice, or strategy. This framework has two distinct sections.

1. The stages: *Decide, Plan and Prepare, Implement*, and *Spread and Sustain*

2. The human- and learning-centered design elements: inclusion, meaningful leadership, professional learning, assess and adjust, collective efficacy, and team (IMPACT)

Human- and learning-centered design is an approach that places the needs, experiences, and perspectives of the human participants at the forefront of the change effort. It emphasizes the creation of learning experiences and materials that are deeply engaging and responsive to the diverse needs of adult learners. Human- and learning-centered design places andragogy at the center of all training and scaling efforts. This approach is integral to the IMPACT implementation framework, as it ensures that educational strategies are effective not only in theory but also in practice, where the nuances of individual learning needs are considered. Research supports this approach, indicating that when educational tools and programs are designed with a deep understanding of the learners' context, they are more likely to be adopted, implemented with fidelity, and sustained over time (Penuel & Gallagher, 2017).

Figure I.1 illustrates the framework you will use throughout the book. Chapter 1 discusses the foundational components and elements in detail.

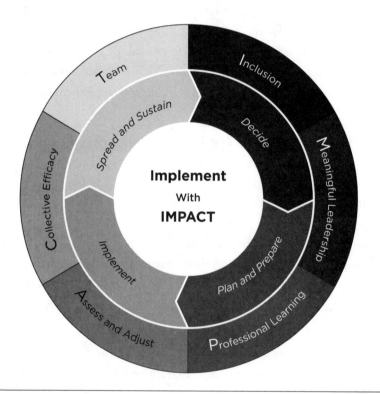

Source: © 2021 by Jenice Pizzuto and Steven Carney.

Figure I.1: IMPACT implementation framework.

Mapping Out Your Learning Journey in This Book

We wrote this book with educational leaders, staff developers, and change agents in mind. We also crafted it with the understanding that each learning organization operates within its own unique context, climate, and culture that influence readiness for change and implementation.

We trust that as you navigate these pages, you will chart a course that resonates with your specific needs and objectives. The insights and strategies presented here are designed to bridge the knowing-doing gap, propelling you and your team toward accelerated implementation and tangible results. Implementation-literate teams, which this book aims to cultivate, are adept at monitoring and adapting their approaches to align with the cultural, climatic, and contextual nuances of their environments.

Through this book, you will deepen your understanding of how effective implementation teams operate. You will learn how to:

- Strategically and effectively build and utilize implementation teams to support change efforts

- Design an implementation plan that incorporates human- and learning-centered design elements and results in efficacious implementation

Let this book be your guide as you lead your implementation team (or teams) toward a future where every educational innovation is not just a plan but a well-implemented reality that positively impacts students' lives.

A learning journey is a planned experience that leads to growth, opportunity, and action. We, the authors, recognize that you come with your own unique experience and expertise with change, implementation, and teams. Your learning organization and the teams you support have their own context, climate, and culture associated with change and implementation readiness. Therefore, we designed this book trusting that you will map out your learning journey through this book, identify your entry points, and glean helpful knowledge and skills that mitigate the knowing-doing gap and accelerate implementation and results.

Implementation-literate teams regularly monitor implementation and rapidly adapt the implementation and innovation to meet cultural, climatic, and contextual needs. In this book, you will learn how implementation teams use deliberately developmental implementation to identify all critical components of change. You will see how implementation teams use this shared knowledge to accomplish the following.

- Strategically and effectively plan and facilitate organizational readiness

- Develop strategies to overcome barriers and maximize facilitators

- Use professional learning designed to capitalize on the promise of human development

In short, you'll learn ways implementation teams can strategically grow a culture that embraces change and increases implementation capacity and fidelity by providing deliberately developmental implementation.

This book is divided into two parts. Part 1 (chapters 1–3) answers the question, "Why are building implementation literacy, focusing on the human elements of change, and harnessing the power of the collective (team) foundational to getting change done right?" Each chapter in part 1 begins with a vignette on the theme of "tripping over the truth" based on direct experiences we've had working with, coaching, and training school districts. While the vignettes are authentic, they do not represent a specific school or district; rather, they are compilations of our experiences. Use these vignettes to foster your thinking and reflection on past and current practices, as they represent real problems educators encounter in implementing change. The vignettes can serve as reflection and discussion tools for you and your team. Each chapter of the book concludes with reproducible tools, activities, and resources.

Chapter 1 provides a foundation for understanding implementation science and sets the stage for exploring its application in the education sector. As we make the case for embracing implementation science, building organizational implementation literacy, and using implementation teams in learning organizations, we try to create relatable experiences that lead you to trip over the truth about implementation in education.

Chapter 2 delves into change theories and implementation frameworks to equip you with essential knowledge to drive effective and sustainable change in schools. In this chapter, you will have the opportunity to explore and unpack the components needed to develop deliberately developmental implementation.

Chapter 3 explores the significance of implementation teams and how to select, build, and empower these teams to drive improvement efforts in your organization. We will outline how implementation teams differ from traditional school-based teams and make a call to repurpose existing leadership teams.

Part 2 (chapters 4–7) walks you through the stages of the IMPACT implementation framework, focusing on highly effective practices and strategies for leading and sustaining deliberately developmental implementation of evidence-based practices.

Chapter 4 offers practical insights and firsthand experience in navigating the crucial first stage of implementation, where you define problems, assess resources, select evidence-based innovations, and establish readiness. This chapter addresses the common errors educational organizations make in identifying the right evidence-based practices and ensuring organizational readiness to implement the selected innovation.

Chapter 5 teaches you how to strategically plan and prepare for implementation through comprehensive road maps, human-centered design, and effective communication strategies. In this chapter, we provide detailed road maps for implementation teams to create a strategic implementation plan guided by human- and learning-centered design.

Chapter 6 explores the roles and responsibilities of implementation teams during the *Implement* stage, utilizing data and cycles of improvement to adapt and ensure successful implementation. This chapter introduces learning walks and fidelity and monitoring tools to build toward sustainability and maintain integrity in the innovation.

Chapter 7 uncovers research and evidence that guide the decision-making process for transitioning from the *Implement* stage to the *Spread and Sustain* stage of implementation. This chapter supports the transition from learning the work to doing the work successfully.

We recommend using a learning journey plan to prepare for and plan your team's learning sequence. This is a tool you can return to throughout your learning journey to record the following.

- Your learning sequence
- Your observations and insights about your own leadership and your organization's implementation efforts
- The skills, practices, and strategies you want to learn and practice
- Your reflections
- Implementation strategies you want to sustain over time

Consider the plan in figure I.2 as an example of how a team might map their learning journey through the first four chapters of the book.

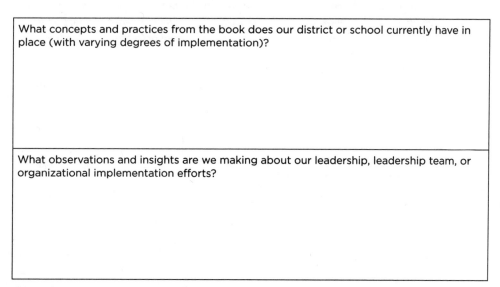

Figure I.2: Learning journey map.

continued →

Chapter	Team Takeaways	Team Commitment	Team Practice	Team Reflection	Team Goals
	New learning, insights, and notices	*Concepts, ideas, and practices we commit to developing*	*Strategies, processes, and tools we plan to learn and practice*	*Strategies, processes, tools, concepts, ideas, and so on we want to go deeper into and share early successes on.*	*Strategies, processes, tools, concepts, ideas, and so on we want to fully operationalize through a commitment of time, resources, and policy*
1	Recognized the need for a shared vision that aligns with our school's commitments to teaching and learning	Develop a shared language around change and innovation within our school	Develop a shared language around change and innovation within our school	Reflect on how our personal biases and school structures impact our approach to change	To have a fully articulated and shared vision for change that is understood and embraced by all stakeholders within the next six months
2	Identified gaps in our team's composition that need to be addressed to ensure diverse perspectives are included	Recruit and train additional team members who bring needed expertise and represent the diversity of our student population	Implement team-building activities that promote trust and understanding	Consider how team dynamics are contributing to or hindering our progress	To have a fully functioning, diverse, and inclusive implementation team in place by the end of the academic year
3	Acknowledged the importance of collaboration across different roles within the school for successful implementation	Foster partnerships with community stakeholders to support our initiatives	Schedule regular cross-functional meetings to ensure alignment and shared understanding of goals	Assess the effectiveness of our communication and collaboration efforts	To establish a robust network of support for our change initiatives that includes teachers, administrators, students, families, and community members within the next year

	Understood the need to align our decisions with the specific needs of our students	Use data-driven decision making in selecting and implementing new programs	Integrate a regular review of student data into our decision-making processes	Evaluate the impact of recent decisions on student outcomes	To have a set of criteria based on student needs that guides all future program and practice decisions
4					
5					
6					
7					

*Visit **go.SolutionTree.com/schoolimprovement** for a free reproducible version of this figure.*

A learning journey map template also appears as a reproducible at the end of each chapter to create a space for you to pause, reflect, and plan.

Thank you for joining us to shine a light on the importance of implementation teams in education. Thank you for being a trailblazer willing to get implementation of EBPs right and build implementation literacy in the education sector. Together, we are better; we are thrilled to have you join us on this journey!

PART 1

Welcome to part 1 of *Implement With IMPACT: A Strategic Framework for Leading School and District Initiatives*. In this first part of the book, you'll build your background knowledge and skills in:

- Defining *implementation science*—understanding what it is and why you should care

- Understanding the IMPACT implementation framework and the importance of the human- and learning-centered design elements

- Managing complex change and paying attention to the people doing the work

- Assembling your guiding coalition of champions (your implementation team)

Think about part 1 as building your foundation to meaningfully and robustly engage in the work of implementing your change initiative.

chapter 1

IMPLEMENTATION IS A SCIENCE

Why leave outcomes to chance when effective alternatives (purposeful implementation supports) are available to realize intended outcomes?

—Dean L. Fixsen, Karen A. Blase, and Melissa K. Van Dyke

In his book *Think Again: The Power of Knowing What You Don't Know*, popular science author Adam Grant (2021) articulates the power of rethinking when he states, "The purpose of learning isn't to affirm our beliefs; it's to evolve our beliefs" (p. 26). Grant's concept of thinking again is powerful for schools embracing the process of implementing change. The following vignette is an example of how one school district reflected on current and past practices regarding change and was willing to think again. Those in the district shifted their mindsets and embraced implementation science.

> *Charbonneau School District was not quite inner city but definitely urban—surrounded by cement, traffic, and crowded streets. The district lay in what could be called a food desert, and as students came to and from school, they had to navigate through challenging environments.*
>
> *Although it had some bright spots and an award-winning elementary school, the district struggled to meet state standards and had a number of schools in improvement status. The district's eleven elementary schools had low reading scores: on a state benchmark reading assessment for basic proficiency, one elementary school's students scored 28 percent, another school's students scored 68 percent, and the remaining elementary schools' students*

scored between 40 and 52 percent. These reading data from state assessments aligned with the district's universal screening and classroom data. Charbonneau School District had a severe problem in meeting students' needs in reading; it was failing to meet the needs of between 48 and 72 percent of its elementary students.

While the Charbonneau leadership team had identified the problem of intransigent low reading scores and knew it needed to change, the team felt stuck. Charbonneau School District had spent well over $150,000 on new materials and various training and strategies but continued to fail to get all students to read by the end of elementary school. The district was ready to move forward with radical open-mindedness. To begin the journey, it did two things right off the bat.

1. Hired a teaching and learning department administrator, Shonda, to champion the work of improving student achievement in the area of reading

2. Partnered with experts in the field of reading and implementation to support the important work moving forward

Based on outside expert recommendations, Shonda built a diverse team of key stakeholders with various instructional, data-collection, and data-analysis expertise. The team included diverse members who had institutional knowledge and were highly credible with principals and their respective school staff. They got straight to work with their partners to improve core literacy instruction in each of the elementary schools.

Upon the recommendation of their collaboration partners (a state technical assistance partner and coach), Charbonneau School District conducted an initiative inventory for reading across all elementary schools. It sought to answer the following questions.

- What evidence-based programs, practices, and materials are universally used during core reading instruction? To what degree are they implemented?

- Are there non-evidence-based practices that are universally used?

- What variations in programs, practices, and materials exist, and to what degree?

- Are there prevalent antiquated approaches?

To answer these questions, the district utilized multiple methods of gathering data, including teacher and administrator surveys; observations of school and grade-level team planning, grade-level intervention, and classroom instruction; material review and counts; and staff, student, and family interviews. The collaboration partners helped design this rigorous inventory to ensure the team could truly discover what was happening in reading instruction across the district.

The data revealed that teachers were not universally implementing any of the three board-adopted program options for providing core reading instruction with integrity or fidelity. In fact, over fifteen programs were in use across the district, and teachers utilized only bits and pieces of all the different programs and strategies. In short, the team discovered curricular chaos.

The data also revealed that, over the years, principals and specialists had been given tremendous leeway to attend trainings, purchase materials, and use their professional judgment upon integrating programs, practices, and materials into the core literacy curriculum. The district office seldom gave them any formal direction, follow-up, or support, believing in school autonomy and a decentralized approach to instruction. Despite individual teacher successes, all schools poorly implemented many programs and practices, even some in opposition to each other. In short, they threw everything they could get their hands on at the problem without knowing if the solution even matched the problem or if the school district had the capacity or resources to implement the new program or practice.

Shonda, her team, and the school district wanted to move beyond isolated bright spots of success. They wanted to move past the "kitchen sink" approach, gain focus, and impact results. The collaboration partners introduced them to the concept of implementation science and how to implement an evidence-based practice right and well for maximum impact.

To provide district leaders with a clear picture of what could be and to expose the research derived from implementation science, the collaboration partners introduced the formula for success. The formula—originally developed by the National Implementation Research Network and articulated by Fixsen, Naoom, Blase, Friedman, and Wallace (2008)—captures the three pivotal components required for achieving substantial outcomes.

1. Effective innovation, *which encompasses any evidence-based program, practice, or guideline that is designed to make a positive impact*

2. Effective implementation with fidelity, *which merges the strategic application of the innovation with the precision and consistency of its execution*

3. Enabling context, *which acknowledges the importance of a supportive environment that facilitates the implementation process*

The formula for success is foundational in implementation science and works like a mathematical equation. The absence of one element in the formula results in a sum of 0. In other words, as shown in figure 1.1 all three formula components—an effective innovation (the thing you are adopting), effective implementation (getting the thing you are adopting firmly in place), and enabling contexts (coaching, resources, policies, and learning supports)—must be present to gain intended results from a selected evidence-based innovation.

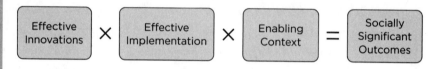

Source: Fixsen et al., 2008, p. 2. Used with permission.

Figure 1.1: The formula for success.

With urgency to find a solution to its problem, Charbonneau School District had ignored effective implementation and enabling contexts. It had kept adding new innovations to the schools without ever fully implementing any of them right and well to get results. The district tripped over the truth that students and teachers benefit greatly when school leadership puts as much energy into planning and supporting effective implementation as it does into identifying and adopting the innovations.

Charbonneau School District went on to embrace implementation science concepts to build a comprehensive literacy instruction framework utilized across its elementary schools. Within two years of using implementation science processes and concepts, all eleven of these schools began to show improvement in reading scores. Some schools improved by as much as 30 percent. All schools improved by at least 15 percent. Charbonneau then used those implementation science concepts and processes for all innovations it adopted.

> *Additionally, Charbonneau School District presented its journey and the importance of using implementation science when implementing new programs, practices, or strategies at national conferences, such as the Northwest Positive Behavior Intervention and Supports Conference or the Learning Forward Conference. The district's willingness to think again enabled growth, learning, and a path to improvement for the students and community it served.*

In this chapter, we begin by explaining why educators should care about implementation science, defining the term, and identifying what strategic implementation looks like. From there, we introduce the IMPACT implementation framework and discuss how it benefits from human- and learning-centered design.

Caring About Implementation Science

If you have ever used the "kitchen sink" strategy to get things done and been frustrated by a lack of results, then you care about implementation science. If you have been part of a failed implementation, as described in the vignette, then you care about moving from solutionitis to getting results. The fact is we know what works in education. Renowned researcher John Hattie has provided the field with meta-analyses of effective practices that maximize student learning (Fisher, Frey, & Hattie, 2016). The persistent truth before the field of education is that "simply introducing evidence-based approaches into schools does not guarantee they will be implemented meaningfully over time" (Donohoo & Katz, 2020, p. 3).

All educators should care about effective implementation because, quite simply, it matters for students. Meaningful gains in student achievement will remain elusive without a focus on the full and effective implementation of evidence-based practices. As you read in the introduction (page 1), our aim is to create a movement where educators care as much about *how* they adopt new practices as they do about the act of selecting them—that is, care about developing implementation literacy in the organization. The Education Endowment Foundation is doing excellent work in the United Kingdom researching implementation and education. In their guide *Putting Evidence to Work: A School's Guide to Implementation*, chief executive Kevan Collins (2019) states, "Ultimately, it doesn't matter how great an educational idea or intervention is on paper; what really matters is how it manifests into the day-to-day work of teachers" (p. 2). Implementation science matters because it is a key to closing the knowing-doing gap.

So, who uses implementation science? Much of the research and early work in implementation science comes from the health and social welfare fields. Hospitals, health providers, family and human services, and researchers have been utilizing implementation science to improve outcomes for clients and innovation beneficiaries since the 1980s. Implementation science researchers Dean Fixsen, Karen Blase, and Melissa Van Dyke (2019) remind us that "with contributions from a variety of fields, implementation is now a discipline unto itself" (p. 4). Implementation science and practice aim to get evidence-based practices firmly in place and utilized as designed to achieve intended results.

If you have ever utilized an automatic handwashing station inside or outside a hospital room or seen instructional handwashing posters and reminders in a hospital, you have been the benefactor of implementation science in the health field. While it is widely understood that handwashing reduces infection and illness, it was, and still is, challenging to implement the innovation in hospitals. Just knowing what to do and how to do it has not been sufficient to get high levels of compliance in hand hygiene. The Centers for Disease Control and Prevention (2023) are still tackling this problem and conducting research on practices to help hospitals get to higher compliance levels. Successfully implementing hand hygiene requires identifying the facilitators and barriers to hand hygiene, making an implementation plan to address barriers, and developing plans to monitor whether people are utilizing hand hygiene as designed. Hand hygiene use in hospitals is one example of how many human service organizations have drastically improved their quality of services and outcomes by using implementation science.

Achieving full and effective implementation of evidence-based practices is high stakes. Poor implementation of evidence-based practices has catastrophic effects for the field of education, its students, and its stakeholders. Improving the transfer-to-practice rate of evidence-based practices in education is critical. From our experience, new innovations fail to take hold without a focus on full and effective implementation; they get implemented haphazardly, fail to reach scale and sustainability, and waste human and capital resources. In the book *Upstream: The Quest to Solve Problems Before They Happen*, Dan Heath (2020) writes, "Surely we'd all prefer to live in the upstream world where problems are prevented rather than reacted to" (p. 3). Becoming an organization focused on deliberately developmental implementation is an upstream solution. Building implementation-literate organizations is an upstream solution that addresses the research-to-practice gap.

Defining Implementation Science

What exactly is implementation science? Implementation science is content and sector agnostic. Implementation science and implementation practice are concerned with getting evidence-based practices implemented right and well regardless of the field, whether that be health care, education, social welfare, or criminal justice. Consider the following widely agreed-on definitions of *implementation science.*

- "Implementation science focuses on producing new, generalizable knowledge about effective techniques for supporting program adoption and sustainment. Implementation practice applies that knowledge to install programs and practices in routine service delivery settings" (Lyon, 2007, p. 1).

- Implementation science is the "application and integration of research evidence into practice and policy" (Glasgow, Eckstein, & ElZarrad, 2013, p. 26).

- "To implement is to use. Implementation practice, policy, and science are concerned with the use of innovations in situations where they can add value. It is a truism that people cannot benefit from innovations they do not experience. That is, if innovations are not used as intended, they cannot produce intended results" (Fixsen et al., 2019, p. 1).

- Implementation science is how "we get 'what works' to the people who need it, with greater speed, fidelity, efficiency, quality, and relevant coverage" (University of Washington, n.d.).

The simplest definition of implementation science we use is this: the study of how to implement evidence-based practices right and well so that they have an impact.

Getting Strategic About Implementation

Effective implementation goes beyond the *what*; it's about the *who, why, where, when,* and *how.* It is the tangible action that springs from planning. Although we in the education field have a rich understanding of what works in schools, considerable learning gaps persist (Dorn, Hancock, Sarakatsannis, & Viruleg, 2020; Hansen, Levesque, Valant, & Quintero, 2018). This discrepancy underlines the need for strategic implementation of evidence-based practices—the cornerstone of introducing any new innovation into your organization.

What is strategic implementation? Figure 1.2 serves as a guide to understanding strategic implementation and discussing what it means for your context. It could spark vibrant discussions among colleagues about how to make informed decisions on an EBP, what changes to make, and how to execute those changes effectively.

Consider the defining characteristics of strategic implementation. Then discuss the questions with your team and take notes in the space provided.	
Strategic + Implementation	
Strategic	**Implementation**
An implementation plan identifies the evidence-based practice (EBP) that meets the needs of the system. It involves the professional practice of strategic planning to document the changes needed to meet the promise of the EBP.	An implementation plan outlines how the strategic changes will be made. It addresses the who, where, when, and how of getting the work done. It involves the professional practice of implementation to document and execute the steps needed to manage and monitor change well.
What EBPs do we need to implement?	Who will be involved?
Why do we need them?	Where and when will the changes occur?
What changes can they bring about?	How will the process unfold?

Figure 1.2: Strategic implementation discussion tool.

Visit go.SolutionTree.com/schoolimprovement for a free reproducible version of this figure.

There is a vast body of research on what it takes to implement an evidence-based program or practice so that it produces the intended results and is sustainable in different settings (Aarons, Hurlburt, & Horwitz, 2011; Fixsen et al., 2019; Metz et al., 2021; Meyers, Durlak, & Wandersman, 2012). Upon synthesis of the literature, several overlapping principles become apparent as being essential to building deliberately developmental implementation and implementation literacy. These principles include the following.

- Implementation is a process and happens in stages.
- Effective implementation takes advantage of implementation teams to actively and adaptively lead implementation efforts.
- Data and feedback drive implementation decision making and continuous improvement.
- Capacity is developed through structures that build meaningful experiences and ongoing opportunities to increase knowledge and skills associated with the innovation.
- The voices of the implementers matter.
- Leadership is adaptive and not label bound.

Implementation science references several strategies that cross into human-centered design. These include, but are not limited to, involving implementers to:

- Identify the problem you need to solve
- Cocreate the solution and be part of the design process
- Plan implementation strategies
- Participate in cycles of improvement to increase implementation effectiveness
- Colearn to increase implementation capacity in innovation effectiveness

Understanding the IMPACT Implementation Framework

K–12 education professionals can benefit from understanding effective implementation practices, especially those practices that put the stakeholders at the center. Various organizations have developed an impressive number of implementation frameworks that include effective practices, many of which have vital implementation components. However, we contend that each implementation stage should include human- and learning-centered design. Therefore, key implementation principles combined with human- and learning-centered design practices form the foundation of the IMPACT implementation framework. The IMPACT framework is grounded in elements that are consistent across implementation research and our experiences leading change and facilitating adults in schools since the 1990s. Our unique research-based framework not only utilizes stages of implementation but also includes the human- and learning-centered design elements we have found to be instrumental in gaining traction with real change in implementation efforts. People—both implementers and leaders—are at the heart of implementation work; embracing and empowering them in the process unleashes optimism, creativity, and inspiration to get better together.

Use the IMPACT implementation framework to organize, support, and plan your change effort. Figure 1.3 introduces the entire framework and the two components it contains: (1) the stages (in the inner circle) and (2) the human- and learning-centered design elements (in the outer circle). You will work with each of the framework components throughout the book.

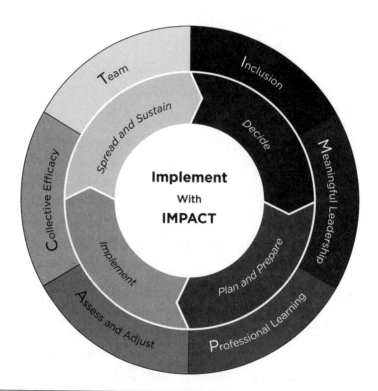

Source: © 2021 by Jenice Pizzuto and Steven Carney.

Figure 1.3: IMPACT implementation framework.

The IMPACT implementation framework is built on two premises.

1. Implementation is a process and happens in four key stages.

   a. *Decide*

   b. *Plan and Prepare*

   c. *Implement*

   d. *Spread and Sustain*

2. The framework is designed with six evidence-based human- and learning-centered elements.

   a. Inclusion

   b. Meaningful leadership

   c. Professional learning

   d. Assess and adjust

   e. Collective efficacy

   f. Team

Implementation is a process that involves identifying and deciding on, planning and preparing for, and carrying out the sustaining changes you want to make. The IMPACT implementation framework is designed to guide your district, school, or team through the four stages of implementation and effectively develop your implementation with evidence-informed strategies that maximize success and sustainability. Within each stage is a collection of suggested activities that you and your team can use to navigate the stage. We developed these activities to include the IMPACT human- and learning-centered design elements. Figure 1.4 (page 28) describes the stages.

Bringing Human- and Learning-Centered Design to Implementation

There are six human- and learning-centered design elements in the IMPACT implementation framework, shown in figure 1.5 (page 29). To improve your implementation efforts, utilize these six human- and learning-centered design elements.

IMPACT
Implementation Process

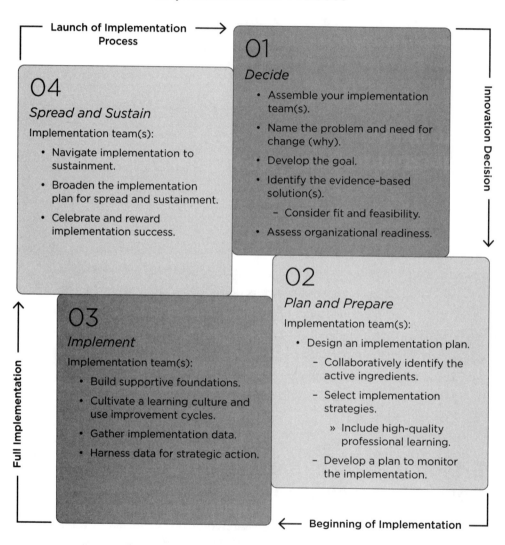

Source: © 2021 by Jenice Pizzuto and Steven Carney.

Figure 1.4: IMPACT implementation framework stages.

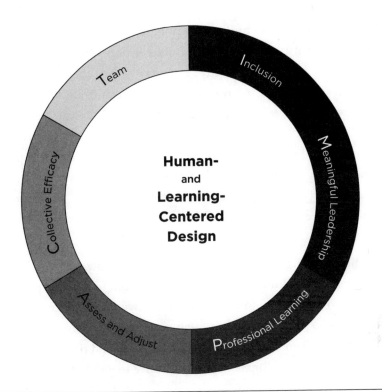

Figure 1.5: Human- and learning-centered design elements in the IMPACT implementation framework.

Implementation is the missing link in education (Fixsen et al., 2019). To be effective, implementation must be relational and must focus as heavily on the quality of implementation as on the selection of an innovation. These human- and learning-centered design elements are what differentiate the IMPACT implementation framework from others available in the field. These elements are components we see as critical in developing organization-wide expertise. The absence of attention to these elements hinders an organization from reaching the full potential of the change effort. The goal of change and implementation is ultimately a transfer-of-knowledge game. Utilizing a human- and learning-centered approach provides tools and mindsets to support the knowledge translation.

Having established why these elements are important, let's unpack the six human- and learning-centered design elements of the IMPACT implementation framework.

Inclusion

Implementers deserve to have a voice in the implementation process. We echo the well-known slogan, "Nothing about us without us." Including implementers in the design of the implementation builds cohesion, helps anticipate barriers, provides equity of voice, and ensures diverse stakeholder group perspectives are included. Implementers have a much more positive experience when they feel they contribute to the success of the adopted innovation. What matters in implementation is not what any one person knows, but what the team knows. As researcher and executive adviser Liz Wiseman (2010) writes, "It isn't just how intelligent your team members are; it is how much of that intelligence you can draw out and put to use" (p. 10). Inclusion means tapping into the intelligence of the organization and recognizing and honoring the people who have something to offer. If you want your implementation to be effective and successful, it must involve the stakeholders; it must be inclusive.

Inclusion means giving stakeholders opportunities to question, challenge, debate, and reflect on what's working and what's not. You need to ask the question, "Who isn't at the table or in the room?" The more inclusive you are, the more likely you will find quality solutions within your system to the problems you are trying to solve. Without inclusive implementation, apathy and rebellion find their way to the surface. Being inclusive produces a climate that is conducive to good implementation.

Meaningful Leadership

Meaningful leadership sets up structures to intentionally and actively involve the people impacted by the change. It is not label bound, and it does not reside in one person or leader. Meaningful leadership structures are horizontal and vertical implementation teams that include implementers' voices on the teams. This inclusive approach is key to nurturing growth and successfully integrating new ideas. Leaders step beyond traditional roles and hierarchies, focusing on the synergy of team dynamics and the importance of routine practice, mentorship, feedback, and common goal setting. By involving team members in developing new practices, meaningful leaders promote a sense of purpose and foster an environment where all contributions are valued. This commitment to collective understanding, continuous learning, clear communication, and problem solving builds an adaptable and knowledgeable organization that values human- and learning-centered design.

We use the term *meaningful leadership* because, from our experience, change and implementation efforts that swiftly lead to intended outcomes directly relate to a learning organization's engagement in ongoing meaningful work. When you disseminate change and leave implementers out of the process of cocreating it, you miss the opportunity to create ownership, understanding, and internal action (Hite & Donohoo, 2021). Without collaborative opportunities to learn and make meaning of the innovation and implementation, shifts in beliefs are minimal. You must realize positive beliefs about and acceptance of the innovation for change to happen.

Meaningful leadership fosters an environment where change is managed with trust and relationships at its core. Kathy Jourdain and Jerry Nagel (2019), authors of *Building Trust and Relationship at the Speed of Change*, suggest that even well-planned and supported changes can fail without trust and strong relationships. To achieve successful change implementation, those responsible for enacting the change—the implementers—must receive opportunities to reflect on and revise their views and beliefs about the change, its implications, and their role in it. Without this reflection, their underlying assumptions and values may obstruct the implementation process, and particularly when challenges arise during the change process, they may blame external factors rather than foster a culture of growth. Meaningful leaders provide safe spaces for failure and reflection that lead to creativity and innovation rather than destruction or oppression.

In essence, meaningful leadership bridges the gap between knowledge and action by establishing structures for shared learning and cocreation across the system.

Professional Learning

Professional learning is not one-and-done (single trainings or workshops); it is ongoing and job embedded. This learning focuses on developing implementers' knowledge, skills, and attitudes; it provides initial training and ongoing follow-up support to build toward mastery. Inclusion of professional learning for *all* staff involved in the change ensures the system supports spreading the new practice. Kegan and Lahey (2016) remind us that "adults, not just children, can and need to keep growing" (p. 87). This is important to note because in an implementation effort, people will be learning and developing. So, you need to know (and sometimes remind them) that learning is possible and appropriate.

Leaders need to sufficiently prepare and plan for collaborative professional learning about the new innovation in order to effectively assist the implementers in adopting and gaining competence in new skills, attitudes, and beliefs for implementation. Researchers Linda Darling-Hammond, Maria E. Hyler, and Madelyn Gardner (2017) note, "Even the best designed [professional development] may fail to produce desired outcomes if it is poorly implemented" (p. 24). The inverse is also true: even the best designed implementation may fail if high-quality, job-embedded, collaborative professional learning about implementation and the innovation is poorly designed.

In a Learning Policy Institute report titled *The Effective Teacher Professional Development*, Darling-Hammond and colleagues (2017) identify seven common design elements of effective professional learning approaches.

1. They are content focused.

2. They incorporate active learning strategies.

3. They engage teachers in collaboration.

4. They use models or modeling.

5. They provide coaching and expert support.

6. They include time for feedback and reflection.

7. They are of sustained duration.

Providing a well-designed, high-quality, collaborative professional learning system that includes all seven of these elements should be considered an essential component of a comprehensive effort to reach full implementation and intended outcomes of a selected innovation. For that reason, the IMPACT implementation framework includes professional learning to build deliberately developmental implementation and implementation literacy. Putting professional learning at the forefront of all implementation practices is critical for success.

Assess and Adjust

Strategic and effective implementation requires continuous assessment and adjustment. It involves making systems better by solving implementation problems and improving change capacity during the implementation process. Implementation leaders must embrace the idea of designing processes that turn failure into learning and growth rather than blame. They do this by trial and error and an iterative improvement or problem-solving cycle, such as Plan-Do-Study-Act, that relies on examining data about the implementation (Leeman et al., 2021; Solution Tree, n.d.). This process provides a structure for teams to examine the implementation and test changes to improve the implementation's quality (Taylor et al., 2014). Even the most comprehensive implementation plans created by diverse implementation teams will have unpredictable holes and gaps impacting implementation integrity and intended outcomes.

Implementation is a learning process, and it involves asking the right questions.

- "What are we trying to accomplish through these implementation strategies?"

- "How will we know if the implementation strategies are effective?"

- "What evidence will we collect to determine implementation effectiveness?"
- "What changes to the implementation do we need to make and why?"
- "How will we know that the new implementation changes we are making are improving implementation quality and effectiveness?"

These questions are part of an ongoing problem-solving and improvement cycle that implementation teams use to monitor, assess, and adjust implementation to increase fidelity to and integrity of the adopted innovation. By learning from implementation efforts and understanding what's working and what's not, practitioners and leaders can refine their implementation to accelerate it and produce significant results.

Collective Efficacy

Collective efficacy is a powerful factor in influencing student achievement. Stanford University psychologist Albert Bandura (1997) coined the term *collective efficacy*, which he defines as "a group's shared belief in its conjoint capabilities to organize and execute the courses of action required to produce given levels of attainment" (p. 477). Bandura discovered that team confidence breeds competence and collective success. Hattie writes the following about collective teacher efficacy:

> Collective teacher efficacy (CTE) is the collective belief of the staff/ faculty in their ability to positively affect students. CTE has been found to be strongly, positively correlated with student achievement. A school staff that believes it can collectively accomplish great things is vital for the health of a school, and if they believe they can make a positive difference then they very likely will. (Visible Learning, 2018)

Hattie's seminal work ranks collective teacher efficacy as having an effect size of 1.57 (Donohoo, Hattie, & Eells, 2018). This effect size signifies that collective efficacy is one of the most powerful influences on student learning. An average effect size is 0.40, which represents typical growth over a year's time—meaning anything at or above 0.40 is effective. Collective efficacy is worth an organization's attention.

In their book *Quality Implementation: Leveraging Collective Efficacy to Make "What Works" Actually Work*, authors Jenni Donohoo and Steven Katz (2020) demonstrate that "the more robust the sense of collective teacher efficacy," the greater the level of student achievement (p. 16). Building collective efficacy is the most potent human-centered thing an organization can do. Beliefs affect behavior. When a team believes in their collective ability to make the necessary changes, their behaviors and actions follow.

Without collective efficacy and a collective belief in the staff's ability to improve outcomes and get results, implementation is often undermined. This is especially true when implementation is challenging. Reverting to what's easy and what you know is a whole lot easier than pushing forward and possibly failing. On the one hand, collective efficacy can be one of the most effective implementation strategies. But, on the other hand, a lack of collective efficacy can be the very thing that keeps an initiative from succeeding. Donohoo and Katz (2020) state that "diminished efficacy is a barrier to quality implementation" (p. 17). According to their findings, a lack of collective efficacy has a negative effect on behavior in the following ways (Donohoo & Katz, 2020).

- Collective efficacy impacts how teams perceive constraints and opportunities afforded in their unique school environments; teams with low efficacy anticipate their efforts will be futile and produce little change.

- When collective efficacy is reduced, teams show a significant reduction in goal setting, impacting motivational investments.

- Collective efficacy beliefs shape experiences; low expectations become self-fulfilling prophecies.

Taking time to build collective efficacy and improve collective beliefs about learning, solution effectiveness, implementation capacity, and goal attainment is human centered and implementer focused.

Team

Strategic and effective implementation requires an implementation team. Implementation teams ensure organizations move from "hoping it happens" to "making it happen." The implementation teams do the work of implementation. In other words, they are responsible for operationalizing your organization's change plans or improvement initiatives. They are groups of individuals, including implementers, who monitor and support the implementation. Implementation teams are accountable for developing the implementation plan and supports, creating organizational readiness, navigating and resolving system and implementation issues, using cycles of improvement to monitor and adjust implementation fidelity and supports, engaging organizational implementers to share and make meaning of the innovation, and fostering enabling contexts, such as collective efficacy. Implementation teams live in both possibility and accountability. Fixsen and colleagues' (2019) summary of the research on implementation teams concludes that "an expert Implementation Team produces about 80% successful use of innovations in about three years. . . . [However,] without the support of an expert Implementation Team, there is about 14% success in 17 years" (p. 62).

Designing a successful implementation plan requires forming strong multilayered teams within the organization. These teams work together both horizontally across the school departments and vertically up through the educational hierarchy (from classroom to district), ensuring implementation knowledge spreads throughout the system. This approach builds a durable and flexible foundation for implementation change.

Building horizontally and vertically means creating teams at the building level and at the systems level. By fostering expertise on deliberately developmental implementation horizontally and vertically, the organization creates a resilient and adaptive framework for change. This strategic implementation move ensures that initiatives and innovations are ingrained in the organization's culture and are not transient or dependent on individuals.

Conclusion

Achieving the full potential of any evidence-based innovation necessitates prioritizing quality implementation. Central to this endeavor is the presence of an implementation-literate team capable of skillfully navigating the stages of implementation, employing human- and learning-centered design principles to develop a deliberately developmental implementation plan, and consistently monitoring and supporting growth and proficient use of the innovation. Through the implementation team's efforts, the innovation thrives, and the individuals and teams responsible for its success are empowered.

Define Implementation Science With Your Team

This activity is designed to build a common understanding of implementation science within the team. It addresses the importance of aligning language and definitions among team members. We invite you and your team to take this activity's powerful steps to build a clear, shared understanding of what implementation science means. We have found this activity to be highly effective in building consensus and energy as teams move toward developing organizations of deliberately developmental implementation.

1. Read the definitions of implementation science.	*Implementation science* is defined as follows. ▪ "Implementation science focuses on producing new, generalizable knowledge about effective techniques for supporting program adoption and sustainment. Implementation practice applies that knowledge to install programs and practices in routine service delivery settings" (Lyon, 2007, p. 1). ▪ Implementation science is the "application and integration of research evidence into practice and policy" (Glasgow et al., 2013, p. 26). ▪ "To implement is to use. Implementation practice, policy, and science are concerned with the use of innovations in situations where they can add value. It is a truism that people cannot benefit from innovations they do not experience. That is, if innovations are not used as intended, they cannot produce intended results" (Fixsen et al., 2019, p.1). ▪ Implementation science answers the question, "How do we get 'what works' to the people who need it, with greater speed, fidelity, efficiency, quality, and relevant coverage?" (University of Washington, n.d.).
2. Write your own definition of implementation science. Write a definition that resonates with you, one that would help you explain implementation science to someone else.	I define *implementation science* as:
3. Share your definition with a partner (partner share). Listen to your partner's definition.	Fully listen to each other's definitions without interrupting or interpreting the messages.

4. With a team of four to eight members, share your definitions (team share).	Use a "whip-around" to share definitions. In a whip-around, one person at a time shares, and all others listen without comment. The sharing rotates in a clockwise progression until all people have had a turn to share. Once all team members have shared, open the definitions up for discussion.
5. With your team, craft one implementation science definition.	Our team defines *implementation science* as:
6. Have each team share its definition with the entire group using the whip-around protocol; once all teams have shared their definitions, open them up for discussion.	Record each team's definition.
7. Post the definitions so that all stakeholders can view them. Note similarities and differences in the definitions.	Similarities and differences in team definitions include:
8. Debrief the process. ○ Did this protocol help build your understanding of implementation science? ○ What worked for you in the protocol? ○ What would you change about the protocol?	Reflect on the process.
9. Optional: Repeat this process with your school site teams, and take notes about what you notice.	Repeating the process with school site teams, we noticed:

page 2 of 2

Assess and Align the IMPACT Framework With Your Organizational Strengths

Share the IMPACT implementation framework with a colleague and describe why human- and learning-centered design elements should be included in implementation design and planning. Identify and discuss processes your organization already has to serve some of these IMPACT areas; for example, you may already have teaming structures or improvement cycles in place.

Framework Discussion Notes	Structures and Supports We Already Have in Place

"Implementation Is a Science"
Learning Journey Map

Use the following two questions to prompt active discussion and thoughtful responses, helping your team assess current practices and plan for future development. This is an opportunity for collective reflection and strategic action.

Together, review the concepts and practices from chapter 1 that your organization has already implemented. Discuss the effectiveness of your leadership and the progress of your implementation efforts. Use the questions to guide a rich conversation, and document your team's insights, commitments, and objectives in the learning journey map.

1. What concepts and practices from chapter 1 does our district or school currently have in place (with varying degrees of implementation)?

2. What observations and insights are we making about our leadership, leadership team, or organizational implementation efforts?

Team Takeaways	Team Commitment	Team Practice	Team Reflection	Team Goals
New learning, insights, and notices	Concepts, ideas, and practices we *commit to developing*	Strategies, processes, and tools we plan to *learn and practice*	Strategies, processes, tools, concepts, ideas, and so on we want to *go deeper into and share early successes on*	Strategies, processes, tools, concepts, ideas, and so on we want to *fully operationalize* through a commitment of time, resources, and policy

chapter 2

IMPLEMENTATION MEANS CHANGE FOR ALL

Believing in the power of some new reform proposal and propelled by a sense of urgency, educational leaders often plunge headlong into large-scale implementation. Invariably, outcomes fall far short of expectations. Enthusiasm wanes, and the field moves on to the next idea without ever really understanding why the last one failed. Such is the pattern of change in public education: implement fast, learn slow, and burn goodwill as you go.

—Anthony S. Bryk, Louis M. Gomez, Alicia Grunow,
and Paul G. LeMahieu

You're likely familiar with Nike's famous slogan: "Just Do It." Despite its popularity, this catchy slogan alone doesn't motivate people to adopt a daily running habit. Most people struggle to alter their entrenched habits and routines. In *Immunity to Change: How to Overcome It and Unlock the Potential in Yourself and Your Organization*, Kegan and Lahey (2009) identify this difficulty in adjusting one's pattern of actions—even in the face of potentially dire consequences—as *immunity to change*. Kegan and Lahey (2016) write the following about an immunity to change:

> If heart doctors tell their seriously ill heart patients they will literally *die* if they do not make changes to their personal lives, such as changing their diet, engaging in regular exercise, or quitting smoking, still, only one in seven is actually able to make the changes. . . .
>
> If people cannot make the changes they dearly want to when their very lives are on the line, then how can leaders at any level, in any kind of organization, expect to successfully support processes of

change—even those they and their subordinates may passionately
believe in—when the stakes and the payoff are not nearly as high?
(pp. 21–22)

Implementation equals change. Given that change is difficult, implementation often presents challenges. This chapter provides implementation teams with tools to support change in the work moving forward, discussing such topics as embracing the need for change, navigating the difficulty of change, supporting people through change, and managing complex change. The vignette in this chapter introduces a school district undergoing a change that proved to be more difficult than anticipated.

Superintendent Amatto was a dynamic leader committed to taking his school district to the next level of performance. He spoke English and Spanish fluently and had been a principal for eleven years, an English language development coordinator, and a teacher for seven years before stepping into the role of superintendent. As a principal, he led and successfully implemented several important initiatives that improved student performance and staff satisfaction.

He spent his first year in the position of superintendent familiarizing himself with the culture and climate of the staff, community, and school board. He was entering a new community and was determined not only to serve as an educational leader, but to intertwine himself and his family with the community. The school district was in a coastal community with a long history of fishing, logging, and tourism, and he was thrilled to call this place his new home for many years to come.

Superintendent Amatto was eager to bring his experience and knowledge to his new district. He felt he had the skills and knowledge to lead the district to adopt new practices that would address the dismal reading scores that had persisted for many years. He began by creating a district literacy team to assess the current situation, audit current practices, and determine the next steps. The team included principals, literacy coaches, teacher representatives, and himself. Superintendent Amatto did not have a top-down management style; his mission was to be inclusive. He was actively involved in statewide improvement initiatives, kept current on educational research, and actively sought out experts to support and grow his knowledge. His goal was to bring the literacy team together, engage in deep learning about evidence-based practices, and improve instruction throughout the district.

Superintendent Amatto and the literacy team spent a year examining current practices for K–5 literacy instruction and determining next steps. The team gathered data by asking questions in small-group interviews, conducting anonymous surveys, and holding listening sessions. Once the entire team felt they had been inclusive, they had taken the appropriate amount of time, and they were ready to report all the findings, they made their recommendations to the school board. They recommended that the district create standards of practice for literacy instruction and develop a literacy instruction framework that followed their state literacy guidelines and aligned with research. The school board adopted the recommendations and funded the purchase of a new reading curriculum to meet the standards of practice.

The adoption process for new materials and the development of the literacy instruction framework were also inclusive and transparent. The literacy team gave the school board quarterly progress updates and provided professional development, coaching, and feedback to staff. It seemed as if everything was moving along smoothly, and Superintendent Amatto and the literacy team were pleased with the progress. Not only did they see changes in teacher practices, but student results improved drastically in some classes. They were curious to see the literacy instruction framework in action and explore more student outcome data. So the literacy team began to conduct cross-group learning walks (principals and staff monitor each other's schools).

During a regularly scheduled cross-group learning walk to monitor the implementation of the literacy instruction framework, the team noticed some worrisome trends. Not all staff were implementing the new framework as designed; in fact, some were not teaching reading during the agreed-on reading time. The cross-group learning walk data indicated that only 62 percent of staff implemented the literacy instruction framework as designed. The team decided to revisit the expectations with the staff at all schools and identify implementation barriers in order to firm up the practices and work toward high-fidelity use of the framework's agreements.

The literacy team and the superintendent had not anticipated that some staff would strongly resist the change. Not only did the resisters openly resent the new clear expectations, but they also created a plan to circumvent the entire literacy instruction framework and its expectations by rallying the community to oppose the school board's decision. One morning, upon arriving at the district office, Superintendent Amatto discovered an article in the local newspaper headlined "New Reading Expectations Threaten Swim Lessons."

Staff members had told the journalist that the new expectations to give students reading time each day put students' access to swim lessons at risk. The school had been providing these Wednesday swim lessons since the 1980s, in response to tragic student drownings at the coast.

Superintendent Amatto was stunned, disappointed, and shocked! This was the first time he'd heard of this alarming concern. He knew there was some resistance to the change in reading requirements, but he had underestimated its potential to cause chaos. In this coastal community, the school-provided swim lessons were seen as sacred, lifesaving, and an important service to the community. But why was swimming being pitted against reading? This was perhaps more than a bump in the road; Superintendent Amatto feared it had the power to unravel all the work he and the literacy team had done to date, particularly as it seemed to oppose the school board's decision.

The superintendent quickly assembled the literacy team, and they began to problem solve. They knew the expectations outlined in the literacy instruction framework were appropriate, backed by research, and aligned with the state's expectations; they were determined not to change the requirements for providing literacy instruction. Meanwhile, they were unsure of how to proceed with the community, staff, and school board. Superintendent Amatto reached out to the team's technical assistance providers, who had helped them draft the plan. The team's coach reassured him—of course, there was time for appropriate reading instruction and swimming instruction! The team was in place to address barriers such as this one. The biggest concern was that the team had missed how challenging the change would be for some staff members. The team had neglected to set things up to meet people's psychological needs, and they had underestimated the emotional underpinnings and resistance associated with change. However, the fact that the team had included stakeholders, the school board, and implementers in the design of the literacy instruction framework from the very beginning would prove invaluable moving forward.

Superintendent Amatto, the literacy team, and the school board arranged an emergency school board meeting; they invited the local press and highly encouraged concerned staff members to attend. In the meeting, the team clarified that swim lessons for students would not be canceled. Additionally, they reassured the board that adequate time would be allotted to reading instruction during the school day. Superintendent Amatto apologized to the entire community for any misunderstandings and pledged to convene a team to help address concerned school staff's feelings about the change. He took accountability for not appropriately anticipating how challenging it was to adopt a new program and gain competence and expertise in new practices. The school board and superintendent went on to design collaborative sessions that supported the voices of concern while maintaining fidelity to the literacy instruction framework.

Although they experienced a bump in the road while implementing the framework, the team quickly recovered due to the strategies they had put in place at the start. The team then put energy and resources into investigating how to support implementers through a change. Superintendent Amatto and his team tripped over the truth that planning and executing a change is challenging, even when that change is inclusive and well planned. Understanding the change process and planning for it can keep an implementation effort on track.

In this chapter, we look at why embracing the need for change is an essential early step in the implementation process, as well as how you can navigate the inevitable difficulties of change. We also share how the IMPACT framework supports implementers through the process of managing complex change.

Embracing the Need for Change

Implementation and change are interdependent. Effective implementation that produces intended results is impossible without change. Change is synonymous with learning. The reciprocal is also true—learning equals change. When implementers are to implement an evidence-based innovation, they need to learn about the innovation and how to implement it right and well. If there is no learning, there is no change. Think about a time when you were asked to make a change. What did you need to learn to be successful with the change?

To implement a large-scale change in a way that produces intended results, that change may require multiple levels that differ in content, speed, and experience. Systemwide implementation of an evidence-based innovation often requires change at the community and family levels, the district and school levels, the team and group levels, and always the individual level. And it often requires more than just change to technical behaviors. Quite frequently, implementation involves examining and possibly changing values, beliefs, and attitudes before the change can effectively manifest. Consider what this chapter's vignette demonstrates about the need to embrace change at various levels.

- To effectively implement the *active ingredients* (the critical components of the literacy framework), change was required at the community and family levels. The community members and families had to embrace the need for change in the instructional model before the literacy team could generate solutions that ensured swimming remained a core offering in the schools.

- At the district and school levels, effective implementation of the newly adopted literacy framework required a vision for change, organizational support, policy changes and development, and implementation planning and support for the life span of the innovation. For change to occur, the literacy team had to adapt the vision and implementation plan to guide the teachers' and intervention support teams' adoption and ongoing maintenance of the required change.

- For the literacy framework to become embedded in the day-to-day work of staff, individual change was required at all levels of the organization. In addition to developing new competencies to implement the change, staff required time to make meaning of the change or, in other words, to develop their understanding of and their feelings about the change.

To navigate and manage the multiple levels and kinds of change, it's helpful to understand the change process and change theories. With that said, change is difficult, and understanding the change process doesn't guarantee implementation success. However, without an understanding of change and its relationship to implementation, an implementation gap or implementation failure is virtually guaranteed.

Changing practice implies implementing new strategies. The research on change suggests many people believe that once you have learned about a new practice, you will use it (Darling-Hammond et al., 2017; Joyce & Showers, 2002). Yet, from experience, almost everyone can tell you this just isn't true. Many more factors are at play, one of which is *organizational readiness for change*—how prepared the organization and its members are to take action. In fact, organizational readiness for change is a powerful and often critical antecedent to successful implementation. Researchers Bianca Albers, Aron Shlonsky, and Robyn Mildon (2020) suggest that at least half of implementation failures result from an organization being insufficiently prepared for change. Readiness for change can include individual and collective attitudes, beliefs, dispositions, capacities, capabilities, and resources.

Change is a process, not an event. Like any complex process, leading the change associated with implementing an evidence-based innovation involves a deep understanding of why the innovation is needed; what skills, knowledge, attitudes, and beliefs need to be developed and by whom; and what processes are needed to facilitate and solicit the required change within the organization, team, and individuals. However, even if the purpose is clear and professional learning opportunities are provided, belief won't always follow. And without the belief that the change is needed and will be effective, the required change won't last, and the implementation gap will remain. Embracing the need for change is an essential first step of the process.

Navigating the Difficulty of Change

Regardless of the depth of change knowledge you have, the number of books you have read, or the number of studies you have reviewed, leading and managing change is extremely complex, and it's virtually impossible to do alone. Managing the complexity of change and facilitating strategic implementation require a collaborative approach to leadership. They require, as leadership expert Michael Fullan (2016) calls it, *shared leadership*. Shared leadership shows up in the field of implementation science in the form of the implementation team.

As you read in the introduction (page 1), an implementation team is a shared team leadership structure charged with supporting, monitoring, and leading the implementation of a new organization-wide innovation; the team navigates the difficulty and complexity of change. Unlike many leadership teams in education, an implementation team uses knowledge of and expertise in improvement and change theory to serve as an instrument for change. Implementation teams endure through the implementation effort. Team membership may ebb and flow, but the framework and the team stay with the work until it is completed. The framework structures and processes ensure that supports are in place in case staff shift. Leaders may come and go, but the system is strong and able to maintain people's focus because the implementation team has built institutional knowledge.

Like most leadership teams working to support change, implementation teams start by identifying strategies to implement change. These strategies are often referred to as *change strategies* or *implementation strategies*. For consistency, we will use the term *implementation strategies*. Identifying the right strategies to fit the organizational culture, climate, and context can be difficult. These specific strategies are what ensure the practices, policies, procedures, programs, and principles of evidence-based innovations move into common use and routine.

To help organizations navigate the challenge of identifying effective and feasible implementation strategies, a team of researchers working with the U.S. Department of Veterans Affairs developed the Expert Recommendations for Implementing

Change (ERIC; Powell et al., 2015). This is a list of recommendations organizations can use to identify change strategies that lead to the successful use of evidence-based programs. The recommendations align nicely with the IMPACT implementation human- and learning-centered design elements. Table 2.1 introduces the IMPACT implementation strategies for change, which assist teams in selecting implementation strategies and paying attention to the human elements of change.

Table 2.1: IMPACT Implementation Strategies for Change

IMPACT Design Elements	Strategy	Definition
Inclusion	Conduct local consensus discussions.	Include all stakeholders and implementers in discussions to unpack the relationship between the identified problem and the proposed program's or practice's ability to address the problem.
	Recruit, designate, and train for leadership.	Recruit, designate, and train leaders for the change effort to build capacity and increase support for implementers to adopt and deliver the new program or practice.
	Create a learning collaborative.	Develop a culture of collaboration, and facilitate collaborative opportunities for everyone to improve the implementation.
	Develop partnerships.	Partner with external experts to bring training or research skills to an implementation project.
	Inform local opinion leaders.	Inform local opinion leaders or influential leaders of the innovation in the hope that they will influence colleagues to adopt it.
	Involve leadership and governing boards.	Involve the board of directors and leadership in the implementation effort, including the review of implementation data.
Meaningful Leadership	Provide building-level incentives.	Provide building-level incentives for schools to participate in districtwide implementation efforts for the new innovation.
	Access new funding.	Identify ways to access new or existing money to facilitate the implementation plan and efforts.
	Change physical structures and equipment.	Evaluate current configurations and adapt, as needed, the physical structure and equipment (changing the layout of a room, adding equipment, and so on) to best accommodate the innovation.

IMPACT Design Elements	Strategy	Definition
	Conduct pilots of change.	Implement the innovation using small pilots before systemwide implementation. This process can continue repeatedly over time if needed; add and record adaptations and refinements to each pilot.
	Conduct educational outreach visits.	Have staff meet with experienced providers in their practice settings to learn about the practice.
	Recruit, designate, and train for leadership.	Recruit, designate, and train leaders for the change effort to build capacity and increase support for implementers to adopt and deliver the new program or practice.
	Remind teachers.	Develop reminder systems that help teachers recall information and prompt them to use the program or practice.
	Tailor strategies.	Tailor the implementation strategies to address barriers and leverage implementation team members through data collection and analysis.
Professional **Learning**	Make professional learning dynamic, and use a variety of professional learning designs.	Vary professional learning designs to be interactive and cater to different learning styles; include observation, reflection, purposeful practice, and feedback.
	Provide ongoing consultation or coaching.	Provide skilled coaching and ongoing modeling, feedback, and support that help staff apply new skills and knowledge in practice.
	Conduct ongoing job-embedded professional learning.	Plan for and conduct ongoing job-embedded professional learning opportunities.
	Develop educational materials.	Develop and format manuals, tool kits, and other support materials to make it easier for staff to learn how to deliver the approach.
	Distribute educational materials.	Develop learning walks and distribute manuals, tool kits, and other support materials for staff to learn how to implement the innovation.
	Use train-the-trainer strategies.	Train implementation team members to provide professional learning and coaching and train others in the innovation.
	Schedule and provide opportunities for purposeful practice and feedback.	Schedule opportunities for staff to practice implementing the innovation and to receive feedback designed to increase implementation fidelity.
	Model the practice.	Prior to implementation, model the practice that will be implemented.

continued →

IMPACT Design Elements	Strategy	Definition
Assess and Adjust	Provide fidelity and feedback data to implementers.	Provide real-time data about key implementation fidelity measures and student outcomes to promote cycles of improvement.
	Develop and use tools for monitoring implementation integrity.	Develop and apply implementation fidelity measures to monitor active ingredients of the innovation.
	Use collaborative teams to engage in cycles of improvement.	Use existing collaborative teacher structures to improve implementation and outcomes through iterative cycles of improvement.
	Promote adaptability.	Articulate ways the innovation can be adapted to best meet the organization's culture, climate, and context.
Collective Efficacy	Identify and prepare a coalition of champions.	Identify and prepare individuals who can motivate colleagues and model effective implementation, overcoming indifference or resistance to innovation.
	Obtain formal commitments.	Obtain written commitments from stakeholders and implementers that articulate what they will do to foster effective implementation.
	Revise professional roles.	Shift and revise roles among implementers, and modify or edit job requirements.
	Use an implementation adviser.	Seek guidance from experts in implementation.
Team	Create a learning collaborative.	Develop a culture of collaboration, and facilitate collaborative opportunities for everyone to improve the implementation.
	Create an implementation team.	Establish a diverse team of stakeholders and implementers to lead and support all implementation efforts.

Source: Adapted from Powell et al., 2015.

*Visit **go.SolutionTree.com/schoolimprovement** for a free reproducible version of this table.*

Districts and schools use the preceding table to select implementation strategies and plan for the change they are about to embark on. A tool such as this allows implementation teams to ensure they choose from proven strategies in the areas of identified need (inclusion, professional learning, and so on).

Implementation teams are different from typical school leadership teams in that they are responsible for implementing the strategies they identify and develop. In addition to the change planning and preparation, implementation teams employ the implementation strategies and engage in cycles of improvement that lead to monitoring and adapting each strategy for increased effectiveness. By doing so, the implementation teams develop a higher level of collaboration than typically practiced on other school leadership teams (Higgins, Weiner, & Young, 2012). Ultimately, they are responsible for creating readiness for change, preparing and providing resources at all levels of the organization to counter the effects of immunity to change, and developing teams' and individuals' ability to implement and sustain the required changes that lead to intended outcomes.

Supporting People Through Change

Adopting a change theory provides a systematic, collective, and planned approach to navigating the emotions encountered by those experiencing the change. Change theories, when enacted, serve as road maps for when and how to design the active and deliberate supports needed to navigate individual, team, and organizational change. These active, deliberate supports come in many forms (training, coaching, modeling, feedback, and so on). Numerous change theories are available and used throughout education. This chapter offers two change theory tools to support people through change.

When using a change theory to drive your efforts to help change practice, be sure the change theory is backed by research and evidence. The IMPACT implementation framework is a research-informed framework that serves as the underpinning for effective change theories. We believe that effective change theories lead to IMPACT, which stands for the following.

1. **Inclusion:** Strategies that incorporate implementers' needs, assets, and perspectives to generate motivation and collaboration

2. **Meaningful leadership:** Strategies that lead to ensuring all stakeholders routinely engage in ongoing learning and improvement processes

3. **Professional learning:** Strategies that foster job-embedded learning and include the examination and reflection of practice, time for practice, and multiple feedback forms

4. **Assess and adjust:** Strategies that allow for ongoing improvement and adaptation to the change needs

5. **Collective efficacy:** Strategies that set the conditions that foster, support, and increase collective effectiveness focused on shared goals

6. **Team:** Strategies that engage all levels of the organization (community, district, school, teams, and individuals) in collaboratively monitoring, supporting, and adjusting implementation efforts

We recommend that you use the IMPACT lens to evaluate which organizational change theory is most appropriate for your culture, climate, and change context.

Adopting a research-based change theory and utilizing an implementation framework build in support to help execute your plan. These things intentionally build in human- and learning-centered design elements, and a good change process requires a strong focus on the human element. Selecting a change theory is an important step in building deliberately developmental implementation because you are deliberately addressing the psychological needs of the people experiencing the change. Entering a change effort without a change theory to address inevitable emotions, behaviors, and frustrations is like flying a kite without wind; when you get stuck, you hope the next action or strategy will boost your evidence-based practice, like wind lifting your kite to soar. That is no way to meet the moments of challenge that implementation teams will face.

To support you and your team, the following sections share two effective change models for your consideration. The important step of selecting a change model will help your implementation team support your staff.

The Model for Managing Complex Change

An approachable and powerful change process tool is the Lippitt-Knoster Model for Managing Complex Change. We have found this model extremely valuable in managing change at scale in school district settings. The model, developed by Mary Lippitt and adapted by Timothy Knoster, provides a framework to effectively navigate organizational change (Knoster, Villa, & Thousand, 2000). Lippitt and Knoster's collaborative work culminated in a structured model that is widely recognized and utilized across various sectors, including education.

The change management process identifies five elements as necessary for successful change implementation: (1) vision, (2) skills, (3) incentives, (4) resources, and (5) an action plan. What we find powerful about this model is that it indicates what outcome will be experienced when an element is missing. For example, if there is a lack of vision, people involved in the change may experience confusion, or if staff members express anxiety, that indicates a lack of skills. This is particularly useful, as it allows the implementation team to backtrack from the situation and get to the cause of it.

1. **Lack of vision → confusion:** This can stem from poor communication of a vision, an unclear vision, lack of understanding of the vision, lack of buy-in for the vision, and so on.

2. **Lack of skills → anxiety:** This means that the implementers need access to the knowledge, skills, and opportunities to build competence in deploying the work.

3. **Lack of incentives → resistance:** Incentives are important, as they provide motivation and momentum to push through when acquisition of new skills becomes difficult, is time-consuming, or is being adopted widely.

4. **Lack of resources → frustration:** Think of resources beyond the material items necessary to perform the new skills. Consider time, human capital, funding, and capacity for new learning. Lacking resources will impact progress and attitudes; it's very frustrating to see that everything is aligned and ready but doesn't progress.

5. **Lack of action plan → false starts:** An action plan aligns the vision, resources, and timelines and provides a structure for the team to work from and monitor and adjust progress. Without an action plan, efforts falter, and training can be random and lack focus.

In the absence of all five elements, even the most well-intentioned change effort can fail to meet the complex needs of the people involved in the change. The power of the managing complex change process (Knoster, Villa, & Thousand, 2000) is that it gives the team indicators of what psychological safety needs people experiencing the change may display. To learn more about the model and view an illustrated version, visit Sergio Caredda's article about the Lippitt-Knoster model (http://tinyurl.com/yc7a368f). Using this model, which elements do you see as strengths for your organization and which elements are challenging?

Using a change model helps implementation teams identify barriers to change and develop actionable recommendations that address the human elements of change. In short, it helps teams identify the root cause and keeps them from abandoning their plan. Because behavior is such a big part of change, we invite you to think about change by asking the question, "What new behaviors do staff need to learn or change?" We discuss this idea in the next section.

The COM-B Model of Behavior Change

Another change model we have seen teams successfully use is the COM-B (Capability, Opportunity, Motivation-Behavior) model of behavior change (Michie, van Stralen, & West, 2011). The COM-B model is helpful for answering the question, "What needs to change for the desired behaviors to occur?" This model cites three factors to consider when planning change: (1) capability, (2) opportunity, and (3) motivation. Researchers Jen Briselli and Amy Bucher (2021) describe these factors as separate but interrelated because they can influence one another. For example, as people become more skilled or practiced at a behavior (capability), they are more likely to consider it as an option and to prioritize it against other options (motivation). Similarly, if a behavior is easier to perform within a certain context (opportunity), it becomes a more attractive option (motivation; Briselli & Bucher, 2021).

Researchers Susan Michie, Maartje M. van Stralen, and Robert West (2011) describe the three COM-B behavior factors as follows.

1. "Capability is defined as the individual's psychological and physical capacity to engage in the activity concerned." This includes the new knowledge, skills, and abilities the implementer must develop to be able to effectively perform the desired change behavior. To perform well, one needs to feel capable and confident that they have the skills necessary to achieve the desired outcome.

2. "Opportunity is defined as all the factors that lie outside the individual that make the behaviour possible or prompt it." These factors include the physical environments, resources, and social environments that enable the adoption of the new skills and behaviors associated with the change.

3. "Motivation is defined as all those brain processes that energize and direct behaviour, not just goals and conscious decision-making. It includes habitual processes, emotional responding, as well as analytical decision-making." Motivation is often overlooked in the implementation of a new change initiative. Just because the leadership team is fully onboard and ready to champion the change does not mean the implementers have the same motivation.

We have found the COM-B model of behavior change to be helpful for implementation teams to utilize in designing the implementation plan and addressing human behavior and needs. When planning to support people through the change, address the factors of capability, opportunity, and motivation, as shown in figure 2.1.

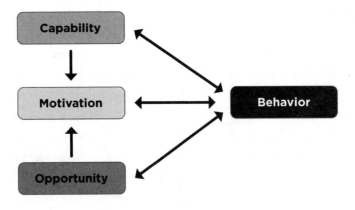

Source: *Michie et al., 2011, licensed under CC BY 4.0.*
Figure 2.1: COM-B model of behavior change.

The COM-B model of behavior change identifies key components to consider within each of the three factors.

1. **Capability**

   › **Physical:** The individual's physical ability to perform the behavior

   › **Psychological:** The mental skills and knowledge necessary to execute the behavior

2. **Opportunity**

   › **Physical:** The external factors that make the behavior possible, such as the environment and available resources

   › **Social:** The social environment, including cultural norms and social cues that can facilitate or hinder the behavior

3. **Motivation**

   › **Automatic:** The unconscious processes that can drive behavior, such as habits, emotional responses, and impulses

   › **Reflective:** The conscious decision-making process, which includes evaluating consequences and making plans

These components work together to influence an individual's behavior, where increasing capability and opportunity can enhance motivation, and strong motivation can increase the effort to improve capability and seek out opportunities.

Conclusion

Changing human behavior is critical to meeting the challenges of implementation. And change involves emotion. Understanding that people involved in the change will experience stages of emotion can help you plan for those reactions and support these people through the stages of implementation. Leverage your understanding of change and select and utilize a change process tool. While we have shared two examples with you, there are plenty of research-based change process tools your team can choose from as you embark on your implementation journey.

A few final reminders about change follow.

- Managing change is complex; embracing change and adopting a model or framework that supports how you address behaviors related to change will pave a smoother pathway to successful change. Focusing on the psychological needs of the implementers helps you build deliberately developmental implementation.

- Get comfortable with the fact that people won't get change exactly right the first time. Build an improvement mindset throughout your organization. Communicate clearly and often that getting it right the first time is not what is critical; constantly reviewing, measuring success, adapting, and adjusting is critical.

Change is here. How you plan for and adapt to change is in your hands. Use these foundational concepts and tools to support your system's current change process. Focus on rapid improvement (use a valid process to do so), involve your stakeholders in design and decision making, be kind to one another, lead with your heart, and passionately embrace an improvement mindset.

Evaluate a Change Theory

Choosing and making sense of a change theory to use as part of your implementation effort can be confusing and overwhelming, as there are numerous change theory models, including those developed by your team or organization. The IMPACT implementation framework is a research-informed framework that serves as the underpinning for effective change theories. When investigating and evaluating change theories you might want to adopt to guide your implementation efforts, use this simple assessment tool aligned with the IMPACT implementation framework to identify strengths and gaps in each change theory you are considering.

IMPACT Implementation Framework

Change Theories	**I**nclusion: The change theory leads to incorporating implementers' needs, assets, and perspectives to generate motivation and collaboration.	**M**eaningful leadership: The change theory leads to ensuring all stakeholders routinely engage in ongoing learning and improvement processes.	**P**rofessional learning: The change theory leads to strategies that foster job-embedded learning.	**A**ssess and adjust: The change theory leads to the development of strategies that allow for ongoing improvement and adaptation to the change needs.	**C**ollective efficacy: The change theory leads to creating the conditions that foster, support, and increase collective effectiveness focused on shared goals.	**T**eam: The change theory leads to the development of strategies that engage all levels of the organization (community, district, school, teams, and individuals) in collaboratively monitoring, supporting, and adjusting implementation efforts.
Rank each change theory's inclusion of the preceding human- and learning-centered design elements on a scale of 1 (a gap in the theory) to 5 (a strength of the theory).						
Theory 1						
Theory 2						
Theory 3						
Theory 4						

"Implementation Means Change for All" Learning Journey Map

Use the following two questions to prompt active discussion and thoughtful responses, helping your team assess current practices and plan for future development. This is an opportunity for collective reflection and strategic action.

Together, review the concepts and practices from chapter 2 that your organization has already implemented. Discuss the effectiveness of your leadership and the progress of your implementation efforts. Use the questions to guide a rich conversation, and document your team's insights, commitments, and objectives in the learning journey map.

1. What concepts and practices from chapter 2 does our district or school currently have in place (with varying degrees of implementation)?

2. What observations and insights are we making about our leadership, leadership team, or organizational implementation efforts?

Team Takeaways	Team Commitment	Team Practice	Team Reflection	Team Goals
New learning, insights, and notices	Concepts, ideas, and practices we *commit to developing*	Strategies, processes, and tools we plan to *learn and practice*	Strategies, processes, tools, concepts, ideas, and so on we want to *go deeper into and share early successes on*	Strategies, processes, tools, concepts, ideas, and so on we want to *fully operationalize* through a commitment of time, resources, and policy

---------- *chapter 3* ----------

YOU CAN'T DO THIS
WORK ALONE

Great implementation requires great teams—teams that are built on a foundation of trust, respect, and a shared commitment to making a difference.

—Jenice Pizzuto and Steven Carney

Implementation is, quite simply, getting better at getting better. When we concentrate on the aim stated in this book's introduction (page 1)—to create a movement in education that focuses on how well educators support a new program, practice, strategy, or policy, rather than leaping from initiative to initiative and continuing to get haphazard or limited results—we begin to shift to a culture that puts a premium on learning and asking the question, "How might we improve?"

In this chapter's vignette, you will meet Principal Carter, a talented principal who wanted to improve behavior outcomes by implementing an evidence-based behavior framework in her school. You may recognize some of the pitfalls and missteps along her implementation journey. To develop deliberately developmental implementation, you must focus on learning; Principal Carter's story highlights the critical components of growing the implementers and building an implementation team.

> *Principal Carter got a job serving as an elementary school principal in a small rural district. Her prior school experiences came from serving in much larger cosmopolitan urban settings. So, she had a lot to learn about leading change initiatives in a more tight-knit school culture and community where most staff had lived and worked there for most of their educational careers. Due to the sparse suburban feel, access to a plethora of outdoor activities,*

opportunities to participate in regular community events, and small school and class sizes, this community was one where multiple generations lived and stayed to raise their families. It was common for the parent or grandparent of a new kindergartner to request the same teacher they had when they were in kindergarten.

The community was known for its agriculture, lumber, and other industries that commonly attracted immigrant workers and their families. During her tenure in the district, Principal Carter witnessed the following.

- *About 50 percent of the district student population was identified as low income.*

- *About 13 percent of the district student population was identified as having disabilities.*

- *The average four-year high school graduation rate was 76.58 percent.*

- *On average, 53.60 percent of students met proficiency in English language arts, and 42.38 percent of students were proficient in mathematics.*

Prior to the first day of school, Principal Carter informed the staff she would be present, visible, and available to all staff and students every day. She told them that she built her daily schedule so she could get into classrooms and other educational and play spaces for an average of three hours per day. This practice had been the norm for her at other schools where she served, and it had been essential to her instructional leader role. She believed, like many great school leaders do, that you can't support and grow what you don't observe.

On the first day of school, right after the first bell, Principal Carter began the best part of her day: walking into classrooms and making herself visible. Within thirty minutes, she received a call from the main office that she had students waiting outside her office. She returned to her office to find three students waiting to see her, all with discipline referrals in hand. She thought it might be a challenging first day for a few students.

Despite the unexpected influx of students, Principal Carter initially chose not to draw conclusions; she waited a month to see if the pattern persisted. Remarkably, the number of office referrals she encountered in her first month as an elementary school principal surpassed that of her entire four-year tenure at a middle school. It became clear that she was witnessing the manifestation of a deeply ingrained cultural norm within the district: a zero-tolerance approach to discipline. This approach, while not formalized in written policy, was a legacy of the previous administration's unwritten expectation that the principal handle all disciplinary matters. Consequently, teachers routinely sent students to the principal's office for a wide array of issues. In keeping with this established cultural expectation, Principal Carter initially adhered to the official district and school policies when disciplining students.

Before long, Principal Carter realized that maintaining the current cultural norm wouldn't work. The same students kept coming back to her over and over again. For a majority of the students, the school's zero-tolerance approach was ineffective, detrimental, and illogical. She knew that punitive responses to inappropriate behaviors, particularly for the students who faced adverse childhood experiences, would not resolve the issues. She quickly discovered that many of her school's students carried the burden of trauma. Based on the school faculty's collective knowledge of students, Principal Carter believed about one in four students in her school had encountered or was currently encountering traumatic experiences.

Principal Carter phoned a principal friend, who told her to look into positive behavioral interventions and supports (PBIS) and trauma-sensitive practices. So, she took a small team, the school counselor and behavior specialists, to a local PBIS conference and training on how trauma impacts behavior and learning. Principal Carter and her team heard story after story of how PBIS has addressed and dramatically improved student behavior in schools across the globe. She learned how trauma-sensitive practices improve student learning and increase positive behavior. She heard stories of principals increasing their time in classrooms and their focus on instruction and spending less time on behavior issues and discipline. PBIS and trauma-sensitive practices had a strong research base and impressive evidence demonstrating their effectiveness in improving learning environments and reducing unwanted behaviors across classrooms, schools, and school systems. Principal Carter and her team had found a solution to the problem they were experiencing with behavior: PBIS combined with trauma sensitivity.

Principal Carter's small team arranged to share their new learning with the staff at the beginning of the upcoming year. They let the staff know they were sending a team of staff members to get trained in PBIS and trauma-sensitive practices so they could serve as trainers and supporters for the rest of the staff. Staff responses were less positive than Principal Carter had hoped; some staff voiced opinions that PBIS wouldn't work while others shared their belief that "this too will pass." Despite the resistance, Principal Carter spent all her school's professional learning budget on training, travel to training, and resources for the small team of trailblazers, including the school counselor. After Principal Carter's team developed skills and expertise in PBIS, they devoted the remaining professional learning days in the school year to becoming a PBIS school.

By the end of year one, very little had changed; the school's resident experts were frustrated, Principal Carter's staff were disenfranchised, and she was still spending the majority of her time on office referrals. An end-of-year fidelity review showed that Tier 1 components of PBIS were evident in public areas (the halls, cafeteria, playground, and so on) but minimally implemented in individual classrooms, which was where the tier truly mattered. Principal Carter knew that when Tier 1 isn't fully implemented with fidelity, Tier 2 and Tier 3 lose their intent and are deemed ineffective; all three tiers of the framework are necessary for full and effective change to take hold. The year's funding, personnel efforts, and time spent had been ineffective. This attempt to spread an evidence-based practice had failed. Principal Carter knew PBIS was the right approach to improve student behavior and well-being, but she felt alone in this endeavor.

Principal Carter surveyed the staff and community at that year's end and learned something valuable. Even though she was ready for change, most of her career educators and support staff expressed that they were unprepared for such drastic change in managing behavior. The top readiness barrier identified was individual and collective beliefs associated with a framework like PBIS and trauma-sensitive strategies. Most of the school staff and the community held strong beliefs about behavior and discipline, and many of these generation-old beliefs contradicted the PBIS and trauma-sensitive practice research and evidence. A year's worth of training, coaching, and communication to parents, staff, and students dramatically clashed against the deep-rooted values, beliefs, and strategies associated with student discipline and adult actions that existed in the school, district, and community. Principal Carter realized that, had she gathered a team of implementers—a guiding coalition of stakeholders to cocreate the readiness supports and colead the implementation—she would likely have learned about, planned for, and addressed the contrasting belief systems and needs in her school from the beginning.

Principal Carter tripped over the truth. She learned that implementing PBIS is a whole-school approach; it recommends that the school establish a Tier 1 team, comprising representatives from the school community, administration, and behavioral experts, to act as an implementation team. The team's single responsibility is to lead the implementation and monitor schoolwide behavior support.

That summer, Principal Carter formed an implementation team for PBIS and trauma-sensitive practices. They met once a week to design and monitor implementation support. Within a year, referrals dropped by 84 percent; detentions became almost nonexistent; and culture and climate survey results demonstrated a sudden improvement in parent, student, and staff satisfaction.

In this chapter, we discuss gathering a guiding coalition of champions—your implementation team—and define what exactly an implementation team is. Next, we discuss the characteristics and behaviors you'll want to look for when choosing team members. We share how to build successful team configurations at the systems level and building level. Finally, we note that implementation teams are different from other kinds of teams within districts and schools; while forming implementation teams is an investment, their unique qualities support them to achieve successful implementation.

Gathering Your Guiding Coalition of Champions

Have you heard of the term *guiding coalition*? We absolutely love this term and use it profusely when supporting and leading change efforts. The research and background on the term *guiding coalition* is found in the fields of implementation science, leadership, and professional learning communities. Educators and authors Mike Mattos, Richard DuFour, Rebecca DuFour, Robert Eaker, and Thomas W. Many (2016) define a *guiding coalition* as:

> An alliance of key members of an organization who are specifically charged with leading a change process through predictable turmoil. Members of the coalition should include opinion leaders—people who are so respected within the organization that others are likely to follow their lead. (p. 21)

This concept of a guiding coalition is foundational to building deliberately developmental implementation. We take the concept further and advocate that organizations build a guiding coalition of champions. These coalition members champion the implementation effort; they are respected opinion leaders within the organization who are willing to learn, embody a growth mindset, and lead the charge with enthusiasm and tenacity. This guiding coalition, your implementation team, is not recruiting the naysayers or defiant persons opposed to the new practice. This team helps influence and inspire those staff members to embrace the innovation.

Change is hard and personal, especially in schools where autonomy and agency are sometimes valued to the point of overshadowing best practices for students. Implementation team members clearly understand *why* a new program, policy, strategy, or initiative is being adopted. They help bring clarity and encourage colleagues to stay the course when challenges arise. For this reason, it is crucial to select implementation team members who work from a learning and improvement mindset. These champions understand why the innovation is a priority and help navigate the system to problem-solve when the implementation stutters, stalls, or is not working and identify bright spots within the organization.

Building a guiding coalition of champions embodies a human- and learning-centered design approach. This approach cultivates meaningful leadership that spans across the organizational structure, both horizontally and vertically. In his 2021 book *Powerful Guiding Coalitions*, educator and author Bill Hall captures the essence of this philosophy: "Powerful guiding coalitions release the leadership potential within the team" (p. 4). In this context, the guiding coalition is not separate from the implementation team; rather, it is the same group of dedicated individuals who champion and execute the change process. This unified team not only accelerates growth for implementers and the organization, but also catalyzes a cultural shift toward a focus on learning and improvement. By leading and championing innovation with human- and learning-centered design elements, the team embeds these values into the implementation effort, ensuring that the guiding coalition fully realizes its transformative potential through its direct involvement in implementation.

Defining Implementation Teams

So, what exactly is an implementation team? It is a group of staff who are responsible for ensuring that individuals horizontally and vertically across the organization build competencies and skills to embrace and enact the change. The implementation team does not do all the work but works together to create the conditions to support the deliberately developmental implementation. These champions create capacity and coherence within the system. Fundamentally, the implementation team systemically develops and sets into motion the implementation plan, which includes coordinating activities, monitoring progress, and developing steps to modify the plan based on relevant data. The team ensures the implementation is not left to chance.

Let's look at a few more definitions. The leading organization studying implementation science and practice, the National Implementation Research Network (2015), defines an *implementation team* as follows:

> An implementation team focuses its energy on developing and sustaining capacity to assure identified student, staff, and/or family outcomes are achieved. . . . Implementation teams are actively involved in facilitating the work of improving the competency and confidence of educators' use of effective programs or practices in their classrooms. (pp. 2-3)

Professorial research fellow Jonathan Sharples and the team at the Education Endowment Foundation describe implementation teams in a way that aligns with our vision and the work you are about to embark on:

> [Implementation teams] draw together multiple types of expertise and skills, from a range of different perspectives, to guide and support the implementation process. They build local capacity to facilitate and shepherd projects and innovations, and continuously remove the barriers that get in the way of good implementation. (Sharples, Albers, Fraser, & Kime, 2019, p. 10)

Additionally, the Colorado Department of Education (n.d.) affirms the importance of implementation teams in its implementation guide:

> A strong implementation team can mean the difference between an initiative that persists and gets refined through difficulty and one that gets dropped when challenges arise. Having a team in place before the implementation begins will help you remain nimble and responsive as the plan progresses and the context evolves. An existing team (e.g., Instructional Leadership Team) may serve the role of Implementation Team, as long as the team has adequate capacity to dedicate to implementation activities. (p. 4)

Implementation teams serve as a conduit to scale evidence-based practices. They are commonly used in health care, social welfare fields, and business industries.

The goal is that they advance the dissemination of the new practice being Introduced into the organization. The Active Implementation Research Network (n.d.) describes the purpose of using implementation teams as follows:

> Expertise is required to purposefully, effectively, and efficiently support using innovations as intended to produce desired outcomes reliably and repeatedly. This expertise is developed in Implementation Teams that are formed by reassigning and repurposing current staff in organizations and systems.

In chapter 1 (page 17), you learned the pivotal role expert implementation teams play in successful adoption of educational innovations. Building on that foundation, it's essential to understand that the process of implementation is inherently a learning journey. It's not merely about individual adoption but about the cultivation of a collective capacity for change. Fostering implementation teams not only aims for widespread adoption but also nurtures ecosystems where change becomes synonymous with learning, growth, and systemic improvement. This strategic investment in team development is what enables systems to realize an average success rate of 80 percent in the adoption of evidence-based practices within a three-year time frame, a stark contrast to the prolonged and often ineffective efforts that occur in the absence of such teams (Fixsen et al., 2019).

The implementation team is key to addressing intransigent problems that are usually overloaded with solutions and underresourced with implementation plans and actions. We like to say that implementation teams are the secret sauce for getting implementation right. Implementation teams are action oriented and solution focused; if your system is not getting the results it should from innovations, it is time to embrace the implementation team concept. Developing an implementation team (your guiding coalition of champions) ensures that the new work is not person or leader dependent. Staff turnover and leadership shifts leave an organization vulnerable when leading the change resides with one or two members of a school or district. With the average tenure of a school leader being four years, leaders and staff shift, grow, and move on, leaving the change effort stalled (Levin & Bradley, 2019). Building expertise, skills, and capabilities across a broad spectrum of staff ensures the innovation lives on when leaders and staff assigned to implement the initiative are absent or depart the organization. With an implementation team in place, team learning and commitment to the change overcome staff changes and turnover. Ultimately, the change initiative is owned by the organization rather than by an individual or small group of staff members.

An implementation support structure is essential for strategic and effective implementation in learning organizations. From our experience, very few schools develop implementation-literate teams as they embark on the work of planning, monitoring, supporting, and sustaining the implementation of evidence-based practices. An implementation team fills this need. The implementation team is your organization's guiding coalition of champions who work together to support your innovation throughout each stage of implementation.

Identifying Team Characteristics and Behaviors

Members of the guiding coalition of champions exhibit and embody a willingness to tackle implementation—and they do so with energy, enthusiasm, and engagement. We call this the *three Es*. Because implementation is relational, these seemingly fluffy components of team members not only are useful but can pull an implementation team through tumultuous times and help overcome barriers. The implementation team is not the place for naysayers and recalcitrant staff members. Team members are open to shifting their opinions; they do not tie their identity to their opinions. We mention this because we see harnessing these characteristics as a gap in implementation and school change efforts. We find that omitting or ignoring the relational pathways, including human- and learning-centered design elements, results in frustration and resistance from implementers and fails to shift the culture to believe in and practice the new work with fidelity.

Speaker and writer Patrick Lencioni (2016) describes the virtues of team members who embody characteristics necessary to lead change.

- **Humble:** Humility is the most indispensable attribute of a team player.

- **Hungry:** Hungry people almost never have to be pushed by a manager to work harder because they are self-motivated and diligent.

- **Smart:** *Smartness* simply refers to a person's common sense about people.

Building your implementation team is an important step you take in designing implementation. Including humble, hungry, smart people will benefit the team. Experience has shown us this is a step you cannot overlook. Even one or two team members saddled with a fixed mindset and a negative attitude can drastically reduce a team's productivity.

Many books, articles, and briefs address the logistics of what a team is, how many people may comprise the team, when they should meet, and perhaps what the team should do while meeting. However, experience shows us that those logistic elements alone are insufficient to get to full and effective change, especially because the implementation team is charged with building systemwide coherence, establishing why the change is happening, gaining the staff's trust, and shifting the culture. As Michael Fullan and Mary Jean Gallagher (2020) write in their book *The Devil Is in the Details: System Solutions for Equity, Excellence, and Student Well-Being*, "For the system to be effective, education leaders need to interact with the system up and down and sideways" (p. 37). It is the same with implementation teams.

Table 3.1 compiles the characteristics and behaviors we believe teams should include to ensure members reflect a human- and learning-centered mindset. Note that this is not a checklist, and no one person should encompass all these ideals. Your team should embody a broad set of the characteristics and behaviors among its members.

Before you build your team, become familiar with these behaviors and characteristics. Worth noting is that while not all team members will hit the mark on all characteristics and behaviors, the team interactions and behaviors will support the cross-development of traits. Aim to build a diverse implementation team of varied stakeholders who *collectively* embody as many of the ideal team characteristics and behaviors as reasonably possible. Do not expect any one individual to embody all characteristics and behaviors; build a guiding coalition of champions who will be empowered with the skills and attitudes each team member can contribute. Use the reproducibles at the end of this chapter (page 86) to help you identify and leverage implementation team characteristics and behaviors.

Building Teams and Configurations

In the landscape of educational change, positional leaders—superintendents, principals, and other administrators—are often perceived as pivotal. They set the vision and framework for implementation. However, the essence of sustainable change lies within the broader school community. Teachers, support staff, and specialized departments are the linchpins of this transformative process, applying the strategic vision to the nuances of daily school life. Their inclusion in implementation teams is not merely beneficial—it is indispensable for the nuanced understanding and practical application they bring to the table.

For these reasons, we persistently and pervasively push for including implementers as active members of the implementation team. While they do not comprise the entire team, their voices must be included early in the process. Implementers

Table 3.1: Ideal Team Characteristics and Behaviors

Characteristic	Behavior
Curious	Demonstrates curiosity over closure
Humble	Exhibits humility over pride
Collaborative	Operates with a mindset of cocreation
Learning	Reads widely, is eager to learn, and applies new learning as rapidly as possible
Inclusive	Is interested in hearing other people's views and revising their own
Growth minded	Uses a growth mindset and has cognitive flexibility and mental agility
Multifaceted	Has a variety of strengths (This way, the team as a whole can be successful.)
Championing	Champions innovation
Actively participating	Participates in the design of the implementation plan
Capacity building	Creates capacity, coherence, and alignment, and builds shared understanding
Experienced	Has deep expertise in the innovation (or is a committed learner)
Change making	Catalyzes change by diagnosing problems before, during, and after initial implementation
Supportive	Provides solutions, supports the process, and contributes resources
Systems thinking	Does systems-level planning and site and building development work
Data driven	Uses data to solve problems and address context issues, site-based barriers, or resource needs
Facilitative	Uses protocols, facilitation tools, improvement cycles, and the IMPACT implementation framework to support the implementation
Adaptive	Anticipates and prevents issues, identifies risks, and develops strategies
Implementation focused	Is involved in the change and deserves to have a voice in the change; is the communication loop and support for the implementers
Insightful	Considers contextual factors that executive leadership may not be aware of
Unifying	Clarifies goals, establishes collaborations, supports the development of resources, and communicates readiness for change
Resourceful	Helps system leaders and stakeholders anticipate resource and organization needs and plan for resources, including human and capital resources
Problem solving	Resolves issues as new ways of working are being developed
Creative	Creates supportive conditions that improve implementation of the innovation

Source: © 2023 by Jenice Pizzuto and Steven Carney.

are the people actually doing the work. Their firsthand experiences are invaluable for navigating the complexities of change and for seizing opportunities that arise during implementation. The diversity of these team members—in roles, tenures, and perspectives—creates a resilient structure capable of fostering innovation and facilitating rapid improvement.

As we delve into the construction of these teams, we must recognize that they are dynamic entities requiring continuous development. These teams will naturally vary in structure, but the core principle remains: to combine strategic oversight with practical expertise, ensuring that those who enact change have a voice on the team.

The active participation of implementers at both the district and school levels is essential. Their roles may differ—with systems-level implementers shaping overarching policies and building-level staff tailoring these to on-the-ground realities—but their contributions are equally critical. When direct involvement is not feasible, teams should employ alternative methods such as surveys and forums to capture the implementers' valuable perspectives.

Recognizing the distinct contributions of systems- and building-level implementers is fundamental. Systems-level insights can highlight systemic needs, while building-level experiences reveal the day-to-day realities of implementing change. Together, they form a comprehensive view for fostering a culture of continuous improvement and equitable change. By valuing these perspectives from the beginning, you set the stage for a well-informed and equitable implementation journey.

Building on our commitment to inclusive implementation, the composition of implementation teams must be diverse. This diversity isn't just about numbers—it's about the breadth of perspectives, experiences, and expertise that members bring to the table. Consider the following elements of diverse implementation teams.

- **Cognitive diversity is key:** A diverse team has greater cognitive flexibility than a nondiverse team, is willing to challenge the status quo, and brings a wealth of information and resources to the fore. This cognitive diversity is the engine of the team's growth and adaptability.

- **Tenure diversity adds depth to team insights:** By bringing together individuals who have served the organization for varying lengths of time, the team gains a blend of fresh eyes and seasoned wisdom.

- **Role representation values each team member's unique expertise and the voice they provide for their group:** It ensures that every impacted facet of the community is heard and team members can each speak on their group's behalf (Higgins et al., 2012).

- **Constituent representation means that teams must mirror the racial and gender diversity of the student body and wider community:** This is non-negotiable; it's at the heart of the team's commitment to equity.

- **Organizational representation requires that teams are structured both horizontally and vertically:** This ensures that ideas and innovations flow through every level of the system, and that feedback loops are quick and effective, driving continuous improvement.

The formation of these teams is not a one-size-fits-all process. It involves creating a structure that works for each organization's unique context. In smaller systems, this might mean dual roles for leaders like superintendents and principals. In larger systems, it might require additional layers to ensure inclusivity without unwieldiness. The essence of implementation team creation is to form a coalition of champions, representative of the entire system, ready to roll up their sleeves and get to work.

Focus on the specifics of team configurations, composition, availability and commitment, time, roles and expectations, and communication. Remember not to get bogged down by titles or structures. Every team member is empowered to contribute to the success of the implementation effort. You're building teams that are not just capable of navigating the challenges ahead but also equipped to seize the opportunities that come with them. With intention, inclusivity, and a focus on the transformative power of collective action, you're setting the stage for a journey of meaningful change.

Ideal Implementation Team Configurations

To ensure you implement innovations right and well, forming implementation teams at the district and school levels is crucial. Throughout the book, we refer to these levels as the *systems level* and *building level*.

Remember the following when creating a systems-level implementation team.

- This team should include representatives of the organization's leadership, key stakeholders, the community, and relevant departments.

- The team will benefit from having a member who is directly impacted by the change and can offer a perspective that team members may otherwise overlook.

Remember the following when creating a building-level implementation team.

- A school leader, such as a principal or assistant principal, is essential for aligning the innovation with school policies and practices.

- Teachers and staff who are directly involved with or leading the innovation provide practical insights and ensure the change is manageable and meaningful at the classroom level.

- Specialists such as academic coaches or intervention support staff contribute their expertise to the implementation process.

- The team should maintain a manageable size while ensuring representation across different roles within the school.

The building-level team must include at least one building administrator, in addition to appropriate representation of the building staff. Along with ensuring that practices are active and effective, the implementation team ensures policy and legal requirements are met. This is why we suggest an administrator (the principal or assistant principal) be present on the team; maintaining fiscal, legal, and policy requirements is a primary role of school leadership. Note that you would need to construct additional state-, province-, or region-level implementation teams for state, provincial, or regional implementation efforts.

While it is essential to keep the group small enough to ensure productivity, it is equally vital that all staff know someone represents them on the team. Research by Monica C. Higgins, Jennie Weiner, and Lissa Young (2012) challenges the notion that team size is a main determinant of effectiveness, highlighting instead the importance of socio-structural conditions. These conditions include a cohesive team with clear boundaries, a compelling direction, an enabling structure, a supportive organizational context, and access to effective coaching. Although some literature suggests smaller teams of three to five members for efficiency, our experience in educational implementation has shown that a range of four to ten members often proves more practical. This allows for a diverse array of skills and perspectives, ensuring that stakeholder and community insights are fully integrated. Ultimately, the goal is to foster a team environment that transcends numbers, one in which team members can adeptly navigate barriers, uphold equity, and cultivate widespread engagement.

The formation of horizontal and vertical team configurations is strategic, aiming to do the following.

- **Leverage diverse strengths:** By drawing on the unique abilities and experiences of team members, you create richer, more capable teams.

- **Foster positive cross-functioning:** Encourage collaboration across different functions and departments to break down silos and promote a more integrated approach.

- **Build intentional communication loops:** Establishing clear channels for feedback and dialogue ensures that information flows effectively throughout the organization.

- **Contextualize operations:** Tailor processes and practices to fit the specific context of the organization, ensuring relevance and applicability.

- **Align resources and training:** Coordinate resources and professional development efforts to support the implementation and sustain the practice.

- **Model evidence-based practice:** Demonstrate the use of evidence-based practice across the system to reinforce its value and effectiveness.

- **Facilitate skill development:** Provide opportunities for team members to develop the necessary skills to seamlessly integrate the innovation into their daily work.

In closing this section, we would like to leave you with a quote from NFL coach Vince Lombardi: "The achievements of an organization are the results of the combined effort of each individual" (BrainyQuote, n.d.). Building deliberately developmental implementation happens together, with intention, in small increments, and over time using implementation teams.

Team Composition

Take the time to identify the right team members. In developing your implementation team, remember to be inclusive, create team diversity, and have implementers' voices on the team. There are several things to consider when identifying your implementation team members. These include but are not limited to:

- Availability and commitment
- Motivation to participate
- Skills in—
  - › Analyzing and synthesizing data
  - › Facilitating adults and adult learning
  - › Developing data collection tools, data-informed presentations, or both
- Knowledge of—
  - › School climate, culture, and context
  - › School programs and practices

> Specific content

> Supervision and leadership

> District and school policies

> School funding and budgeting

> Equity and inclusion

> District and school support services

> Organizational and systems thinking

- Respect commanded in their colleagues

When planning and resource gathering for the implementation team begin, keep the preceding items in mind.

Team Availability and Commitment

An implementation team's success hinges on the balance between additional responsibilities and the regular workload of its members. Educators are often prepared to take on extra tasks, especially when these efforts align with their contracted hours and professional development schedules. To honor this balance and support the team's dedication, consider the following.

- Provide coverage for staff to participate in meetings during school hours.

- Offer stipends for contributions made outside the school day.

- Manage team members' class responsibilities to afford them additional preparation time.

- Relieve team members of routine duties so they can focus on implementation tasks.

Clearly articulate the team members' roles, functions, and time commitments. This ensures each member can contribute effectively, demonstrates the value the institution places on this work, and prevents misunderstandings. This clarity not only facilitates a shared understanding but also showcases the commitment to the initiative, reinforcing its significance to all staff members.

Time for Implementation Teamwork

Finding time for implementation teamwork requires careful consideration and collaboration among team members. Consider the following process teams can use to explore different approaches to time allocation.

1. **System reflection:** Begin by conducting a system reflection to spot potential areas where you can carve out time for the implementation team's work. This involves analyzing current schedules, routines, and practices to identify opportunities for adjustments.

2. **Team discussion:** Facilitate a team discussion to gather input and ideas from team members. Encourage open and honest dialogue about time constraints and potential solutions. Consider the following questions as starting points for reflection.

   › "In what ways might we streamline or eliminate current meetings or commitments to create additional time for this project?"

   › "How could we redistribute tasks or responsibilities among team members to enhance our collective availability for this initiative?"

   › "What nonessential activities or practices could we consider reducing or pausing to focus our efforts on the implementation work?"

   › "What alternative meeting formats could we explore to overcome scheduling challenges and ensure effective communication?"

3. **Prioritization and trade-offs:** Engage in a collaborative process to prioritize implementation teamwork and identify trade-offs. Recognize that finding time for teamwork may require sacrificing or reprioritizing certain activities or tasks. It's important to align on the most critical and impactful areas where the team should focus its time and energy.

4. **Flexible scheduling:** Explore flexible scheduling options that accommodate different team members' availabilities. These options might include utilizing noninstructional time, planning periods, before- or after-school hours, or dedicated professional learning days. Consider rotating meeting times to accommodate varying schedules and ensure equitable participation.

5. **Team reflection protocol or tool:** Develop a team reflection protocol or tool to regularly assess and adjust the team's effectiveness and time management strategies. This tool can include questions such as the following.

   › "How well are we managing our time as a team?"

   › "What recurring challenges or constraints impact our ability to find time for implementation work?"

> › "What adjustments or improvements can we make to optimize our use of time?"

> › "What creative or innovative solutions can we explore to enhance our time management?"

By engaging in ongoing reflection and adaptation, the team can continuously refine its approach to time management and ensure that the necessary time and resources are allocated for effective implementation work.

Team Roles and Expectations

Once your implementation team is identified, this team should define the tasks and expectations associated with working together. These include the following.

- Identify and define the purpose and core values of the implementation team.

- Articulate and accept the goals and responsibilities of the implementation team.

- Adopt norms and agreements that the implementation team members will follow. For example, use the seven norms of collaborative work from the Adaptive School (Garmston & Wellman, n.d.):

  1. **Pausing:** Pausing before responding or asking a question allows time for thinking and enhances dialogue, discussion, and decision-making.

  2. **Paraphrasing:** Using a paraphrase starter that is comfortable for you—"So . . ." or "As you are . . ." or "You're thinking . . ."—and following the starter with an efficient paraphrase assists members of the group in hearing and understanding one another as they converse and make decisions.

  3. **Posing Questions:** Two intentions of posing questions are to explore and to specify thinking. Questions may be posed to explore perceptions, assumptions, and interpretations, and to invite others to inquire into their thinking. For example, "What might be some conjectures you are exploring?" Use focusing questions such as, "Which students, specifically?" or "What might be an example of that?" to increase the clarity and precision of group members' thinking. Inquire into others' ideas before advocating one's own.

4. **Putting Ideas on the Table:** Ideas are the heart of meaningful dialogue and discussion. Label the intention of your comments. For example: "Here is one idea . . ." or "One thought I have is . . ." or "Here is a possible approach . . ." or "Another consideration might be . . ."

5. **Providing Data:** Providing data, both qualitative and quantitative, in a variety of forms supports group members in constructing shared understanding from their work. Data have no meaning beyond that which we make of them; shared meaning develops from collaboratively exploring, analyzing, and interpreting data.

6. **Paying Attention to Self and Others:** Meaningful dialogue and discussion are facilitated when each group member is conscious of self and of others, and is aware of what [they are] saying *and* how it is said, as well as how others are responding. This includes paying attention to learning styles when planning, facilitating, and participating in group meetings and conversations.

7. **Presuming Positive Intentions:** Assuming that others' intentions are positive promotes and facilitates meaningful dialogue and discussion and prevents unintentional put-downs. Using positive intentions in speech is one manifestation of this norm.

- Determine how team members will reach consensus in the decision-making process, whether through voting or other means. We advocate for the Fist to Five consensus-building tool, originally designed by the American Youth Foundation (Fletcher, 2002)—a straightforward yet effective method for gauging agreement on proposed solutions. This tool not only surfaces the level of agreement but also facilitates open discussion and dissent, which are vital steps toward achieving consensus. When employing the Fist to Five method, team members express their support using the following gestures.

  > **Closed fist:** "I am in complete opposition. This blocks consensus."

  > **One finger:** "I have major concerns or unresolved issues."

  > **Two fingers:** "Minor issues exist that I would like to discuss."

  > **Three fingers:** "Minor issues exist that can be resolved later. I'm comfortable enough to move forward with the proposal."

> **Four fingers:** "It's a good idea, and I can work with it and support it."

> **Five fingers:** "I'm all in. This is a great idea, and I'm willing to lead the implementation of it. I'll champion it."

Team members showing fewer than three fingers are invited to voice their objections, which allows the team to address concerns. This process continues until a consensus is reached (all members show three or more fingers) or the team decides to move on.

- Agree on the frequency and scheduling of implementation team meetings. We recommend getting started with weekly meetings and moving to monthly to monitor and support progress.

- Create ways for implementation team members to share information and resources (including agendas, meeting minutes, and notes) within and outside the team.

- Define and assign roles individuals will play to support team efficiency and effectiveness. Consider the following suggested roles and responsibilities as a starting point.

  > **Facilitator:** Starts and chairs each meeting, reviews the purposes of the meeting, facilitates the team by taking them through the agenda, and fosters the team's implementation literacy

  > **Minute taker:** Takes the minutes and updates the implementation action plan

  > **Timekeeper:** Monitors the amount of time available and keeps the team aware of time limits

  > **Data analyst:** Reviews and organizes implementation and improvement data prior to each team meeting to share the data with the team

  > **Administrator:** Facilitates implementation team activities and recommendations; provides planning time and feedback; serves as the point person for communication with and between the district, community, parents, staff, and students; and ensures implementation integrity of identified interventions

Successful implementation teams are teams in their truest form, as the roles and tasks are distributed equitably. Meetings that lead to strategic implementation planning and effective decision-making processes have key roles designated to help make team meetings and processes run smoothly. Although the names and descriptions of these roles can vary from team to team, the suggested roles are commonly known to contribute to success. Interests and specific skill sets often contribute to the roles individual team members gravitate toward or are assigned. An excellent way to build team capacity is to rotate the prominent roles among all the implementation team members to increase each member's experience and skills. By rotating roles, you can avoid overreliance on a few and prevent any perception of concentration of power or favoritism. Commitment to using roles and effective team protocols and processes that improve team effectiveness is more important than the specifics of the roles.

Team Communication

Your implementation team must consider how to keep all stakeholders informed of implementation activities as they unfold. Figure 3.1 provides a tool to help your team design and build a robust communication plan.

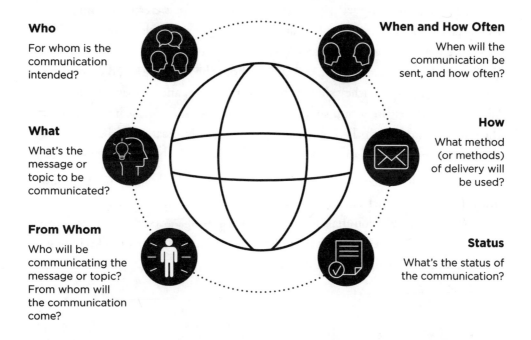

IMPACT
Communication Map

Use this map to plan your communication.

Who

For whom is the communication intended?

When and How Often

When will the communication be sent, and how often?

What

What's the message or topic to be communicated?

How

What method (or methods) of delivery will be used?

From Whom

Who will be communicating the message or topic? From whom will the communication come?

Status

What's the status of the communication?

Source: © 2021 by Jenice Pizzuto and Steven Carney.

Figure 3.1: IMPACT implementation team communication map.

We recommend that the systems-level implementation team take on the task of communication to align and keep clear, coherent messaging. The goal is to keep others informed of what is happening with the innovation, what actions are in place, and what impact they are having. Successful districts design a communication plan that includes who will be informed, when they will be informed, what method of communication will be used (digital communication, face-to-face communication, districtwide communication, presentation, and so on), and which team members will provide the communication. We advise implementation teams to consider three broad areas when developing a strategic and intentional communication system: (1) sharing initial decisions and ongoing progress at regular intervals, (2) presenting data, and (3) obtaining feedback from stakeholders.

Figure 3.2 is a sample communication plan detailing tasks at both the systems level and the building level to plan and direct communications.

Taking time at the start to draft a communication plan is time well spent. We have seen implementation teams use a plan such as this to communicate a clear, concise, and comprehensible (the three Cs!) message about why the innovation is happening, what it is exactly, and how it will unfold. This type of planning includes communicating with the school board and the community. Mapping out the activities prevents surprises, questions, and feelings of being left out or uninformed about changes.

In one change initiative we witnessed, a team of principals created a common slide deck to share with all staff members at all their district's schools at the beginning of the school year. They even partnered up and shared in pairs at each other's schools. This ensured cohesive and clear messaging about the new work and commitment to mission and purpose (they shared the rationale, data, and implementation plan). Additionally, the entire group shared the same information with the school board. The school board was thrilled to get such strong communication and excited about a clear implementation plan to address identified issues.

By thoughtfully updating and sharing with staff, you build and maintain buy-in and sustain commitment to the work. Communicate early, share the rationale, use data to back your decision making, communicate using varied methods on various platforms, be transparent, and have an overall communication plan to keep messaging clear and not miss important details.

COMMUNICATION PLAN

Systems Level

Information to Be Communicated	Who Needs to Know	When and How Often	Method of Communication	Team Member Responsible	Completion Dates	Completed?
Introduction of a new reading intervention program	Teachers, students, parents	Initial announcement, then monthly updates	School assembly, letters home, school website	Literacy coordinator	Start of term; monthly thereafter	Yes
Training sessions for new educational technology	Teachers, IT staff	Two weeks before training sessions	Email, staff meetings	Tech integration specialist	Prior to training dates	Yes
Policy changes regarding homework	Teachers, students, parents	As changes are implemented	School newsletter, parent-teacher meetings, school website	Vice principal	Upon policy change approval	No
Results from student assessments	Teachers, administration	After each grading period	Email, staff meetings	Assessment coordinator	End of each grading period	Yes
Opportunities for extracurricular activities	Students, parents	Start of each term, then as activities are scheduled	Morning announcements, flyers, school website	Extracurricular activities director	Start of term; ongoing as scheduled	Yes
Updates on school facility improvements	Teachers, students, parents, staff	As developments occur	Bulletin boards, email blasts, PTA meetings	Facilities manager	As each phase of improvement is completed	No

continued ↓

Figure 3.2: Sample implementation team communication plan.

Building Level						
Information to Be Communicated	Who Needs to Know	When and How Often	Method of Communication	Team Member Responsible	Completion Dates	Completed?
Introduction of the new literacy program	Teachers, students, parents	Initial announcement, then biweekly updates	School assembly, letters home, school website	Implementation team	Start of term; biweekly thereafter	Yes
Training schedule for the literacy program	Teachers	One month before training; reminder one week prior to training	Email, staff meetings	Reading specialist	One month before training; one week before training	No
Progress updates on literacy program implementation	Teachers, administration	Monthly updates	Email, staff meetings	Implementation team	End of each month	No
Feedback request on the literacy program	Teachers, students, parents	After first month; end of each term	Surveys, parent-teacher meetings, school website	Reading specialist	After first month; end of each term	No
Showcase of student work from the literacy program	Parents, community members	End of each term	School newsletter, school website, local newspaper	Administration	End of each term	No
Literacy program's impact on student learning	School board, donors	End of the academic year	Presentation at school board meeting, annual report	Administration	End of the academic year	No

Visit **go.SolutionTree.com/schoolimprovement** for a free reproducible version of this figure.

Recognizing How Implementation Teams Are Unique

You may be thinking, "How am I going to get another team going in my already over-burdened multi-team system?" While implementation teams differ from other teams, the work of implementation teams can and should be done. Researchers Higgins, Weiner, and Young (2012) describe the essential difference: "Implementation teams are unlike other conceptions of teams in that members both develop and implement a strategic vision" (p. 366). Their findings and this description align perfectly with our vision of the implementation team as your guiding coalition of champions.

Implementation teams' sole responsibility is to assist in scaling the new innovation and ensure full and effective implementation. They operate as the lever for building knowledge, skills, and attitudes about the change effort. While they do not do all the work, they align resources, contact experts or bring in technical assistance, and use a plan to drive the improvement effort. They utilize aligned teams (systems level and building level) and the implementation plan as tools to hold the system accountable for ensuring adequate implementation support is present. They understand and use stage-based planning to build knowledge and skills.

Unlike other teams, implementation teams primarily focus on developing and enacting a strategic vision for new innovations, ensuring that these are embedded into daily practice. This is not just an operational necessity but a growing expectation in the educational landscape. Increasingly, grant funders and new program initiatives are recognizing the importance of dedicated implementation teams and requiring detailed plans that outline how such teams will execute programs to achieve intended outcomes. This shift underscores the critical role of implementation teams in translating strategic plans into tangible results. Without a committed team to shepherd these new initiatives, the likelihood that they successfully integrate into the fabric of daily educational practice significantly diminishes.

At the onset, an implementation team may be a small group of key stakeholders who will work together to complete the tasks associated with the *Decide* stage of the IMPACT implementation framework (chapter 4, page 93). However, once implementation moves into the *Plan and Prepare* stage, you will likely need to expand the team to include implementers, especially those who have influence with their role group. Many schools may not have the time nor the capacity to create yet another team; in this case, they might sunset existing teams or repurpose team structures to add the implementation responsibilities. Regardless of the team's genesis, it is important that schools expressly protect the implementation process from the mundane tasks that often find their way onto agendas.

Additionally, implementation teams aren't the same as professional learning communities (PLCs). Implementation team members commonly encounter misunderstandings between implementation teams and the kinds of collaborative teams found in PLCs. PLCs are "schools that empower educators to work collaboratively in recurring cycles of collective inquiry and action research to achieve better results for the students they serve" (Solution Tree, n.d.). While PLCs include collaborative teams, they should not be reduced to those teams and, therefore, should not be conflated with implementation teams. The skills and dispositions necessary for success in PLCs and implementation teams often align, but their purposes, structures, and intended outcomes differ. Figure 3.3 provides an at-a-glance reference you can use to explain the differences to colleagues and other stakeholder groups.

Conclusion

Team member learning is an essential component of the implementation of an evidence-based program. At its core, then, an implementation team is rooted in a learning and improvement mindset. This team learning approach enhances participation and improves the propensity to spread and sustain the new work. Educators and authors Fullan and Gallagher (2020) remind us, "You have to treat implementation as a learning proposition, not as a matter of executing policy" (p. 118). Implementation teams are charged with supporting the change and ensuring that implementers gain the knowledge and skills to deploy the innovation systematically and systemically.

Having administration and staff work together across the system horizontally and vertically is a collaborative venture. Teams of people who have diverse perspectives and different functions within the organization ensure that the innovation can become firmly established in the day-to-day practice of the implementers. Building implementation teams requires focusing not only on roles, responsibilities, and logistics but also on team behaviors and characteristics. As you saw in this chapter's vignette (page 59), Principal Carter tripped over the truth that her school needed to not only focus on the what of positive behavioral interventions and supports, but also build an implementation team to scale their implementation.

IMPLEMENTATION TEAM

A collaborative team of people accountable to
the success of the implementation

versus

PLC

Schools engaging in the ongoing process of working collaboratively
using collective inquiry and action research to improve
teaching skills and students' academic performance

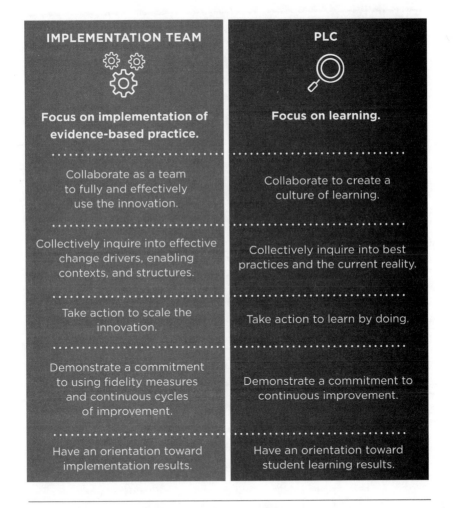

IMPLEMENTATION TEAM	PLC
Focus on implementation of evidence-based practice.	**Focus on learning.**
Collaborate as a team to fully and effectively use the innovation.	Collaborate to create a culture of learning.
Collectively inquire into effective change drivers, enabling contexts, and structures.	Collectively inquire into best practices and the current reality.
Take action to scale the innovation.	Take action to learn by doing.
Demonstrate a commitment to using fidelity measures and continuous cycles of improvement.	Demonstrate a commitment to continuous improvement.
Have an orientation toward implementation results.	Have an orientation toward student learning results.

Source: © 2020 by Jenice Pizzuto and Steven Carney.

Figure 3.3: Implementation teams versus PLCs.

Reflect on Building Effective Implementation Teams

Begin this activity by completing the template independently. Then partner up with a teammate, share your responses, and discuss any differences and similarities. Make revisions as necessary to reach full understanding of the concepts.

Describe the importance of building implementation teams.	
Define what implementation teams are.	
List voices and groups that need representation.	

Map Essential Team Behaviors and Characteristics

This systems-level team activity will help your organization determine which of the implementation team behaviors and characteristics are necessary for the design of implementation teams. Complete the following process to build equity of voice and surface different perspectives.

1. Independently review the team characteristics and behaviors list in chapter 3 (page 69).

2. Independently list team characteristics and behaviors you feel are critical to your organization in scaling the new work.

3. Form pairs (partner A and partner B). Or if you have a large team, consider using triads (partners A, B, and C).

4. Have partners take turns sharing their lists and listening.

5. Once they've completed sharing their lists with each other, have the partners discuss their lists for five to ten minutes.

6. Have each pair or triad create an agreed-on list of ideal critical attributes using the following diagram as a brainstorming and discussion guide.

**The Most Critical Implementation Team Behaviors
and Characteristics to Your Organization**

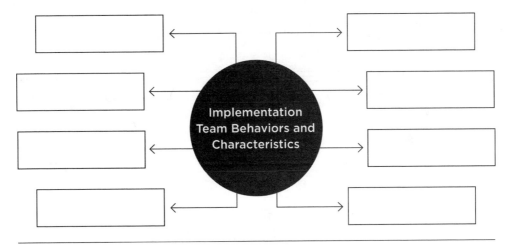

Source: © 2022 by Jenice Pizzuto and Steven Carney.

7. Reconvene with the wider team to share the lists. Use the Fist to Five consensus-building tool (page 77) to gauge agreement and identify the essential behaviors and characteristics that the whole team aligns with.

8. Discuss implications and opportunities based on the agreed-on attributes.

9. Document the final list of essential behaviors and characteristics for future reference and action planning.

Assess Individual Characteristics and Behaviors

Once your team has identified the most critical team characteristics and behaviors, use the following chart to self-reflect and determine your areas of strength, as well as opportunities for growth. Remember, this is *not* a checklist; no one person is going to fulfill all areas.

Ideal Team Member Characteristics and Behaviors			
Characteristic	Rocking It *"This is me!"*	Striving *"I'm trying!"*	Not Me *"We can't all be everything!"*
Curious: Demonstrates curiosity over closure			
Humble: Exhibits humility over pride			
Collaborative: Operates with a mindset of cocreation			
Learning: Reads widely, is eager to learn, and applies new learning as rapidly as possible			
Inclusive: Is interested in hearing other people's views and revising their own			
Growth minded: Uses a growth mindset and has cognitive flexibility and mental agility			
Multifaceted: Has a variety of strengths (This way, the team as a whole can be successful.)			
Championing: Champions the innovation			
Actively participating: Participates in the design of the implementation plan			
Capacity building: Creates capacity, coherence, and alignment, and builds shared understanding			
Experienced: Has deep expertise in the innovation (or is a committed learner)			
Change making: Catalyzes change by diagnosing problems before, during, and after initial implementation			
Supportive: Provides solutions, supports the process, and contributes resources			
Systems thinking: Does systems-level planning and site and building development work			

page 1 of 2

Characteristic	Rocking It "This is me!"	Striving "I'm trying!"	Not Me "We can't all be everything!"
Data driven: Uses data to solve problems and address context issues, site-based barriers, or resource needs			
Facilitative: Uses protocols, facilitation tools, improvement cycles, and the IMPACT implementation framework to support the implementation			
Adaptive: Anticipates and prevents issues, identifies risks, and develops strategies			
Implementation focused: Is involved in the change and deserves to have a voice in the change; is the communication loop and support for the implementers			
Insightful: Considers contextual factors that executive leadership may not be aware of			
Unifying: Clarifies goals, establishes collaborations, supports the development of resources, and communicates readiness for change			
Resourceful: Helps system leaders and stakeholders anticipate resource and organization needs and plan for resources, including human and capital resources			
Problem solving: Resolves issues as new ways of working are being developed			
Creative: Creates supportive conditions that improve implementation of the innovation			

Source: © 2022 by Jenice Pizzuto and Steven Carney.

"You Can't Do This Work Alone" Learning Journey Map

Use the following two questions to prompt active discussion and thoughtful responses, helping your team assess current practices and plan for future development. This is an opportunity for collective reflection and strategic action.

Together, review the concepts and practices from chapter 3 that your organization has already implemented. Discuss the effectiveness of your leadership and the progress of your implementation efforts. Use the questions to guide a rich conversation, and document your team's insights, commitments, and objectives in the learning journey map.

1. What concepts and practices from chapter 3 does our district or school currently have in place (with varying degrees of implementation)?

2. What observations and insights are we making about our leadership, leadership team, or organizational implementation efforts?

Team Takeaways *New* learning, insights, and notices	Team Commitment Concepts, ideas, and practices we *commit to developing*	Team Practice Strategies, processes, and tools we plan to *learn and practice*	Team Reflection Strategies, processes, tools, concepts, ideas, and so on we want to *go deeper into and share early successes on*	Team Goals Strategies, processes, tools, concepts, ideas, and so on we want to *fully operationalize* through a commitment of time, resources, and policy

PART 2

You've made it to part 2 of *Implement With IMPACT: A Strategic Framework for Leading School and District Initiatives*! We applaud you and your team (or teams) for taking the time to build your knowledge, skills, and attitudes through the foundational content you encountered in part 1. By cognitively engaging in the activities and tools in chapters 1–3, you and your team have intentionally been developing a learning and improvement mindset. Bring this attitude of learning and improvement to your team and to your system.

When people in the system have space to learn, grow, fail, learn, and improve, they can master new skills. Invariably, they will encounter setbacks and challenges on the path to mastery. However, this supportive culture will maximize sustainable growth.

Part 2 is about learning by doing. Here, you and your team will engage in activities and use tools to identify your change and get it implemented right and well. You'll encounter the IMPACT implementation planning template, which you'll use to plan, track, and support the implementation along the way. Each chapter of part 2 introduces one stage of the IMPACT implementation framework and provides a list of key objectives to complete for that stage. The four stages of the IMPACT implementation framework are:

1. *Decide*

2. *Plan and Prepare*

3. *Implement*

4. *Spread and Sustain*

Use all you learned in chapters 1–3 about change and the construction of an implementation team (your guiding coalition of champions) as you move through the implementation process. Remember, using a framework and planning tools keeps the system from getting stuck in analysis paralysis. Providing a clear, comprehensive approach in an engaging, positive, and respectful manner will build a team that collaborates and comes to agreement at each stage of the implementation. Use the tools, set the expectations, and get ready to collaborate!

――――――― *chapter 4* ―――――――

THE *DECIDE* STAGE

The closer you can match a practice or program to your students'
needs, the greater the possibility it will lead to the desired outcome.

—IRIS Center

Do you know the parable of the blind men and the elephant? The gist of it is a group of blind men encounter an elephant and try to imagine what the animal is like by touching it. Each man grabs hold of a different part of the elephant and describes what the elephant is like to the other blind men.

- One man grabs hold of one of the elephant's tusks and declares an elephant is like a spear.

- Another grabs hold of the elephant's trunk and declares an elephant is like a snake.

- Another touches one of the elephant's ears and declares an elephant is like a fan.

- Another feels the elephant's knees and declares an elephant is like a tree.

- Another holds the elephant's tail and declares an elephant is like a rope.

- Finally, the last blind man feels the elephant's side and declares an elephant is like a wall.

The parable illustrates how important perspective is when a group needs to see the whole picture. Each member's personal perspective is built from their limited experiences; thus, when you rely too heavily on any one person's perception of what is right, you are only capable of seeing a portion of the whole. It can be easy to get stuck in your own individual work within the learning organization. If the blind men had put all their experiences together, they would have come to a better understanding of what the elephant actually looked like.

The parable of the blind men serves as an apt metaphor for the *Decide* stage of the implementation process. Just as the blind men each had a different perspective on the elephant based on the part they touched, team members may have varying perspectives on the need for and nature of change within the organization. Much like piecing together the comprehensive picture of the elephant, the *Decide* stage involves combining each team member's unique insights to form a well-rounded understanding of the situation and identify the problem, the solution, and associated factors of success. Together, you are better, and with a strong team, you can see the entire elephant before you. In the *Decide* stage, you will take steps to see the whole picture and include diverse perspectives.

In this chapter, we start by identifying key activities and objectives of the *Decide* stage, as well as introducing the IMPACT implementation planning template and providing guidance about assembling implementation teams. We then provide a variety of tools teams can choose from to facilitate naming the problem and the need for change in their organization. Once they've accomplished this, teams turn their focus to developing the goal and identifying evidence-based solutions. Finally, we note that teams must assess their organization's readiness for implementation to ensure successful adoption of new initiatives.

Gearing Up for Success

This chapter focuses on the first stage, the *Decide* stage. Consider figure 4.1, which reintroduces the IMPACT implementation framework stages you encountered in chapter 1 (page 28). Review each of the four stages and get ready to dig into the *Decide* stage.

The *Decide* stage launches your implementation effort and builds the road map for your implementation. During this stage, your team engages in several processes that will lead to consequential decisions throughout the entire implementation effort. The five steps of the *Decide* stage are as follows.

1. **Assemble your implementation team:** Gather a team (or teams) that will lead and support the implementation effort.

2. **Name the problem and need for change (*why*):** Clearly articulate the issue that needs to be addressed, and understand the underlying reasons for the need for change.

3. **Develop the goal:** Define specific, measurable goals for what the implementation seeks to achieve.

4. **Identify the evidence-based solutions:** Explore and select evidence-based solutions or strategies that will help reach the defined goals.

5. **Assess organizational readiness:** Determine if the organization is prepared to effectively support and engage in the change process.

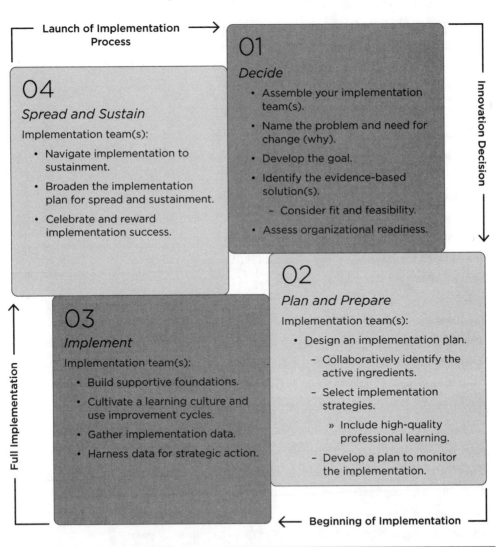

IMPACT
Implementation Process

Launch of Implementation Process →

Innovation Decision ↓

Full Implementation ↑

← Beginning of Implementation

04
Spread and Sustain

Implementation team(s):

- Navigate implementation to sustainment.
- Broaden the implementation plan for spread and sustainment.
- Celebrate and reward implementation success.

01
Decide

- Assemble your implementation team(s).
- Name the problem and need for change (why).
- Develop the goal.
- Identify the evidence-based solution(s).
  - Consider fit and feasibility.
- Assess organizational readiness.

03
Implement

Implementation team(s):

- Build supportive foundations.
- Cultivate a learning culture and use improvement cycles.
- Gather implementation data.
- Harness data for strategic action.

02
Plan and Prepare

Implementation team(s):

- Design an implementation plan.
  - Collaboratively identify the active ingredients.
  - Select implementation strategies.
    » Include high-quality professional learning.
  - Develop a plan to monitor the implementation.

Source: © 2021 by Jenice Pizzuto and Steven Carney.

Figure 4.1: IMPACT implementation framework stages.

The *Decide* stage is the time to build infrastructure to make sure the system can do what the implementation plan intends it to do. As the team embarks on the *Decide* stage, leaders must create the conditions for success by planning for the implementers' learning: adopting a learning and improvement mindset, being ready to make and fund decisions, including the school board and key stakeholders early and often, using the team to address setbacks, and being deliberate in the endeavor.

Taking these important steps, and addressing all the critical elements in the *Decide* stage, helps steer the organization toward success and away from the graveyard of good ideas. You probably know of or have been part of adoption processes that have ended up being abandoned, put aside, or stalled. This happens when well-meaning organizations make hasty decisions and latch onto inappropriate solutions before they thoroughly understand the problem to be solved and the human, financial, and physical resources that are available to address the issue. These organizations must understand the problem well before innovation implementation takes place. While the work completed during this stage can seem arduous, methodically completing these tasks is a valuable investment of time and energy.

The *Decide* stage is all about understanding the problem to be solved, selecting the best possible solution, and ensuring that the solution can be implemented. This chapter covers the steps in the *Decide* stage. Table 4.1 introduces the *Decide* stage's key activities and objectives through the IMPACT lens. You and your team will find this tool valuable to prepare for the stage. It describes what outcomes result from the major activities that take place. Use this overview to help key stakeholders or staff understand the purpose of the stage and build deliberately developmental implementation. Although this table covers the key activities to include in an IMPACT implementation plan, the table is not comprehensive. There are other activities involved in this stage, as described throughout the chapter. Review the activities in the table and check your plan to ensure you have built-in protocols, time, and resources to meet each objective.

Decide Stage Decisions

Now is the time to make decisions, select staff, identify and allocate funding sources, communicate with key stakeholders, and select your implementation team. This is the time to ensure the team understands your organization, utilizes systems thinking, and pays attention to and plans for the human elements of change. If the team has not done so yet, now is the time for it to select a change theory to utilize as the team designs the implementation plan (see chapter 2, page 41).

Table 4.1: *Decide* Stage Key Activities and Objectives

IMPACT	Key Activities	Key Objectives
Inclusion	Identify stakeholders responsible for the change, and engage them throughout the process to determine needs and readiness.	Foster a sense of shared responsibility and buy-in among stakeholders; identify needs and readiness for change.
Meaningful Leadership	Identify infrastructures that provide time and processes designed to support systems change, practice, team development, and resources for the innovation.	Develop systems that support effective implementation of the innovation; build capacity for leadership at all levels.
Professional Learning	Identify support (for example, time allocated and coaches) and plan for professional learning to occur in an ongoing and embedded manner, and provide structures that support learning about the change.	Plan to build knowledge and skills among implementers to effectively implement the innovation; ensure ongoing support for professional learning.
Assess and Adjust	Identify the problem to be solved, conduct audits, and assess the current system infrastructure and the fit and feasibility of the identified solution or EBP.	Develop a deep understanding of the problem to be solved; identify potential solutions, and determine feasibility and fit within the current system.
Collective Efficacy	Identify and recognize the problem as a shared problem, collectively evaluate possible solutions, and cocreate shared goals to solve the problem.	Foster a sense of shared responsibility for the problem and its solution; develop a shared vision and goals for addressing the problem.
Team	Identify implementation teams to serve the system throughout all stages, up and down the organization.	Develop an effective implementation team to support the innovation at all stages of the implementation process.

Visit *go.SolutionTree.com/schoolimprovement* for a free reproducible version of this table.

During this stage, the leadership team clarifies and approves the implementation's purpose, need, and key outcomes. The organization will engage in several processes that lead to multiple decisions.

Figure 4.2 (page 98) lists the major decisions to include during the *Decide* stage (in no particular order) and provides room for teams to record notes about their progress. It's important to note that this is *not* a checklist to assign to a team member but a series of discussions the implementation team will collectively engage in and make decisions about. If you'd like to note when items have been completed, you may list the date in the space indicated for each decision. While this list is robust, you may encounter other items to address to match your climate, culture, and context. We like to say *T.I.R.*: "Thinking is required." Meet as a team, think, discuss, and decide together.

Decide Stage Decisions		
Decisions	**Notes**	**Date Completed**
Identify and decide who will be on the systems-level and building-level implementation teams.		
Conduct a needs assessment, audit current practices, or conduct a survey (collect multiple data).		
Build clarity on the why. Why is this important work?		
Identify the problems that need to be solved.		
Explore solutions (EBPs) to address the identified problems; explore several alternatives and ensure they meet the need as determined by data.		
Collectively identify and agree on the solution to address the identified problems; consider capacity (human and capital), culture, and climate before final selection.		
Identify and decide on the fit and feasibility of the innovation. Can it be implemented as designed? Does it fit the climate, culture, and context of the organization?		
Identify and decide who will be implementing the innovation and who is involved in the change.		
Identify the collective strengths of the implementers to inform implementation planning. Do the staff have innovation-specific knowledge? Do teams have the skills to scale the new behaviors?		
Identify organizational facilitators, and link them to the solution (for example, coaches, funding allocated, time dedicated, and materials purchased).		
Identify organizational barriers, and note to address them in the *Plan and Prepare* stage.		
Decide how the implementation team will work together (how often, how long, funding to work, and use of agendas and tools).		
Identify and decide on team communication structures.		

Figure 4.2: *Decide* stage decisions.

*Visit **go.SolutionTree.com/schoolimprovement** for a free reproducible version of this figure.*

Each stage contains a decisions chart to guide your team to capture progress and identify next steps. Looking at the chart, consider this: "Are there items that are strengths for my organization? Are there items that are stretches for my organization?" Figure 4.2 features the major decisions to be made during the *Decide* stage, and if your team covers them all, you will be on your way to sustainability.

IMPACT Implementation Planning Template

Implementation plans are widely used across sectors to provide road maps for successfully introducing new initiatives and ensuring they are effectively integrated into the system. In K–12 education, an implementation plan is essential to guide decision making, manage resources, ensure stakeholder buy-in, and achieve the desired outcomes. Using a planning template ensures the implementation is not person or leader dependent, and it supports scaling the innovation while adjusting to changes in staff or context. Developing the implementation plan sets the stage for implementing the new innovation successfully and with integrity.

The implementation planning template provides space to describe how the new innovation aligns with the school or district's mission and vision, identify the initiative's specific goals and objectives, and establish measurable outcomes to assess the initiative's effectiveness. The plan also allows for the identification of potential barriers to implementation and the development of strategies to overcome them. By utilizing the implementation planning template, school leaders can ensure that the new innovation is integrated into the existing infrastructure and that staff, students, and other stakeholders are prepared for the change.

The IMPACT implementation planning template provides space to record and describe the following.

- **The goal:** The team should answer the question, "Where are we going?" Stating a goal that is collectively agreed on and widely understood by the practitioners and leaders experiencing the change is paramount to gaining and maintaining momentum to address the identified problem.

- **The problem and rationale:** A well-defined problem statement is critical to the success of the change, so the team must identify why the challenge or issue needs to be addressed through change implementation. This occurs during the *Decide* stage and serves as the foundation for effective planning and execution of the initiative.

- **Evidence-based solutions:** This process includes the identification of a solution's active ingredients—the non-negotiable elements that underlie its effectiveness. Understanding these active ingredients is critical to successful implementation and evaluation of the innovation's effectiveness.

- **Implementation strategies:** Implementation of an evidence-based innovation requires using strategies that prioritize human-centered design. The IMPACT implementation framework offers guidelines for developing effective implementation strategies. By applying this framework, organizations can better navigate the complexities of implementation, optimizing their chances of success.

- **Monitoring strategies:** Assessing and monitoring implementation fidelity is crucial to ensuring that an evidence-based innovation is implemented as intended, particularly in the context of K–12 education, where students are the primary stakeholders. It helps identify any deviations from the intended implementation process and ensures the team takes corrective action where required. Ultimately, this guarantees that the innovation is executed with high integrity, which leads to positive outcomes for students and supports the overarching mission of the educational institution.

The IMPACT implementation planning template is a living document that all teams follow throughout the implementation process. Therefore, during each of the four stages (*Decide, Plan and Prepare, Implement,* and *Spread and Sustain*), implementation teams will record their major actions and decisions in the template. Figure 4.3 shows how a team might complete the IMPACT implementation planning template.

The planning template is a systems-level document that all teams access. While building-level implementation teams may make adapted versions (or make building-specific plans) to meet their contexts, they maintain adherence to achieving the overall goal. In this way, context and culture are honored. For example, we have seen IMPACT implementation plans that maintain the same goal but have individual elementary, middle, and high school versions. While the schools all work toward the same goal and even identify the same EBP, they customize the plan to the needs of each level. The critical commonalities are the shared goal and adherence to the plan components.

The systems-level implementation team reviews the plan at least three times a year with the building-level teams until the innovation is successfully in place. Feedback and data from the building-level teams, which meet at least monthly in the beginning, inform the system of necessary adaptations and adjustments as well as

Inclusion | Meaningful Leadership | Professional Learning | Assess and Adjust | Collective Efficacy | Team

Implementation Planning Template

Implementation Team Members: ☑ System ☑ School

- **System:** *Dr. Jane Smith, director of curriculum*
- **School:** *Mr. John Doe, principal*

Goal: Where are we going? (State the goal in SMART format.)

By the end of the academic year, increase student reading proficiency in the third grade by 15 percent, as measured by standardized reading assessment.

Stage	Problem	Evidence-Based Solutions	Implementation Strategies	Monitoring Strategies
Decide	*Reading proficiency in third grade has stagnated, affecting students' long-term academic success.*	*Implementation of a structured literacy program*		
Plan and Prepare		*Direct instruction, phonemic awareness, phonics, vocabulary, and reading comprehension strategies*	*Professional development for teachers, literacy coaching, and classroom resource allocation*	*Regular formative assessments, teacher feedback sessions, and literacy coaching check-ins*
Implement		*Tailoring instruction to individual student needs, integrating culturally relevant texts*	*Parental engagement workshops, reading buddies program*	*Reading progress tracking software, monthly reading proficiency dashboards*
Spread and Sustain		*Funding for ongoing teacher training, updated reading materials*	*Community literacy events, ongoing teacher collaboration sessions*	*Annual standardized assessments, continuous professional development logs*

Source: © 2022 by Jenice Pizzuto and Steven Carney.

Figure 4.3: Sample IMPACT implementation planning template.

recognize accomplishments and progress. Together, the teams record all adaptations on the plan and maintain progress toward the goal.

In the *Decide* stage, the systems-level implementation team will complete the following sections of the planning template.

- List team members' names.
- Name the problem and why change is needed.
- Develop the goal.
- Name the proposed solution (EBP).

Because the IMPACT implementation planning template is intended to be used in all four stages of the implementation effort, it appears at the end of each chapter in part 2 for teams to record their actions and progress. Have teams utilize this organic tool at least three times a year to support, guide, and monitor the implementation of the selected EBP.

Assembling Your Implementation Team

Implementation teams guide implementation efforts. They plan the implementation with the leadership team. Including implementers in designing the implementation empowers organizations to uncover barriers, maximize facilitators (things that make the work easier and propel its success), and build buy-in and clarity. Exploring and acknowledging the resources currently in place—such as staffing, funds, previous training, policy, beliefs, and culture—is powerful. Acknowledging what is in place supports the change effort, avoids taking unnecessary actions, and recognizes staff for previous work. Quite often, teams find that they already have a number of necessary resources in place; they may not necessarily need to start from scratch. Approaching the implementation process through an appreciative inquiry lens builds credibility for what the educational institution has already put into place, recognizes and honors the people and the work completed to pave the way for new work, and brings team members together.

Recognizing and naming the facilitators already in place also keeps the teams going when the work can feel overwhelming. Consider the following examples of facilitators.

- Coaching structures that are in place for staff training
- Funding that is in place to provide substitutes for staff training
- Time that is allocated for professional learning

- Building leadership that aligns with the vision and onboarding
- Funding that is available for new materials

During the first stage of implementation, you may only have a leadership-level implementation team formed; this is the team that will do the work of the *Decide* stage. While building-level teams do not have to be actively involved in the *Decide* stage, the systems-level implementation team must have building-level representatives. For example, when working with school districts, we often see the districts form systems-level implementation teams to understand the problem to be solved and select an appropriate evidence-based practice, but these teams always include a good representation of the implementers' voices. (For a refresher on the ideal implementation team configurations at the systems level and building level, see page 68.)

Implementation team selection is a critical step in the *Decide* stage. Review the components in chapter 3 (page 59)—ideal team configurations, team composition, team availability and commitment, time for implementation teamwork, team roles and expectations, and communication—as you prepare to select your implementation team members. And consider the following tips for designing and forming the implementation team.

- Explicitly outline the scope of work, and develop a job description for team members.
- Develop an application process that provides interested colleagues with an opportunity to share their interest, experience, and expertise specifically related to the scope of work.
- Identify if, and how, you will incentivize participation on the implementation team.
- Identify potential funding sources for the new program.
- Remove barriers to meeting, and allocate time and space.
- Establish a meeting schedule and expected time commitment.

Once you've formed the team, take time to identify why the team has been formed and to become crystal clear on the team's purpose (that is, to develop and support the implementation plan). The implementation team will develop a clear, concise, and comprehensible plan that moves from identifying the problem and solution to designing implementation strategies, monitoring implementation, and fully implementing and sustaining the new program, practice, or strategy.

A final note on including implementers' voices in the design process: Once the implementers are on the team, their representation is equally valued in the decision-making process. The systems-level implementation team is an egalitarian decision-making body. The implementers are there not to say yes to everything but to identify barriers, surface new opportunities and solutions, monitor and adjust the plan, and make intelligent adaptations with the team. Systems-level implementation team members collectively analyze data and adjust the implementation plan as needed.

In closing this section, we want to call attention to an exciting outcome of cocreating an implementation plan with horizontal and vertical implementation teams: the power of acquiring skills together. An embedded feature of colearning and growing toward a shared goal of increased implementer capacity and innovation effectiveness is it inspires staff and uplifts the organization. Implementation teams become adept at learning together and asking staff, "How is it going?" and "What do you need?" to get to the next level of implementation. The implementation teams intentionally and collectively build their knowledge, skills, and attitudes and support the development of the staff's knowledge, skills, and attitudes.

Naming the Problem and the Need for Change (the Why)

One reason improvement efforts fail is that schools spend inadequate time understanding the problem they are trying to solve. Increasingly high expectations and shrinking resources often lead to expedited solutions that may or may not effectively address the real problem. Jumping to quick fixes and searching for silver bullets are issues educational organizations constantly face. Additionally, educational organizations fail to take the time to determine the right evidence-based solutions to address the problem and improve outcomes. This often leads to initiative overload and the adoption of multiple programs and practices that are, consequently, implemented poorly. The adopt-and-abandon cycle continues.

To stop initiative overload and end the adopt-and-abandon cycle, learning- and improvement-focused organizations spend the necessary time in each implementation stage, especially the *Decide* stage. Fixsen, Blase, and Van Dyke (2019) note that "implementation will take an average of two to four years to reach sustainability and significant results" (pp. 62–63). To get lasting change from the right innovation designed to accurately address the real problem, avoid the quick-fix trap, and give implementation time.

Refer to your IMPACT implementation planning template ("Name the problem and *why* this problem needs to be solved"). It is time that you and your systems-level implementation team decide on the problem that needs to be solved. To avoid what researchers Anthony S. Bryk, Louis M. Gomez, Alicia Grunow, and Paul G. LeMahieu (2015) describe as *solutionitis*, "the propensity to jump quickly on a solution before fully understanding the exact problem to be solved" (p. 24), we suggest using a robust problem identification process. Several resources and tools are available to support a rigorous and valid problem identification process. Which tool you use is not as important as making sure that the process addresses all the areas we have discussed and that the team avoids solutionitis. Resist the urge to move forward with a hunch or feeling. To avoid relying on hunches or letting biases filter into the process, it is paramount that you gather the team, select a problem identification process, and utilize that process to identify the problem. Ensure the tool you select includes (1) identifying the problem, (2) assessing the magnitude of the problem, and (3) exploring the root causes of the problem (auditing current practices).

Let's consider a few tools you might use to support problem identification. The first is a simple four-step process (Chevallier, 2016).

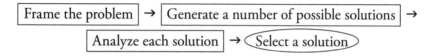

The objective here is to pinpoint the problem through data analysis, propose multiple evidence-based solutions, assess each for fit and feasibility (considering resources like staffing, funding, and overall capacity), and select the most suitable evidence-based solution.

Figure 4.4 (page 106) illustrates the fishbone diagram, a causal diagram commonly used to examine critical influencing factors. This problem-solving tool, developed by professor Kaoru Ishikawa (1990) and published in his book *Introduction to Quality Control*, supports a group to clearly identify a problem and its root causes in a team format. The tool honors and engages multiple stakeholders' points of view. Once completed, the diagram resembles the skeleton of a fish. Teams undertake the following steps to complete the diagram.

1. Identify the problem on the head of the fish.

2. Label possible root causes of the problem on the ribs, which branch out from each side of the spine.

3. Consider three basic types of causes.

   a. Physical causes (Tangible, material items failed in some way.)

   b. Human causes (People did something wrong or did not do something that was needed; these may lead to physical causes.)

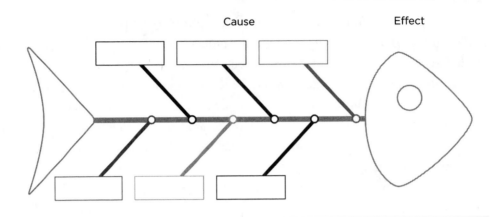

Figure 4.4: Fishbone diagram.

*Visit **go.SolutionTree.com/schoolimprovement** for a free reproducible version of this figure.*

    c.   Organizational causes (A system, process, or policy used for making decisions or doing the work of an organization was faulty.)

  4. Investigate patterns of negative causes to find hidden flaws in the system and discover specific actions that contributed to the problem. This means that root cause analysis often reveals more than one root cause.

Author and coach Tony Jeary's (2011) SWOT analysis is a helpful tool for understanding the internal factors (strengths and weaknesses) and external factors (opportunities and threats) influencing an organization's vision, goals, and student learning outcomes. Teams discuss the questions in each quadrant to identify the organization's strengths, weaknesses, opportunities, and threats. Figure 4.5 shares a sample SWOT analysis.

Detailed descriptions of how to use each problem identification protocol are easily accessed via the internet. Select a problem identification tool and follow the process with the implementation team.

Once the systems-level implementation team has completed the problem identification process, go back to the IMPACT implementation planning template and complete the section prompting you to name the problem and why the problem needs to be solved. We highly recommend taking time to define the why (the need for change) of the innovation selection and the change your organization is embarking on. In his 2009 TED Talk titled "How Great Leaders Inspire Action," author and motivational speaker Simon Sinek introduces the Golden Circle model as an explanation of why some organizations flourish. Sinek argues that an organization's

Strengths	Weaknesses
What positive internal factors are in our control?	*What do we need to do to improve?*
What strengths does our system have or show?	*Do the staff have the necessary knowledge, skills, and attitudes?*
What evidence do we have that this is true?	*Have training or learning events been conducted? How do we know?*
	Is mastery present? How do we know?
	What are our weaknesses?
Opportunities	**Threats**
What are the best opportunities to make an impact and improve?	*What barriers will stop, stall, or impede progress?*
What do student data indicate is a priority need?	*Is there adequate staffing available?*
What do surveys indicate is a priority need?	*Is there capacity for new learning (human and capital) available?*
What do the state or province, community, school board, and stakeholders see as a priority need? What facilitators are in place to support a change?	*Is leadership onboard? Will it change?*
What new or redistributed funding may be available?	

Figure 4.5: Sample SWOT analysis.

*Visit **go.SolutionTree.com/schoolimprovement** for a free reproducible version of this figure.*

constituents are motivated not by the features, functions, or benefits of its products or services (the what) but by the underlying problem that those products or services solve (the why). He emphasizes that organizations that cannot articulate their why cannot successfully define the need for their products or services.

Sinek's (2009) Golden Circle model is grounded in neuroscience research showing that messages that communicate with the limbic system—the part of the brain responsible for behavioral and emotional responses—tend to elicit more positive responses. This is because the limbic system processes information based on feelings rather than facts or details. Therefore, starting with the why of a product or service taps into the part of the brain that influences behavior and inspires action. By connecting to the emotional part of stakeholders' brains, the *why* statement can be an effective tool for building passion and urgency for change and ensuring successful implementation of an innovation.

Developing the organization's why comes after understanding the problem during the *Decide* stage. The *why statement* (or problem statement) serves as the basis for identifying the evidence-based program, practice, or policy. The statement should deeply resonate with stakeholders and connect with their emotional response system.

The statement should also provide a clear understanding of the change the organization is trying to bring about and the implementation strategies that the organization will use to achieve the change. It is important to draft multiple versions of the *why* statement if needed and land on the one most team members can *feel*. Team members must feel motivated and inspired to understand the required change and to support effective implementation strategies.

The *why* statement should connect with the hearts and minds of the team members and build passion and urgency for the change. The statement should resonate with stakeholders, and anyone on the implementation team should be able to easily describe it to community members, staff members, or colleagues. Overly complex statements can lead to confusion, misinterpretation, or a general lack of buy-in. Be sure to give the statement the elevator test: can you clearly and succinctly describe the rationale on a one-way elevator trip to the sixth floor? If not, tighten it up and try again!

For example, let's see how a school district embarking on implementing response to intervention (RTI) in elementary English language arts took time to unpack their *why*. The implementation teams used a data protocol to examine the past three years' systems-level reading data and collectively reviewed all English language arts training and professional development over the same time period. Each person then crafted their own definition for why RTI would meet the problem stated; they shared their definition first with a partner and then with their table team. Next, each table team collectively wrote out one definition and shared it with the entire group of five table teams. In this way, all ideas surfaced, all voices were acknowledged, and collective agreement and alignment developed.

Now, the school district had five solid definitions that utilized data, implementer input, evidence of previous training and learning opportunities, and the climates and cultures of all buildings. The teams each took these definitions back to their respective buildings for review and final input. After the building-level implementation teams shared and refined their versions, all teams reconvened with the systems-level implementation team to craft one definition that articulated their why: they were adopting RTI to address intransigent low reading scores across elementary schools.

Finally, each building-level team took the final version of the district's why back to their building and shared it with all impacted staff members. To emphasize the systems-level commitment to adopting this new evidence-based practice, building leaders from the other implementation teams (principals and coaches) copresented the rationale at each school. The teams wanted to communicate the cohesive and collective agreement on the implementation effort. This process empowered the teams to stay the course when barriers arose, competing initiatives were proposed, or problems surfaced. Their why for using RTI was clear across all buildings and a multitude of staff members, and it allowed participants to own and embrace the vision with clarity.

When it's time to develop your why, use the following process as a guide.

1. **Understand the problem:** Before developing the why, the organization should have a clear understanding of the problem to solve. The organization can do this by conducting research, gathering data, and engaging stakeholders.

2. **Draft multiple versions of the why:** The organization should draft multiple versions of the *why* statement, ensuring that the why connects with stakeholders on an emotional level and inspires action (Sinek, 2009). The statement should be clear, concise, and easy to understand.

3. **Refine the why:** The organization should review and refine the *why* statement based on feedback from team members and stakeholders. The team should revise the statement until it resonates with its members.

4. **Test the why:** The organization should test the *why* statement by giving it the elevator test. Can team members clearly and succinctly describe the why on a one-way elevator trip to the sixth floor? If not, the statement needs to be tightened up and revised (Sinek, 2009).

5. **Communicate the why:** Once the team has developed the *why* statement, they should communicate it to all stakeholders, including staff members, community members, and colleagues. The statement should be used as a tool to build passion and urgency for change and to ensure successful implementation of the organization's innovation.

By following this process, an organization can develop a clear and compelling *why* statement that inspires action and drives positive change.

Developing the Goal

Now that you have identified the problem and identified *why* change is needed, it is time to collectively develop the goal. Collectively developing the goal to address the identified problem supports buy-in and builds goal credibility. Write the goal as a SMART goal; that is, the goal is *strategic and specific, measurable, attainable, results oriented*, and *time bound* (Conzemius & O'Neill, 2014). Consider the following example SMART goal, broken down into its components: by the end of year two of implementing the evidence-based practices, the school district will increase its graduation rate by 10 percent through the implementation of a comprehensive student support program.

- **Strategic and specific:** The goal is clearly defined, with a specific target of increasing the graduation rate by 10 percent.

- **Measurable:** The goal can be quantified by tracking the graduation rate before and after the implementation of the support program.

- **Attainable:** The goal is achievable based on the organization's resources and capabilities.

- **Results oriented:** The goal addresses the district's low graduation rate, which is a significant issue that needs to be resolved.

- **Time bound:** The goal has a specific timeline of achieving the 10 percent increase by the end of a two-year implementation period, which provides time for the plan to take hold and creates a sense of urgency and accountability.

The district will provide support to reach this goal by implementing a comprehensive student support program, such as MTSS and the PLC process. By implementing these EBPs, the district can increase its graduation rate and provide students with the necessary support to succeed academically.

With your systems-level implementation team, develop a SMART goal based on your identified problem. Record the SMART goal in your IMPACT implementation planning template.

Identifying the Evidence-Based Solutions

Once you've developed the goal, it is time to gather evidence and identify the evidence-based solution (that is, the innovation, program, practice, or strategy) that addresses the problem, causation, and needs. Once the implementation team members understand the gap between current practices and identified goals, they can begin exploring and identifying key resources and potential programs and practices that meet evidence requirements. We cannot overemphasize the importance of making an evidence-informed decision about which program, practice, policy, or principle you will implement to address the problem. Examining various resources, including online clearinghouses like the What Works Clearinghouse (https://ies .ed.gov/ncee/wwc), the Education Endowment Foundation (https://education endowmentfoundation.org.uk), Visible Learning (https://visible-learning.org), or the Best Evidence Encyclopedia (https://bestevidence.org) will help you identify possible improvement strategies for potential evidence-based practices. Be thorough in this process; there is absolutely no point in selecting a solution if the system does not have the capacity, skills, or implementation supports necessary to gain the intended results. This is *not* a time to pick what a neighboring district selected or what someone heard about at a conference. It is a time to be a discerning consumer focused on selecting a data-informed solution to the identified problem.

Figure 4.6 provides a chart your team can use to refine your search for an EBP.

Key Questions to Consider as You Gather and Assess Evidence for an EBP	Yes	No	Don't Know	Notes
Is the evidence-based innovation designed to support the population we intend to serve?	☐	☐	☐	
Do we know what type of program or practice we are looking for (for example, one that addresses foundational mathematics skills, reading skills, bullying, social-emotional learning, or development)? How do we know this? What data indicate the need?	☐	☐	☐	
Have we identified the skill or behavior that needs to be addressed (for example, overall mathematics or reading achievement, reading fluency and phonics, or self-regulation)?	☐	☐	☐	
Does the evidence-based innovation allow for intelligent adaptations while maintaining the program's integrity?	☐	☐	☐	
What system, staff, and student implications will the evidence-based innovation have if we implement it?	☐	☐	☐	
Has research that applies to our population been conducted on the evidence-based practice?	☐	☐	☐	
What evidence is available about the EBP?	☐	☐	☐	
What learning gaps is the EBP designed to address? Does it match the identified problem?	☐	☐	☐	
How, by whom, and at what frequency is the EBP designed to be delivered?	☐	☐	☐	
Is the EBP aligned with our learning standards and objectives?	☐	☐	☐	
Other questions the team feels are important:	☐	☐	☐	

Figure 4.6: Key questions to consider to assess an evidence-based practice.

*Visit **go.SolutionTree.com/schoolimprovement** for a free reproducible version of this figure.*

Once you have, as a systems-level team, identified possible EBPs to solve the identified problem, it is time to apply a fit-and-feasibility lens to the proposed solutions. While this step is often minimized and even overlooked, we have found skipping it to be a major cause of later abandonment of selected evidence-based practices. While different proposed solutions may be equally strong, a certain new practice may be too big a lift or simply not a fit for staff's daily routines or the district or school culture. Understanding the students and the culture, climate, and context in which the program or practice will be implemented is important to identifying the right EBP.

Figure 4.7 contains a chart your team can use to assess fit and feasibility.

Key Questions to Process Fit and Feasibility	Yes	No	Don't Know	Notes
Does the EBP fit and align with the culture and values?	☐	☐	☐	
Will the EBP fit with existing programs, practices, and innovations in the school or district?	☐	☐	☐	
Are implementation materials available to guide the implementation of the EBP (manuals, procedures, workbooks)?	☐	☐	☐	
Is technical support available to support the implementation?	☐	☐	☐	
Are professional learning designs provided for staff facilitating and implementing the innovation?	☐	☐	☐	
Are fidelity or monitoring tools available to measure implementation and EBP outcomes?	☐	☐	☐	
Are there current policies or procedures that might hinder or get in the way of effective implementation of the innovation?	☐	☐	☐	
Are human and capital resources available to feasibly implement the innovation with high integrity?	☐	☐	☐	
How much time will it take? Will we have to adjust schedules?	☐	☐	☐	
What are the short-term and long-term costs associated with the EBP?	☐	☐	☐	
Can staff master the required skills? Will they need to gain new knowledge, skills, and attitudes? Who will do this work? How long will it take?	☐	☐	☐	
Is the EBP replicable across our system?	☐	☐	☐	
Can all staff gain mastery of the skills necessary to use the innovation?	☐	☐	☐	

Figure 4.7: Key questions to process fit and feasibility.

*Visit **go.SolutionTree.com/schoolimprovement** for a free reproducible version of this figure.*

Once the team has considered fit and feasibility and determined the solution can successfully be replicated across the system, record the solution to the problem in your IMPACT implementation planning template.

Assessing Organizational Readiness

Assessing readiness for the implementation of evidence-informed innovations is essential in promoting the uptake of EBPs and technologies in K–12 education.

Studies highlight the importance of systematically gauging system and staff willingness and ability to engage in a change process. Planning for and gathering these valuable insights has been shown to better ensure innovative practices' successful adoption and provide for their long-term sustainability. Researchers James-Burdumy and colleagues (2021) conducted a study to assess K–12 schools' readiness to implement EBPs related to social-emotional learning (SEL). These researchers found that schools were most ready to implement SEL practices if they had high levels of teacher and student engagement, as well as great support from school leaders. This study emphasizes the importance of assessing schools' readiness to implement EBPs, particularly in SEL, to improve student outcomes related to social-emotional development.

Researchers Penuel and colleagues (2020) assessed schools' readiness to implement new technology-based innovations for teaching and learning. They found that schools were most ready to adopt technology-based innovations if they had a culture that valued innovation and risk taking, as well as effective professional learning opportunities for teachers. This study emphasizes how a comprehensive readiness assessment helps to ensure that an innovation is compatible with the school's context, goals, and values and to identify potential barriers to and facilitators of implementation.

In conclusion, comprehensive readiness assessment is key to ensuring the successful adoption and sustainability of innovative practices. K–12 schools can assess their readiness and identify areas for improvement in the implementation of evidence-informed innovations.

Figure 4.8 (page 114) contains the K–12 implementation readiness tuning protocol, a great tool implementation teams can use to assess readiness and identify areas they must attend to prior to and during the implementation process.

K–12 Implementation Readiness Tuning Protocol

Purpose: The K–12 implementation readiness tuning protocol is a time-efficient method for understanding your organization's readiness to implement a new evidence-based innovation (a new program, practice, principle, procedure, product, or policy). It allows team members to share their perceptions of organizational readiness so that the team can collectively generate information for implementation planning and preparation.

Intention: This tool gives individual team members a chance to consider the challenges and strengths associated with research-informed organizational readiness components. It provides focus points for discussion and develops a system's view of readiness to implement. This tool offers perspectives for change and implementation readiness strategies, implementation readiness issues, and decision-making trends.

Background: *Organizational readiness for implementation* is the degree to which the organization is able and willing to implement and sustain an innovation. Organizations with high degrees of readiness have fewer implementation challenges and obstacles and greater implementation success. Readiness to implement is impacted by the organization's motivation and its capacity and resources to implement the innovation as designed. Schools can increase their readiness to implement by assessing key organizational readiness components and using that information to develop actions to prepare and implement successfully.

The items associated with readiness, which are informed by change and implementation science, are organized by the following components.

- **Motivation:** Implementers' willingness or desire to change, adopt, and effectively implement a new innovation
- **Innovation-specific capacity:** The specific knowledge, skills, infrastructure, supports, systems, and resources needed to successfully implement the new innovation
- **General capacity:** Your organization's general functioning and ability to support the innovation (for example, context, culture, climate, use of resources, leadership, infrastructure, and organizational processes)

$$R = MC^2$$

Readiness = Motivation × Innovation-Specific Capacity × General Capacity

Instructions for the Implementation Team Facilitator

1. **Provide an overview:** Provide an overview of the evidence-informed innovation and a brief description of the problem the innovation is designed to help solve (four minutes).

2. **Pair participants:** Create work groups (pairs or larger), and provide a recording sheet for each group.

3. **Complete the readiness thinking tool:** Ask group members to work individually first, completing the Dawn Chorus Group's brief readiness thinking tool by considering whether each area is an organizational challenge or strength as it relates to the new innovation (ten minutes).

4. **Facilitate partner or small-group discussions:** After a designated amount of time, structure small- or full-group interaction exploration of the individual responses through the provided discussion questions (fifteen minutes).

5. **Lead a full-group discussion:** Lead the full group in discussing next steps (actions or tasks) to help prepare the organization for implementation of the new innovation (thirty to sixty minutes).

Motivation	The Degree to Which We Want the Innovation to Happen	It's a Challenge	It's a Strength	I'm Unsure
Relative advantage	This innovation seems better than what we currently do.	☐	☐	☐
Compatibility	This innovation fits with how we do things.	☐	☐	☐
Simplicity	This innovation seems doable.	☐	☐	☐
Ability to pilot	This innovation can be tested and experimented with.	☐	☐	☐
Observability	We are able to see that this innovation is leading to outcomes.	☐	☐	☐
Priority	This innovation is important compared to other things we do.	☐	☐	☐
Innovation-Specific Capacity	**What Is Needed to Make This Particular Innovation Happen**	**It's a Challenge**	**It's a Strength**	**I'm Unsure**
Innovation-specific knowledge and skills	Sufficient abilities to do this innovation	☐	☐	☐
Supportive climate	Necessary supports, processes, and resources to enable this innovation	☐	☐	☐
Interorganizational relationships	Relationships between organizations that support this innovation	☐	☐	☐
Intraorganizational relationships	Relationships within an organization that support this innovation	☐	☐	☐
General Capacity	**Our Overall Functioning**	**It's a Challenge**	**It's a Strength**	**I'm Unsure**
Culture	Norms and values of how we do things here	☐	☐	☐
Climate	The feeling of being part of this organization	☐	☐	☐
Innovativeness	Openness to change in general	☐	☐	☐
Resource utilization	Ability to acquire and allocate resources, including time, money, effort, and technology	☐	☐	☐
Leadership	Effectiveness of our leaders	☐	☐	☐
Internal operations	Effectiveness of communication and teamwork	☐	☐	☐
Staff capacities	Having enough of the right people to get things done	☐	☐	☐
Process capacities	Ability to plan, implement, and evaluate	☐	☐	☐

Brief Readiness Thinking Tool
Use the chart to think about the organization's readiness to implement a program or change. Consider whether these elements are challenges or strengths for your innovation. Discuss this with your colleagues also involved in implementation.

Figure 4.8: K–12 implementation readiness tuning protocol.   continued →

Principles of Readiness	Discussion Questions
1. Readiness isn't one thing; it is a combination of motivation, innovation-specific capacity, and general capacity. 2. Readiness can change over time. 3. Readiness is important throughout implementation. 4. Readiness is innovation specific. 5. Readiness can vary across levels of implementation. 6. Readiness can be built.	What is the greatest implementation challenge currently? What is the greatest strength? Where would more information and data be helpful? How can you get these data? Where do you have differences with your colleagues? Which areas do you think would be most important to address early on in your project?

Source: Adapted from Dawn Chorus Group, n.d.

*Visit **go.SolutionTree.com/schoolimprovement** for a free reproducible version of this figure.*

Conclusion

Give the *Decide* stage the time and energy it deserves! Identify your guiding coalition of champions, and get them on board early in the process to nurture enthusiasm for the change, build buy-in, and strengthen the process with multiple skills and viewpoints. With your implementation team, take the necessary time to identify the problem that needs to be addressed, and write a SMART goal to address the problem. Through the explicit use of thinking and engagement protocols, gather multiple forms of data, and explore the options of solutions that would be feasible to implement as designed in your system. Then select the one that your team agrees best fits and meets the needs of your organization to ensure you get the results you are seeking to achieve.

Record the actions and decisions in your IMPACT implementation planning template. Completing these sections as a team will build a shared understanding of the problem to be solved and the solution selected and empower the organization to move forward with clarity.

Let's move beyond solutionitis practices and routines and on to actively and intentionally selecting innovations that can make an impact in your organization. Build deliberately developmental implementation and use the IMPACT implementation planning template and the tools introduced to set the stage for a successful implementation. Remember to use the *Decide* stage's key activities and objectives on page 97 to guide your work during this stage.

Decide Stage IMPACT Implementation Planning Template

Complete the appropriate sections of the template with your team, recording your decisions in the space provided.

Inclusion | Meaningful Leadership | Professional Learning | Assess and Adjust | Collective Efficacy | Team

Implementation Planning Template

Implementation Team Members: ☐ System   ☐ School

Goal: Where are we going? (State the goal in SMART format.)

Stage	Problem	Evidence-Based Solutions	Implementation Strategies	Monitoring Strategies
Decide	Name the problem and why this problem needs to be solved.	Name the proposed solution (EBP).		
Plan and Prepare		Identify the active ingredients of the EBP. What is the EBP and its associated active ingredients?	How will we skill up to scale up? List implementation strategies here.	Are we doing what we said we would do? Identify the monitoring tools.
Implement		What intelligent adaptations to the EBP are needed based on culture, climate, and context?	Adapt existing implementation strategies or add new ones here.	Adapt existing monitoring tools or add new ones here.
Spread and Sustain		Identify resources needed to sustain implementation of the innovation.	Identify implementation strategies to support, spread, and sustain effective implementation.	Identify ongoing monitoring tools to inform implementation integrity.

Source: © 2022 by Jenice Pizzuto and Steven Carney.

The *Decide* Stage Learning Journey Map

Use the following two questions to prompt active discussion and thoughtful responses, helping your team assess current practices and plan for future development. This is an opportunity for collective reflection and strategic action.

Together, review the concepts and practices from chapter 4 that your organization has already implemented. Discuss the effectiveness of your leadership and the progress of your implementation efforts. Use the questions to guide a rich conversation, and document your team's insights, commitments, and objectives in the learning journey map.

1. What concepts and practices from chapter 4 does our district or school currently have in place (with varying degrees of implementation)?

2. What observations and insights are we making about our leadership, leadership team, or organizational implementation efforts?

Team Takeaways *New* learning, insights, and notices	Team Commitment Concepts, ideas, and practices we *commit to developing*	Team Practice Strategies, processes, and tools we plan to *learn and practice*	Team Reflection Strategies, processes, tools, concepts, ideas, and so on we want to *go deeper into and share early successes on*	Team Goals Strategies, processes, tools, concepts, ideas, and so on we want to *fully operationalize* through a commitment of time, resources, and policy

—————— *chapter 5* ——————

THE *PLAN AND PREPARE* STAGE

*The implementation process is an active process and
requires planning and engagement from the start.*

—Steven Carney and Jenice Pizzuto

Imagine a bridge—a robust, thoughtfully constructed link between two critical points. In your school or district, this bridge is more than a mere structure; it's a metaphor for the vital connection between the evidence-based practices you understand and the effective actions you must execute. It's a call to transform knowledge into practice, ensuring that what you know doesn't just stay within the pages of research or in the repository of best practices but comes alive in the classrooms and hallways of your school.

This chapter is about answering that call. It's a guide to constructing the bridge that will carry the weight of your aspirations and allow them to materialize into outcomes that matter. During this stage, you lay the foundation with the evidence, raise the framework with strategic planning, and pave the walkway with steadfast preparation. Every step is deliberate, every action intentional, ensuring that the journey from theory to practice is not left to chance.

As you embark on this chapter, think of yourself and your team as both architects and builders. You are tasked with not just envisioning but actualizing the bridge that links *what we know* to *what we do*. It is a journey from the abstract to the concrete, from high hopes to high impact. With implementation science and human- and learning-centered design as our foundation, we will explore how to raise the framework with strategic planning and pave the walkway with steadfast preparation so that every step taken is a step toward measurable success. Let this chapter serve as your blueprint, offering strategies and insights essential for bridging the implementation gap and ensuring the journey from innovative ideas to effective practice is both clear and achievable.

In this chapter, we explore key activities and objectives in the *Plan and Prepare* stage. At this stage, teams identify the active ingredients of the solution they've chosen for their organization and select implementation strategies. To assess implementation progress, teams also develop a plan to monitor implementation, including fidelity checklists, observation protocols, self-report measures, and fidelity assessments.

Building the Foundation

As any builder knows, a sturdy foundation is essential for constructing a building that will stand the test of time. Similarly, planning and preparation are crucial when implementing evidence-based innovations to ensure that the innovations can deliver their intended outcomes and sustain their impact over time. Without a solid foundation and planning, failure is likely; the implementation risks failing to achieve its intended outcomes, resulting in wasted resources and frustration for stakeholders. The *Plan and Prepare* stage moves you and your team from knowing why and what you are implementing to adding structure to your road map for implementation. This stage develops your organization's capacity to implement the identified change effectively and efficiently. It lays the groundwork for success.

During the *Plan and Prepare* stage, an implementation team completes the components of the IMPACT implementation plan, which is designed to fully prepare an organization for the successful implementation of any evidence-based innovation. By taking the time to plan and prepare effectively, you can help ensure that you build your innovation on a solid foundation and you are ready to face the challenges and opportunities that lie ahead.

The ability to embrace change in the educational landscape varies across classrooms, grade levels, departments, schools, and districts. The most common explanation for this difference is the absence of a comprehensive implementation plan and organizational readiness for change and implementation. The schools most successful in implementing evidence-based initiatives and achieving intended results are those that treat change not as an isolated event to be managed but as a continual opportunity to evolve and improve. They have established a shared ability and responsibility to continuously plan for, initiate, and respond to change in advantageous ways;

minimize risk; and sustain performance. They have achieved this through meticulous planning and preparation.

Table 5.1 introduces the *Plan and Prepare* stage's key activities and objectives through the IMPACT lens. You and your team will find this tool valuable to prepare for the stage. It describes what outcomes result from the major activities that take place. Use this overview to help key stakeholders or staff understand the purpose of the stage and build deliberately developmental implementation. Although this table covers the key activities to include in an IMPACT implementation plan, the table is not comprehensive. There are other activities involved in this stage, as described throughout the chapter. Review the activities in the table and check your plan to ensure you have built-in protocols, time, and resources to meet each objective.

Table 5.1: *Plan and Prepare* Stage Key Activities and Objectives

IMPACT	Key Activities	Key Objectives
Inclusion	Develop stakeholder competencies through learning together; develop a purposeful practice schedule with implementers.	Increase buy-in from stakeholders; improve implementation fidelity; foster more effective communication and collaboration between stakeholders.
Meaningful Leadership	Develop infrastructures that provide time and processes designed to support practice, reflection, meaning making, and change.	Increase capacity for leadership; more effectively implement the innovation; improve alignment of stakeholders for the innovation.
Professional Learning	Develop professional learning designs and structures that support learning about the change.	Increase knowledge and skills among implementers; improve implementers' ability to effectively implement the innovation.
Assess and Adjust	Use fidelity assessments to inform implementation, assess gaps in implementation and implementation readiness, assess team competencies, and develop success criteria and fidelity assessments.	Improve implementation fidelity; increase the effectiveness of the innovation; better understand the innovation's impact and how to sustain it.
Collective Efficacy	Develop mastery criteria and milestones (goals); engage in joint implementation planning with positive interdependence.	Increase sense of ownership and shared responsibility; make collaboration more effective; improve implementation fidelity.
Team	Develop implementation team competencies, obtain resources needed to support the innovation and the implementation, and develop the implementation plan.	Foster more effective coordination and communication among team members; increase team members' ability to identify and obtain needed resources; improve implementation fidelity.

*Visit **go.SolutionTree.com/schoolimprovement** for a free reproducible version of this table.*

Throughout the *Plan and Prepare* stage, it is crucial to keep the IMPACT model in mind. Additionally, it is critical that the systems-level or building-level implementation team dedicate careful attention and time to setting the organization on a successful path for rolling out the innovation and implementation strategies.

Figure 5.1 lists the major decisions to include in your IMPACT implementation plan and includes space your team can use to take notes. It's important to note that this is *not* a checklist to assign to a team member but a series of discussions the implementation team will collectively engage in and make decisions about. If you'd like to note when items have been completed, you may list the date in the space indicated for each decision.

Plan and Prepare Stage Decisions		
Decisions	**Notes**	**Date Completed**
Develop a compelling why to be shared throughout the organization.		
Identify the innovation's active ingredients.		
Identify implementation strategies.		
Use the Expert Recommendations for Implementing Change and other resources to identify and select implementation strategies that will best support the school culture, climate, and context.		
Develop a professional learning plan to support ongoing job-embedded learning and mastery development, considering the following. • Include a variety of professional learning designs to support change. • Allocate or capture time for team and staff learning. • Develop an infrastructure and a schedule to support innovation practice and feedback.		
Develop a staff communication plan that fosters shared understanding of the following. • Innovation vision and mission • Incentives • Guiding champions		

Decisions	Notes	Date Completed
Establish integrity agreements by considering the following questions. • "How good is good enough?" • "How do we know we are getting it done as designed?"		
Develop an implementation-monitoring plan that includes the following. • Innovation-monitoring processes that include implementers • A schedule of three times per year for the first year of implementation, and two times a year following year one		
Develop professional learning impact monitoring and adjustment processes and a schedule that includes the following. • Innovation-monitoring processes and a schedule • Professional learning impact monitoring and adjustment processes and a schedule • Implementation strategy monitoring and adjustment processes and a schedule • Data collection, format, and analysis protocols		

Figure 5.1: *Plan and Prepare* stage decisions.

*Visit **go.SolutionTree.com/schoolimprovement** for a free reproducible version of this figure.*

Looking over the *Plan and Prepare* stage decisions list, what items do you notice are strengths for your organization? What items are stretches for your organization? Keep these decisions in mind as you read through the remainder of this chapter. Use the "*Plan and Prepare* Stage IMPACT Implementation Planning Template" reproducible (page 148) to guide your team in your implementation process.

Note that the *Plan and Prepare* stage should not be skipped or underestimated, as this stage, done right and well, sets the conditions for success. It takes time to identify, establish, and institutionalize the resources, procedures, protocols, and policies to support implementation. Skipping steps or omitting procedures can result in poor implementation and will most likely require circling back to repair the missed steps, resulting in delayed implementation effectiveness. Because the *Plan and Prepare* stage is critical to the ultimate success of the new innovation, it is essential to spend an appropriate amount of time focused solely on getting the necessary support in place before starting implementation. Additionally, some of the activities associated with the *Plan and Prepare* stage may continue to occur (or be revised) as implementation begins.

During the *Plan and Prepare* stage, implementation teams build on the work they began in the *Decide* stage, creating many parts of the IMPACT implementation plan. Completing the template collaboratively is important because, as our friend Stefani Hite always reminds us, "We build collective efficacy while working together around shared work" (personal communication, March 28, 2023). The IMPACT implementation planning template is a living, organic document teams utilize in all phases of the implementation process. For a template customized to this stage, see the reproducible at the end of this chapter (page 148).

In this stage, implementation teams complete the Evidence-Based Solutions, Implementation Strategies, and Monitoring Strategies sections of the template. We recommend providing a digital copy (for ease of updating and sharing across buildings) or a hard copy of the template for each team member. This is a learning-by-doing book. Collaboratively designing the implementation plan and adhering to the IMPACT implementation planning template provides teams with a cocreated goal and process to guide the implementation effort during this stage.

Identifying the Active Ingredients

The next step of completing the IMPACT implementation planning template is to identify the active ingredients of the solution selected by the team. According to the Education Endowment Foundation (2021), it is crucial to pinpoint and comprehend the key elements (active ingredients) within evidence-based programs, as these core components are responsible for the programs' efficacy. Active ingredients are the most significant elements of an innovation that you must implement faithfully in order to attain the desired results; they encompass the critical behaviors and content that enable the innovation to function effectively (Sharples, Albers, et al., 2019). When implementers deeply understand these components and execute them with fidelity, the likelihood of successful implementation increases. Identifying a core set of active ingredients required for successful implementation will help the implementation team monitor and build capacity more effectively.

Some evidence-based innovations come with a clearly defined set of core components that you must implement as designed to produce the intended outcomes. If your district or school has purchased an innovation, check with the program's or practice's authors to see if they have identified a set of active ingredients that must be implemented with fidelity or high integrity. Ask what active ingredients you can adapt to fit organizational culture, climate, and context. Also, inquire about which components of the innovation have little or no bearing on achieving the intended results. If the innovation's authors or publishers cannot provide this information, the implementation team should develop the organization's own clear and concise set of active ingredients required for successful implementation. Even if the authors or publishers provide what they believe are the most critical components of the innovation, the implementation team should still identify the components where the organization will be tight and where it will be loose. Having a set of author- or publisher-provided active ingredients jump-starts the process of defining the change.

Whatever process the implementation team uses to identify the innovation's active ingredients, ensure the team can answer this question: "If we were looking through a one-way window into a classroom or space that was implementing the innovation right and well and getting the intended results, what critical behaviors or activities would we consistently see and hear? How would we describe those behaviors or activities?" You might also ask, "What resources, materials, or tools would we see used as part of this description?"

In defining the active ingredients, think about what it looks and sounds like (that is, teacher moves, student actions, and so on) when the innovation is implemented as designed and produces results. Be specific but not too verbose here. This is where having implementers' voices on the team is especially helpful. Lean into the implementers' experience and expertise in defining the active ingredients. We recommend that the identified active ingredients meet the three Cs rule: they should be clear, concise, and comprehensible. Ensuring they meet the three Cs rule provides the clarity implementers need to succeed in their implementation. For example, if the evidence-based innovation is an SEL program, the active ingredients could include training teachers on specific SEL competencies, establishing consistent routines for implementing the program, providing SEL interventions for students based on their needs, and developing strong family-school partnerships to support the program's implementation. Figure 5.2 (page 126) outlines a process for identifying the active ingredients of an evidence-based innovation, including space for the team to indicate the date of completion.

Once the team has selected the active ingredients, record them in your IMPACT implementation planning template (locate the Evidence-Based Solutions column, and record the active ingredients in the *Plan and Prepare* row).

Step	Description	Date
Conduct a comprehensive review of the literature.	Conduct a comprehensive review of the literature on the evidence-based innovation to identify the key ingredients of the innovation and the factors that facilitate or hinder successful implementation.	
Check with the program or practice authors.	If the district or school purchased the innovation, check with the program or practice authors to see if they have identified a set of active ingredients that must be implemented with fidelity or high integrity. Ask what active ingredients can be adapted to fit organizational culture, climate, and context, and inquire about which components of the innovation have little or no bearing on achieving the intended results.	
Involve stakeholders.	Engage in stakeholder consultation to ensure that the identified active ingredients are feasible, acceptable, and relevant to the context of implementation. This can involve gathering feedback from a range of stakeholders, including implementers, administrators, and program beneficiaries.	
Define the active ingredients.	Define the active ingredients, ensuring that they are clear, concise, and comprehensible and therefore meet the three Cs rule.	
Test the active ingredients.	Test and refine the active ingredients through iterative cycles of implementation and feedback. Use qualitative and quantitative methods to assess the impact of the active ingredients on outcomes and gather feedback from stakeholders on their experiences of implementing the active ingredients.	
Refine the active ingredients.	Refine the active ingredients based on the testing and feedback to ensure that they are effective and appropriate for the context of implementation.	

Figure 5.2: Process for identifying active ingredients.

Visit ***go.SolutionTree.com/schoolimprovement*** *for a free reproducible version of this figure.*

Selecting Implementation Strategies

The success of any implementation effort is knowledge translation. How will implementation teams ensure staff have the knowledge and abilities to carry out the change? What strategies will be deployed to ensure all practitioners have the opportunity, time, and motivation to gain any new skills required to perform new tasks? We call this *skill up to scale up*—provide varied strategies and multiple opportunities for staff to develop proficiency in deploying the new innovation. This means identifying the right implementation strategies, involving all stakeholders in the implementation process, and investing in ongoing professional learning (not random acts of training) and development. By doing so, we can ensure that evidence-based innovations are implemented with integrity and fidelity. We honor the implementers by providing time to build toward mastery and by putting supportive learning structures in place.

Implementation strategies are the specific methods, techniques, or approaches aimed at ensuring the successful adoption, integration, and sustained execution of evidence-based programs or practices. They address potential barriers and enhance factors that influence the effective implementation and longevity of these innovations, such as adapting to the school's culture, managing resources, building capacity, and engaging stakeholders. These strategies are the concrete actions that school leaders, implementation teams, and teachers undertake to transition an innovative idea into regular practice. They are the dynamic elements that activate the implementation process and are crucial for the success of any educational initiative.

For example, one school might adopt an implementation strategy of *peer coaching*, where experienced teachers mentor their colleagues in applying a new teaching method and provide guidance and feedback to ensure they use it effectively in the classroom. Another school might develop *implementation checklists* that educators use to self-assess whether they are applying the new methods as intended, ensuring consistency and fidelity to the program's design. These strategies are not just theoretical concepts; they are the practical steps that bring about real change in the day-to-day operations of schools, ensuring that innovative practices are not just introduced but fully integrated.

Implementation efforts often fail because implementation strategies were missing or not well planned (Fixsen et al., 2019). Thus, it is essential to take time to design implementation strategies that are evidence based and human and learning centered to ensure successful implementation.

Implementing educational innovations can be complex and challenging, and implementing change is never easy. Therefore, teams must use evidence-based implementation strategies that have proven effective in implementing educational innovations. Evidence-based implementation strategies can help to overcome common implementation challenges, such as resistance to change, lack of resources, and inadequate training and support for implementation teams and implementers, as researchers Byron J. Powell and colleagues (2015) suggest; these strategies should be specified and reported to facilitate their use and evaluation.

We advocate for the use of implementation strategies that are designed to meet an organization's needs and are aligned with the IMPACT human- and learning-centered design components. These components provide a road map for effective implementation by promoting the successful adoption of educational innovations in a human- and learning-centered way. By using evidence-based implementation strategies, educational institutions can increase their chances of successfully adopting and sustaining educational innovations.

Expert Recommendations for Implementing Change

The Expert Recommendations for Implementing Change, a compilation of more than seventy implementation strategies identified by change and implementation experts, provide a comprehensive set of strategies relevant to the implementation and sustainability of educational practices (Powell et al., 2015). As mentioned in chapter 2 (page 41), we have selected strategies from this framework that align with the IMPACT human- and learning-centered design components: inclusion, meaningful leadership, professional learning, assess and adjust, collective efficacy, and team. Consider the following examples of strategies aligned with each component.

- Inclusion strategies entail involving stakeholders from diverse backgrounds in decision making and planning, which has been shown to increase the success of implementation efforts (Bryk et al., 2015).

- Meaningful leadership involves leaders who support the new initiative and create a positive environment for change.

- Professional learning strategies focus on providing relevant and ongoing professional development to educators (Darling-Hammond et al., 2017).

- Assess and adjust strategies involve engaging in ongoing monitoring and evaluation of the initiative's progress and making necessary adjustments.

- Collective efficacy strategies aim to build a sense of shared responsibility and collective efficacy among educators (Donohoo, Hattie, & Eells, 2018).

- Team strategies involve collaboration among educators, who work in groups to support each other (Hord, 2009).

By adopting these evidence-based implementation strategies, educational institutions can increase their chances of successfully adopting and sustaining educational innovations in a human- and learning-centered way.

Using the Expert Recommendations for Implementing Change list, an adaptation of that list (such as the IMPACT implementation strategies for change found in table 2.1, page 48), or similar tools, educational systems and institutions can identify and select effective implementation strategies tailored to their specific context. This can help teams ensure they successfully implement evidence-based innovations and have a positive impact on student outcomes.

For example, let's say a school district used a tool called the Expert Recommendations for Implementation Framework to select implementation strategies for a new science curriculum. The district identified a range of potential implementation strategies, including providing professional development and support for educators, using data to inform instruction, and fostering a culture of continuous improvement. It evaluated the strength of the evidence supporting each strategy, assessed the feasibility and acceptability of each strategy, and selected and tailored the implementation strategies based on the local context. The district then monitored and evaluated the implementation using both quantitative and qualitative data. As a result of this process, the district was able to successfully implement the new science curriculum and improve student outcomes in science.

Professional Learning Plan

Professional learning involves providing ongoing opportunities for implementers to learn and develop the necessary skills and knowledge to effectively adopt innovations, and it is a *critical component* of effective implementation. This includes providing training tailored to the unique needs of implementers, such as coaching, mentoring, and job-embedded professional development. High-quality professional learning is the path to building educators' knowledge, skills, attitudes, and, ultimately, competence and confidence in using the new strategies.

In identifying implementation strategies and zeroing in on high-quality job-embedded professional learning, some teams find it valuable to extend their implementation plan to include a separate professional learning plan. A well-crafted professional learning plan illustrates a commitment to educators' growth and development. Such a plan is not just a schedule of activities but a strategic approach to building capacity and ensuring the seamless integration of new practices into the daily rhythm of teaching. Figure 5.3 (page 130) is a concrete example of a professional learning plan designed to be embedded within the professional duties of educators, fostering continuous learning and mastery development.

Developing a professional learning plan that supports ongoing job-embedded learning and mastery development is critical to successful implementation. The professional learning plan should include a variety of professional learning designs, such as team learning, text-rendering activities and protocols, video watching or review sessions, coaching, mentoring, job-embedded professional learning, and collaborative learning communities, to support change. These professional learning designs should be tailored to the unique needs of implementers and aligned with the IMPACT human- and learning-centered design components. By investing in ongoing professional learning, implementers can develop the necessary skills and knowledge to adopt and implement innovations effectively.

Sample Professional Learning Plan for Middle School Mathematics Teachers Implementing Project-Based Learning (PBL)

Objective: To integrate project-based learning into the middle school mathematics curriculum to enhance student engagement and understanding

Duration: One academic year

Key Components

1. **Initial training workshop**

   – A two-day workshop at the beginning of the school year will introduce the concept of PBL, its benefits in mathematics education, and initial strategies for implementation.

   – Activities will include interactive seminars, group discussions, and hands-on sessions where teachers create their first PBL mathematics unit.

2. **Peer observations**

   – Teachers will be paired to observe each other's classes once a month, focusing on the use of PBL strategies.

   – Postobservation debriefs will be conducted to discuss observations and provide constructive feedback.

3. **Coaching sessions**

   – Each teacher will receive bimonthly coaching from a PBL expert, focusing on lesson planning, student engagement, and assessment of PBL units.

   – Coaches will provide personalized feedback and support for continuous improvement.

4. **Collaborative teams**

   – Teachers will meet biweekly in collaborative teams to share experiences, discuss challenges, and collaboratively work on refining PBL units.

   – Collaborative teams will also review student work and assessment data to inform instructional decisions.

5. **Midyear review seminar**

   – A one-day seminar will occur midyear to reflect on progress, share successes, and workshop challenges faced in implementing PBL.

   – Guest speakers who are experts in PBL will provide additional insights and strategies.

6. **Ongoing resource sharing**

   – An online repository of PBL resources, including lesson plans, assessment tools, and instructional videos, will be created.

   – Teachers will be encouraged to contribute to and utilize the repository throughout the year.

7. **End-of-year showcase**

   – Teachers will present their most successful PBL units and student work in an end-of-year showcase.

   – This event will serve as a celebration of the year's work and a learning opportunity for the entire teaching staff.

Monitoring and Evaluation

- Teachers will complete a self-assessment survey at the beginning, middle, and end of the year to reflect on their growth in implementing PBL.
- Student engagement will be monitored through surveys and classroom observations.
- Student understanding of mathematical concepts will be assessed through pre- and post-tests on PBL units.

Support Structures

- The school will provide substitutes to allow teachers to participate in observations and collaborative teams during school hours.
- A budget will be allocated for resources and materials needed to create PBL units.
- Administration will ensure that the professional learning plan aligns with the school's overall goals for instructional improvement.

Figure 5.3: Sample professional learning plan.

Infrastructure and Schedule

Developing an infrastructure and a schedule to support innovation practice and feedback is also critical to successful implementation. The infrastructure should include the necessary resources—such as technology, facilities, and materials—to support innovation practice. For instance, if a school is implementing a new digital-literacy program, the infrastructure must include updated computer labs with high-speed internet access, digital-literacy software, and training materials for both students and teachers.

Alongside the physical resources, the schedule should provide dedicated time for implementers to practice and refine their implementation of the innovation, receive feedback, and reflect on their practice. For example, a school might set aside two afternoons each month exclusively for teachers to engage in collaborative practice sessions. During these sessions, teachers could work in teams to develop digital-literacy lesson plans, observe each other's classes, and provide constructive feedback. Additionally, quarterly professional development days could be dedicated to refining the digital-literacy curriculum, addressing challenges, and sharing best practices across the school or district. By providing a supportive infrastructure and schedule, educational institutions can ensure that implementers have the necessary support to implement innovations with integrity and fidelity.

Staff Communication Plan

Developing a staff communication plan is also critical to successful implementation. This plan serves as the blueprint for how the vision, progress, and expectations of a new initiative are communicated within the school community. It ensures that all staff members, from teachers to administrative personnel, understand their roles in the adoption and success of this initiative.

We recommend that a staff communication plan include the following elements to ensure successful implementation.

- **Vision and mission communication:** The communication plan articulates how the initiative aligns with and supports the school's vision and mission. This alignment is communicated through various channels, ensuring that the purpose and goals resonate with all staff members.

- **Implementation timeline and milestones:** A clear timeline, including key milestones and phases of implementation, is shared with all staff. This timeline serves as a guide for what to expect and when to expect it, providing a structured overview of the initiative's rollout and staff implementation expectations.

- **Professional development and support:** The plan details the professional development opportunities available to staff, including workshops, training sessions, and support materials. It also outlines the schedule for these opportunities, ensuring that staff can plan their engagement in advance.

- **Opportunities for practice:** The plan should communicate scheduled times and structured opportunities for staff to practice the new initiative, ensuring they can apply what they've learned in a safe and supportive environment.

- **Feedback mechanisms:** Establish channels for providing feedback, encouraging staff to share their insights and experiences. This two-way communication is vital for adjusting the implementation process and ensuring that it meets the needs of all stakeholders.

- **Recognition of efforts:** The communication plan includes a strategy for recognizing and celebrating the efforts and achievements of staff as they engage with the new initiative and demonstrate proficiency. This recognition serves as an incentive and boosts morale.

- **Resource availability:** Clearly communicate information about the resources—such as new technology, additional staffing, or budget allocations—to ensure that staff feel equipped and supported.

- **Policy updates:** Promptly and clearly communicate any changes to school policies or practices that arise from the implementation, explaining how these changes affect daily operations and expectations.

- **Leadership and support structures:** The plan identifies the leaders and support teams responsible for the initiative, providing staff with clear points of contact for questions and support.

- **Ongoing communication:** Schedule regular updates to keep staff informed about the initiative's progress. These updates highlight successes, address challenges, and provide a continuous feedback loop.

By incorporating these elements into a comprehensive staff communication plan, schools can ensure that all members of the educational community are informed, engaged, and collaboratively working toward the successful implementation of new initiatives. This plan is not just a dissemination tool but a framework for fostering a unified and informed school culture.

The Process of Identifying Implementation Strategies

The process of selecting effective implementation strategies involves conducting a needs assessment, identifying evidence-based strategies, evaluating their fit for the specific context, prioritizing them, including them in developing an implementation plan, and monitoring and adjusting the implementation strategies as necessary. By following this six-step process, implementation teams can select implementation strategies that are well suited to their specific contexts, resulting in more effective implementation and improved student outcomes.

1. **Conduct a needs assessment:** Before selecting implementation strategies, implementation teams must conduct a needs assessment to identify the specific challenges and needs of the organization. The needs assessment should consider the context of the organization, the innovation being implemented, and the resources available.

2. **Identify evidence-based implementation strategies:** Once the needs assessment has been completed, implementation teams should identify evidence-based implementation strategies that have proven effective in similar contexts. The adapted IMPACT implementation strategies for change (see table 2.1, page 48) and other implementation frameworks can be helpful resources for identifying evidence-based strategies.

3. **Evaluate the fit of implementation strategies:** Once implementation teams identify a list of potential implementation strategies, they should evaluate each strategy's fit for the specific context in which the innovation is being implemented. This evaluation should consider the organization's resources, its culture, and the specific needs identified in the needs assessment.

4. **Prioritize implementation strategies:** After evaluating the fit of each strategy, implementation teams should prioritize the strategies that are most likely to be effective in the specific context. Prioritization should consider factors such as feasibility, sustainability, and potential impact.

5. **Develop an action plan:** Once teams have selected and prioritized implementation strategies and recorded them in the IMPACT implementation planning template, they should develop a detailed action plan that includes specific actions, timelines, and responsible individuals.

6. **Monitor and adjust implementation strategies:** Throughout the implementation process, implementation teams should monitor the effectiveness of selected strategies and make necessary adjustments to ensure successful implementation. Monitoring and evaluation should include regular check-ins with stakeholders, ongoing data collection, and progress reports.

By following this process, implementation teams can select evidence-based implementation strategies well suited to their specific contexts, resulting in more effective implementation and improved student outcomes.

Once your team has selected its strategies, be sure to record them in the IMPACT implementation planning template (locate the Implementation Strategies column, and record the selected strategies in the "How will we skill up to scale up?" section of the *Plan and Prepare* row).

De-Implementation

After identifying and recording their implementation strategies, implementation team members commonly feel overwhelmed by the amount of work required to implement them successfully. We recommend that implementation teams reflect to identify the things individuals, implementation team members, and the organization need to *stop doing* to make way for the new work of deploying the implementation strategies. By understanding and committing to what needs to stop, you can support your implementation team and organization in preparing for individual and shared actions associated with the newly identified strategies. This process can help ensure that the implementation team members are not overburdened with work and they have the necessary time and resources to implement the strategies effectively. And by committing to this reflective process, the organization can better support the implementation team and improve the chances of successful implementation and sustained change. De-implementation keeps the ghosts of past projects and initiatives from becoming barriers to the current work.

For example, as an implementation team was monitoring its school district, the team discovered that staff were still utilizing their old program alongside their new program. As the team continued this monitoring, the data indicated the problem was not isolated but pervasive in 45 percent of the monitored classrooms. Some staff members were utilizing the Developmental Reading Assessment with every student three times a year and utilizing the newly adopted universal screener three times a year. This practice (overassessing) not only was harmful to the students but also robbed staff and students of precious teaching and learning time and wasted human and capital resources. Additionally, the implementation-monitoring data indicated that some staff were only using parts of the newly adopted reading curriculum as outlined in the district's agreed-on literacy instruction framework, and they were mixing those parts with the previous program or collections of materials from outside sources. The implementation team needed to understand why these barriers to utilizing the new innovation as designed were occurring.

In their regularly scheduled implementation meetings, the team members examined the professional learning plan, the collected implementation data, and the implementation plan to discover why this issue was prevalent in some schools but not in others. The data they reviewed showed that key implementation team members had been absent at several training events. Further, the team members realized they needed to make a plan for how to ensure missing members received any missed training, information, resources, and, most importantly, buy-in and vision for the work. The team's investigation uncovered that some schools covered de-implementing the previous assessments and other schools did not. The implementation team planned to provide the missed learning events to staff as necessary, reinforce the vision and why of the new work with all teams, and conduct an additional round of monitoring. The next round of implementation monitoring saw a 20 percent improvement. While the implementation team members knew they still had de-implementation work to do, they felt confident they were well on their way to systemically implementing the new practices.

Developing a Plan to Monitor the Implementation

Implementing evidence-based innovations is a challenging task, so it's crucial to assess how well implementation is going. Quality implementation is a process that can take two to four years (sometimes more), and it requires routine monitoring of how successfully the new innovation is being implemented and adopted. Measuring implementation progress provides the implementation team with timely data to identify areas for improvement, inform implementation adjustments and innovation adaptations, and achieve intended outcomes more rapidly.

However, before measuring whether an innovation is actually having an impact, it is vital to ensure that the innovation is *fully implemented* (according to implementation science, full implementation occurs when 50 percent of implementers implement with fidelity; Fixsen et al., 2019). Therefore, the IMPACT implementation plan should articulate the degrees of implementation and identify what stakeholders want to see and hear at different future times, such as six months, one year, eighteen months, and two years from now (short term, medium term, and long term). The plan should include descriptions of measures (implementation outcomes) and a plan for regularly monitoring quality implementation.

Assessing implementation progress involves looking into the organization at different future times and examining the implementation outcomes of acceptability, feasibility, fidelity, and reach (Proctor, Powell, & McMillen, 2013).

- *Acceptability* refers to the degree to which stakeholders accept the innovation and associated practices, policies, procedures, and products.

- *Feasibility* is the degree to which the innovation can be successfully used by the staff and fully integrated into the organization's culture, climate, and context.

- *Fidelity* is the degree to which the innovation is implemented as its active ingredients prescribe or as the innovation developers intend.

- *Reach* refers to innovation integration, and can refer to the number of students the innovation is serving or the number of staff who are using the active ingredients (and to what degree they are using them).

We recommend assessing the acceptability, feasibility, fidelity, and reach of the innovation three times in the first year of implementation and subsequently twice a year thereafter. You should maintain this process until at least 80 percent of implementers are applying the innovation with high integrity and consistently achieving the intended outcomes. To assess that, you will need to develop a set of assessment tools that measure the identified implementation outcomes. Unfortunately, quality implementation in the education sector is young and rare, so very few quality evidence- or research-based measures have been developed. If organizations do not have the expertise to develop quality measures that accurately assess implementation outcomes, they can look outside themselves for someone with expertise in developing quality measures, and collecting qualitative and quantitative data might be helpful.

While all four types of assessments—acceptability, feasibility, fidelity, and reach— are crucial to assess implementation progress, focus on fidelity as the primary assessment. This is because an innovation can achieve its intended outcomes only if it is implemented as prescribed by its active ingredients or as intended by the innovation's developers. Assessing fidelity helps the implementation team identify where implementation gaps exist and make necessary adjustments to ensure the innovation is fully implemented. This assessment takes place at the systems level and is never a teacher evaluation. The intent is to answer the following questions.

- "Are we doing what we said we would? If not, what is getting in the way?"

- "How can we help provide more training and learning to ensure staff gain the knowledge, skills, and attitudes to perform the necessary tasks with an acceptable level of competence?"

Therefore, the IMPACT implementation plan should include a robust plan for regularly monitoring fidelity, articulating the degrees of implementation, and identifying the stakeholders' expectations for different future periods. This way, you can ensure your schools implement the innovation with high integrity and achieve the intended outcomes.

Assessing implementation fidelity is important because it allows you to determine whether the outcomes of an intervention are due to the intervention itself or to other factors, such as the quality of the implementation. Additionally, it can help you identify areas for improvement in the innovation's implementation, give valuable feedback to those involved in its delivery, and provide responsive training and learning opportunities for staff to gain the identified skills. This is done through the lens of systemwide scaling and is not to become entangled with any teacher evaluation systems.

There are several ways to assess implementation fidelity, including the use of fidelity checklists, observation protocols, and self-report measures. Let's take a closer look at each of these.

Fidelity Checklists

A fidelity checklist is a tool that outlines the key components of an intervention and allows the observer to rate whether each component was present. The checklist is typically created based on the intervention manual or other relevant documentation. Fidelity checklists are useful because they provide a clear and structured way to assess the fidelity of an intervention, and they can be quickly and easily completed. Figure 5.4 (page 138) contains a sample fidelity checklist for implementing a peer-tutoring program for mathematics.

Strategy: Peer-tutoring program for mathematics

Objective: To improve students' mathematics skills by providing them with opportunities to work with and learn from their peers

Program Implementation

☐ Peer-tutoring sessions are held on a regular basis, according to the established schedule.

☐ The peer-tutoring program is implemented as designed, with tutors following the established procedures and guidelines.

☐ Tutoring sessions are held in a quiet and conducive environment for learning.

Tutor Training

☐ Peer tutors have received appropriate training on the content they will be tutoring on.

☐ Peer tutors have received training on effective tutoring techniques and strategies.

☐ Tutors are monitoring students' progress and providing feedback during tutoring sessions.

Student Participation and Engagement

☐ Students are attending tutoring sessions regularly.

☐ Students are actively engaged and participating during tutoring sessions.

☐ Students are demonstrating improvement in their mathematics skills as a result of participating in the tutoring program.

Data Collection and Monitoring

☐ Student attendance records are being kept.

☐ Student performance data are being collected, such as pre- and post-tutoring assessment data.

☐ Data are being analyzed regularly to assess the effectiveness of the tutoring program.

Figure 5.4: Sample fidelity checklist.

*Visit **go.SolutionTree.com/schoolimprovement** for a free reproducible version of this figure.*

By using a fidelity checklist, educators can ensure the evidence-based practice is being implemented as intended and is effectively improving students' outcomes. If the checklist illuminates any areas of concern, the implementation team can improve the fidelity and effectiveness of the program by giving staff the necessary support to learn and master the skills.

Observation Protocols

Observation protocols involve observing the delivery of an intervention and taking notes on specific aspects of the implementation. The observer may use a predetermined protocol that outlines what they should be looking for, or they may take more open-ended notes. Observation protocols are useful because they allow the observer to capture details of the implementation that a fidelity checklist may not capture (Barwick, Peters, Boydell, Jordan, & Curry, 2021). Figure 5.5 provides a sample observation protocol used for observing the evidence-based practice of project-based learning.

Observation Protocol

Instructions: Use the following four-step process to complete the observation protocol. Record your thoughts in the space provided.

1. **Preparation:** Familiarize yourself with the observation protocol before the classroom visit. Understand each item you will be observing and assessing. Bring a copy of the protocol and additional note-taking materials to the observation.

2. **Observation:** Observe the class without interfering with the natural flow of the lesson. For each item on the protocol, write down specific observations. Avoid yes-or-no answers; instead, provide descriptive notes and examples that capture the essence of what is happening in the classroom. Stay objective and focus on the teacher's and students' actions relevant to the project-based learning criteria.

3. **Postobservation:** Review your notes and summarize key findings for each protocol item. Reflect on the overall effectiveness of the project-based learning implementation, and identify areas of strength and opportunities for improvement. Prepare to share your observations with the implementation team or the observed teacher, offering constructive feedback and suggestions.

4. **Feedback session:** Schedule a feedback session with the teacher or implementation team. Discuss your observations, providing evidence from your notes to support your assessments. Engage in a dialogue about potential strategies for enhancing the project-based learning experience based on the observations.

Consider the following elements during your observation and assessment.

Lesson Preparation

- **Learning objectives and expectations:** How did the teacher communicate the learning objectives and expectations for the project? Provide specific examples.

- **Background knowledge and resources:** What background knowledge and resources did the teacher provide, and how did they support the project?

- **Challenge and alignment:** In what ways was the project challenging and aligned with grade-level standards?

Figure 5.5: Sample observation protocol.

continued →

Student Engagement

- **Engagement in learning:** Describe how students are engaged in the project-based learning experience.

- **Collaborative work:** Observe and note the nature of student collaboration and group effectiveness.

- **Critical thinking and problem solving:** Provide examples of critical thinking, problem solving, and creativity demonstrated by students.

Teacher Facilitation

- **Facilitation of the learning experience:** How is the teacher facilitating the project-based learning experience? Include examples of strategies used.

- **Feedback and support:** What type of feedback and support is the teacher providing? Note the impact on student learning.

- **Monitoring and adjustment:** How is the teacher monitoring progress, and what adjustments are they making in response to student needs?

Assessment

- **Inclusion of assessments:** Describe the formative and summative assessments used and their appropriateness.

- **Alignment with objectives:** How are the assessments aligned with the learning objectives and standards?

- **Use of assessment data:** In what ways does the teacher use assessment data to adjust the project and inform instruction?

By using an observation protocol, implementation team members can effectively assess the implementation and effectiveness of an innovation experience. They can use the protocol to provide targeted feedback to the team and to identify areas for improvement and ongoing learning to gain mastery. The specific items on an observation protocol may vary depending on the teaching strategy or intervention being observed and the age of the students.

Self-Report Measures

Self-report measures involve asking those delivering the intervention to rate their fidelity to the intervention, usually via surveys or interviews. Self-report measures are useful because they allow those delivering the intervention to reflect on their own practice and provide feedback on areas where they may need additional support.

Figure 5.6 (page 142) features a sample self-reporting worksheet educators can use to evaluate their use of explicit instruction—a structured, systematic, and effective teaching strategy. The worksheet prompts educators to consider various aspects of their teaching, from planning and implementation to assessment and student engagement.

Each section of the figure asks educators to rate their frequency of using explicit instruction strategies on a Likert scale from 1 (rarely) to 5 (always). It also requests that they provide qualitative evidence by describing specific instances that illustrate their use of these strategies. This dual approach of quantitative and qualitative self-assessment allows educators to deeply reflect on their practice and identify areas for growth.

For example, under Beliefs and Attitudes, a teacher might rate their belief in the effectiveness of explicit instruction and then describe an instance where this approach led to a noticeable improvement in student understanding. Similarly, in the Differentiation and Individualization section, a teacher could rate how often they use explicit instruction to meet individual student needs and give an example of adapting a lesson to accommodate different learning styles.

The example seen in figure 5.6 is a practical application of self-reporting, enabling educators to actively engage in their professional development by monitoring and documenting their implementation of the active ingredients and their impact on student learning.

Self-Report: Explicit Instruction

Beliefs and Attitudes

I believe that explicit instruction can be effective in improving students' academic achievement.

Rarely   Always

| 1 | 2 | 3 | 4 | 5 |

Evidence: Please describe one example of how you have seen explicit instruction improve students' academic achievement.

Implementation and Fidelity

I use explicit instruction strategies during instruction.

Rarely   Always

| 1 | 2 | 3 | 4 | 5 |

Evidence: Please describe one example of how you have recently used explicit instruction strategies in your instruction.

I monitor my students' progress and adjust instruction as needed.

Rarely   Always

| 1 | 2 | 3 | 4 | 5 |

Evidence: Please describe one example of how you have monitored your students' progress and adjusted instruction as needed.

Assessment and Feedback

I use a variety of assessments to measure my students' progress and provide feedback on their learning.

Rarely   Always

| 1 | 2 | 3 | 4 | 5 |

Evidence: Please describe one example of how you have used a variety of assessments to measure your students' progress and provide feedback.

I provide timely and specific feedback to my students to help them improve their understanding and skills.

Rarely   Always

| 1 | 2 | 3 | 4 | 5 |

Evidence: Please describe one example of how you have provided timely and specific feedback to your students to help them improve their understanding and skills.

Curriculum and Instructional Planning

I plan my instruction using a backward design approach that aligns with content standards and learning objectives.

Rarely   Always

| 1 | 2 | 3 | 4 | 5 |

Evidence: Please describe one example of how you have planned your instruction using a backward design approach.

I use explicit instruction strategies to scaffold learning and build my students' understanding.

Rarely   Always

| 1 | 2 | 3 | 4 | 5 |

Evidence: Please describe one example of how you have used explicit instruction strategies to scaffold learning and build your students' understanding.

Differentiation and Individualization

I use explicit instruction strategies to differentiate instruction based on my students' needs and to promote individualized learning.

Rarely   Always

| 1 | 2 | 3 | 4 | 5 |

Evidence: Please describe one example of how you have used explicit instruction strategies to differentiate instruction based on your students' needs.

Figure 5.6: Sample self-reporting worksheet. continued →

Student Engagement and Motivation

I use explicit instruction strategies to promote my students' engagement and motivation.

Rarely				Always
1	2	3	4	5

Evidence: Please describe one example of how you have used explicit instruction strategies to promote your students' engagement and motivation.

I provide opportunities for my students to actively participate in their own learning.

Rarely				Always
1	2	3	4	5

Evidence: Please describe one example of how you have provided opportunities for your students to actively participate in their own learning.

Classroom Environment and Relationships

I create a positive and supportive classroom environment that promotes academic achievement.

Rarely				Always
1	2	3	4	5

Evidence: Please describe one example of how you have created a positive and supportive classroom environment that promotes academic achievement.

I use explicit instruction strategies to reinforce positive behavior and build trust and respect.

Rarely				Always
1	2	3	4	5

Evidence: Please describe one example of how you have used explicit instruction strategies to reinforce positive behavior and build trust and respect.

Evaluation and Continuous Improvement

I regularly evaluate the effectiveness of my instructional practices and use data to make improvements.

Rarely				Always
1	2	3	4	5

Evidence: Please describe one example of how you have used data to evaluate and improve your instructional practices.

*Visit **go.SolutionTree.com/schoolimprovement** for a free reproducible version of this figure.*

Fidelity Assessments

Regardless of the method teams use, assessing implementation fidelity requires careful planning and attention to detail. It is important to select a method that is appropriate for the intervention being delivered and to ensure that those involved in the assessment are properly trained and clearly understand the intervention and its intended implementation. It is also important to consider the limitations of each method. For example, fidelity checklists may not capture all aspects of an intervention, observation protocols may be influenced by observer bias, and self-report measures may be subject to social desirability bias.

In short, assessing implementation fidelity is a critical step in evaluating the success of educational interventions. By using appropriate methods to assess fidelity, teams ensure that the outcomes of an intervention result from the intervention itself and not other factors, and they identify areas for improvement in the implementation of the intervention.

Consider the following four key steps to designing fidelity assessment measures.

1. **Identify the active ingredients of the innovation:** Start by identifying the innovation components that are most essential for achieving the desired outcomes. You can do this by reviewing the existing literature on the innovation and by consulting with experts in the field.

2. **Determine the implementation strategies:** Identify the critical implementation strategies that are necessary to ensure fidelity to the innovation. This determination might include factors such as training, support, and ongoing monitoring of the implementation process.

3. **Select fidelity measurement tools:** Choose the most appropriate tools for measuring fidelity to the innovation based on the essential components of the intervention and implementation. These tools might include fidelity checklists, observation protocols, and self-report measures.

4. **Establish a fidelity threshold:** Establish a threshold for what constitutes acceptable fidelity to the innovation. This might involve setting a minimum number of components that must be implemented as intended, or specifying the level of quality required for each component.

Let's say that a school district has decided to implement a new reading intervention for struggling readers in its elementary schools. The goal of this innovation is to improve reading outcomes for struggling readers to reduce the achievement gap between struggling readers and their peers. To ensure that the intervention is implemented successfully, the school district needs to design effective fidelity assessment measures to monitor intervention fidelity over time. Let's look at how the school district follows the four steps to design these measures.

1. **Identify the active ingredients of the innovation:** The active ingredients of a reading intervention for struggling readers might include systematic phonics instruction, reading fluency practice, and vocabulary development.

2. **Determine the implementation strategies:** Essential components of implementing the reading intervention might include ensuring that teachers have received adequate training in the intervention, that they have access to the necessary materials and resources, and that they are using a consistent approach to instruction.

3. **Select fidelity measurement tools:** To assess fidelity to the reading intervention, the implementation team might use fidelity checklists to ensure that all the essential components of the intervention are being implemented. They might use observation protocols to capture the quality of instruction and teacher-student interactions. They might use self-report measures to gauge teacher perceptions of fidelity to the intervention.

4. **Establish a fidelity threshold:** A fidelity threshold for the reading intervention might specify that at least 80 percent of the intervention's active ingredients should be implemented with fidelity in order to ensure that the intervention is delivered as intended and is likely to produce the desired outcomes.

By following these four steps, education professionals can accurately monitor fidelity to an innovation, identify areas where the implementation process can improve, and make necessary adjustments to ensure that the innovation is delivered as intended.

The frequency with which schools and districts should assess fidelity will depend on a variety of factors, including the nature of the innovation, the resources available for fidelity assessment, and the goals of the assessment. In general, schools and districts should assess fidelity regularly to ensure that the innovation is implemented as intended and to identify areas where the implementation process can improve. The exact frequency of fidelity assessments will depend on the specific circumstances. For example, if the innovation is a relatively simple intervention (has few active ingredients and minimal skills to acquire), it may suffice to conduct fidelity assessments on a quarterly or biannual basis. If the innovation is a complex intervention (has more human components and requires staff to adopt new knowledge and skills), it may require conducting fidelity assessments on a more frequent basis, such as monthly.

In addition to the frequency of assessments, your implementation team should consider assessment timing. For example, it may be beneficial to conduct fidelity assessments at the beginning of the implementation process to establish a baseline level of fidelity and then to conduct follow-up assessments at regular intervals to monitor progress and identify areas for improvement. Overall, the timing of fidelity assessments should be determined based on the specific context and goals of assessment.

Once your implementation team has decided on and designed fidelity measures, their frequency, and who will utilize the measures, record all these decisions in the IMPACT implementation planning template (locate the Monitoring Strategies column, and record the monitoring plan in the "Are we doing what we said we would do?" section of the *Plan and Prepare* row). Creating a fidelity-monitoring plan addresses one of the "enemies of collective efficacy, ambiguity" (S. Hite, personal communication, March 28, 2023). Getting clear on what they want to have in place and monitoring whether it is in place allows teams to identify and address gaps.

Conclusion

Building a strong foundation for successful innovation implementation is critical. This involves identifying the active ingredients of the innovation, selecting evidence-based implementation strategies, developing a robust professional learning plan, and developing a plan to monitor the implementation. The *Plan and Prepare* stage lays the foundation for successful innovation implementation by ensuring that all key stakeholders understand the innovation's purpose and how it will be implemented. The goal is to build clarity and supports for the next stage to succeed. We want to eliminate the habit of adopting an innovation and jumping right to implementing it without setting up enabling conditions. Follow the *Plan and Prepare* stage to set up enabling conditions that will support the implementation teams, practitioners, and system leaders.

While it may take time and resources to fully implement an innovation, investing in the *Plan and Prepare* stage is critical for ensuring that the innovation is implemented with high integrity and achieves the intended outcomes. Remember to use the *Plan and Prepare* stage's key activities and objectives on page 121 to guide your work during this stage.

Plan and Prepare Stage IMPACT Implementation Planning Template

Complete the appropriate sections of the template with your team, recording your decisions in the space provided.

Inclusion | Meaningful Leadership | Professional Learning | Assess and Adjust | Collective Efficacy | Team

Implementation Team Members: ☐ System   ☐ School

Implementation Planning Template

Goal: Where are we going? (State the goal in SMART format.)

Stage	Problem	Evidence-Based Solutions	Implementation Strategies	Monitoring Strategies
Decide	Name the problem and why this problem needs to be solved.	Name the proposed solution (EBP).		
Plan and Prepare		Identify the active ingredients of the EBP. What is the EBP and its associated active ingredients?	How will we skill up to scale up? List implementation strategies here.	Are we doing what we said we would do? Identify the monitoring tools.
Implement		What intelligent adaptations to the EBP are needed based on culture, climate, and context?	Adapt existing implementation strategies or add new ones here.	Adapt existing monitoring tools or add new ones here.
Spread and Sustain		Identify resources needed to sustain implementation of the innovation.	Identify implementation strategies to support, spread, and sustain effective implementation.	Identify ongoing monitoring tools to inform implementation integrity.

Source: © 2022 by Jenice Pizzuto and Steven Carney.

The *Plan and Prepare* Stage Learning Journey Map

Use the following two questions to prompt active discussion and thoughtful responses, helping your team assess current practices and plan for future development. This is an opportunity for collective reflection and strategic action.

Together, review the concepts and practices from chapter 5 that your organization has already implemented. Discuss the effectiveness of your leadership and the progress of your implementation efforts. Use the questions to guide a rich conversation, and document your team's insights, commitments, and objectives in the learning journey map.

1. What concepts and practices from chapter 5 does our district or school currently have in place (with varying degrees of implementation)?
2. What observations and insights are we making about our leadership, leadership team, or organizational implementation efforts?

Team Takeaways	Team Commitment	Team Practice	Team Reflection	Team Goals
New learning, insights, and notices	Concepts, ideas, and practices we *commit to developing*	Strategies, processes, and tools we plan to *learn and practice*	Strategies, processes, tools, concepts, ideas, and so on we want to *go deeper into and share early successes on*	Strategies, processes, tools, concepts, ideas, and so on we want to *fully operationalize* through a commitment of time, resources, and policy

chapter 6

THE *IMPLEMENT* STAGE

*Leaders who understand the implementation dip know that
people are experiencing two kinds of problems when they are
in the dip—the social-psychological fear of change and the lack
of technical know-how or skills to make the change work.*

—Michael Fullan

Everyone has core memories, moments that deeply resonate and shape their lives. These incidents happen at different times and stick for various reasons. The following story is a core memory that deeply impacted staff at a school in Beaverton, Oregon.

As the August sun shone brightly through its large windows, the school library filled with excited and nervous teaching staff, school psychologists, counselors, paraprofessionals, and office and custodial personnel. Amid the exchanging of pleasantries and tales of summer vacations, colleagues anxiously awaited discovering why they had been summoned together. In their school, it was rare, if not unprecedented, for a leader to gather *all* staff in the same location. Yet Brian Horne, the school's principal, was not an ordinary leader. What he did that day in that school library to launch the new school year made an indelible impact on staff, students, and the community as a whole. He created a core memory.

As the meeting began, Mr. Horne walked throughout the library, passing out a five-dollar bill to every person in attendance. Each bill was individually sealed in a small, clear plastic bag. Aside from a turned corner or small crease, many of the bills appeared unremarkable. However, some of the five-dollar bills were crisp and new, as if they had come straight from the U.S. Mint. Others showed the wear and tear of having been exchanged through numerous acts of commerce. Two of the bills appeared to have been balled up, as if they were found in the bottom of a fifth grader's backpack a week after the book fair. There were even bills that were torn or not fully intact (though the serial numbers were still legible).

This distribution of five-dollar bills engendered conversations as the staff reviewed the condition of the cash each received. The staff with bills that were crisp and new appeared to be much more excited than those with the more tattered money. It was Mr. Horne's next move, however, that gave everyone pause. He asked, "Does each five-dollar bill have the same value? Look at them; some are torn, some only have the serial numbers left, and some are crisp and new. Do they all have the same value?" The resounding response was yes, of course! Everyone in the room agreed it did not matter what condition the bills were in; they held the same value, whether they were crisp and new or torn and tattered.

Mr. Horne went on to describe who would be coming through the school's doors that year: children who had enriched lives full of support, children who were accessing local homeless services, children who were facing behavioral challenges, children who were facing academic challenges—each and every one of them having the same value. At that point, he made it clear to the staff that they could do what they wished with that money. However, he set forth a challenge to the staff: "I ask you to hold onto this five-dollar bill for the school year and put it somewhere to remind you that the value each human who enters our building brings is equal, and our job is to meet them where they are and provide all the support necessary to help them learn and grow."

The bill was a vivid symbol of Mr. Horne's powerful opening-day message and the commitment made to students. It was displayed in the classroom and later in the office, a constant reminder of the inherent value of every individual encountered. As careers progressed, people continued to prominently display their five-dollar bills in their new leadership roles and organizations. Though many years removed from that August day, Mr. Horne's message stayed with many of those he inspired.

This core memory serves as a guiding principle, especially in this chapter about the *Implement* stage. While we do not have a five-dollar bill to give to each reader, we hope that the message in this vignette will be as impactful. As you dive into this chapter, remember the valuable lesson Brian Horne taught everyone at the school that day. In the complex but critical work of implementation and change, it is imperative that teams focus on and value each implementer. Like the bills Mr. Horne distributed to his staff, every colleague is different—and they are all equally worthy of respect and support as professionals and people. Implementation teams' goal during this stage is to model a learning and improvement mindset and bring it to the work and staff they serve.

In this chapter, we identify key activities and objectives of the *Implement* stage. Teams begin this stage by growing the implementers using supportive structures—providing expert coaching or technical assistance, acknowledging resistance to change and supporting staff through it, and securing funding are just a few examples. During this stage, teams also focus on cultivating a learning culture and using improvement cycles. To ensure implementation is proceeding successfully, teams gather data using monitoring tools, surveys and questionnaires, interviews, observations, examination of artifacts, and any documentation that provides evidence of implementation. Finally, teams harness data they've collected to take strategic action that addresses any barriers to successful implementation.

Growing the Implementers

Implementation is about learning how to get better at getting better. Nowhere in the implementation process is this more evident than in the *Implement* stage. You do not think or plan your way to change; you create change through your actions. In other words, merely contemplating or strategizing does not achieve your objectives; instead, actively altering your actions and habits is what truly brings about change (Grant, 2021).

Simply put, the goal of the *Implement* stage is to value the people in the system and grow the implementers. All the prework—building a guiding coalition of champions, adopting a change theory, and completing the *Decide* and *Plan and Prepare* stages—provides the infrastructure to support staff to, as Adam Grant (2021) puts it, behave their way to change.

The *Implement* stage is a vulnerable stage. It's a time of taking risks, which inevitably means emotions will vacillate between highs and lows as implementers develop new skills. Initial implementation needs to be a psychologically safe space, and applying the human- and learning-centered design elements of IMPACT serves as a guide to ensuring your implementation team considers implementers' needs during the *Implement* stage. This stage is critical to achieving the promised results of the selected evidence-based practice. Fully commit to the *Implement* stage with adequate resources (both human and capital) and time to reach the implementation plan goals and make an impact.

Table 6.1 (page 154) introduces the *Implement* stage's key activities and objectives through the IMPACT lens. You and your team will find this tool valuable to prepare

Table 6.1: *Implement* Stage Key Activities and Objectives

IMPACT	Key Activities	Key Objectives
Inclusion	Focus on growing the implementers through varied team learning activities, structures, and opportunities in a psycho-logically safe manner. Utilize feedback loops and focus on purposeful practice.	Increase buy-in; improve attitudes toward the change and willingness to participate.
Meaningful Leadership	Establish supportive structures that recognize implementation team members are leaders in the work. Establish and utilize varied communication loops that provide clarity on shared goals and ensure the implementers' feedback is received.	Create internal capacity, expertise, and high-functioning teams to support the implementation effort; increase participation and willingness to participate.
Professional Learning	Use the implementation plan and strategies to guide acquisition of the knowledge, skills, and attitudes necessary to produce results for the new innovation. Provide varied professional learning in an ongoing and embedded manner to support implementers in developing mastery of the new skills.	Improve levels of expertise within the organization; increase the skills, knowledge, and attitudes of the imple-menters; ensure a majority of implementers are trained in the new practice and are working toward mastery.
Assess and Adjust	Engage in iterative, rapid-cycle problem-solving protocols to strengthen the implementation methods, assess outcomes, and collect data to support fidelity, monitoring, and improvement. Make intelligent adaptations to the intervention as determined by the team members.	Identify barriers and facilitators to the implementation in a rapid and solution-focused, action-oriented manner.
Collective Efficacy	Clearly establish the why with all implementers, and frequently revisit the shared goal of team learning. Collectively ensure there is clarity about the active ingredients of the innovation. Celebrate mastery moments and met milestones.	Increase participation and willingness to adopt the new innovation with a growth mindset.
Team	Establish consistent meeting times, adopt agendas, identify protocols for team learning, and use the implementation plan. Gather implementation data, and support team member growth and learning. Address barriers and challenges, and communicate and celebrate small and large successes.	Across the system, commit to implementing the innovation while learning about what is going well and what is getting in the way and improving the delivery of the implementation plan.

*Visit **go.SolutionTree.com/schoolimprovement** for a free reproducible version of this table.*

for the stage. It describes what outcomes result from the major activities that take place. Use this overview to help key stakeholders or staff understand the purpose of the stage and build deliberately developmental implementation. Although this table covers the key activities to include in an IMPACT implementation plan, the table is not comprehensive. There are other activities involved in this stage, as described throughout the chapter. Review the activities in the table and check your plan to ensure you have built-in protocols, time, and resources to meet each objective.

The *Implement* stage is the time for learning by doing. The most successful schools and districts adopt a culture of learning for *all*, including their leaders, teachers, specialists, school boards, and stakeholders. This stage is collaborative and requires leveraging the implementation teams to codesign, colearn, and cocreate solutions to implementation setbacks as they occur. While this can feel unfamiliar and requires organization and logistics to be successful, authors Stefani Hite and Jenni Donohoo (2021) remind us, "Creating structures that increase the need for teachers to be interdependent encourages individual teachers to think and act as a team" (p. 69). As you move into the *Implement* stage, you have a number of decisions to make and actions to take. It is crucial that you keep the IMPACT model in mind. Additionally, you must recognize and establish the enabling conditions for staff to work toward mastering new skills.

Figure 6.1 (page 156) lists the major decisions that should be part of your IMPACT implementation plan and includes space your team can use to take notes. It's important to note that this is *not* a checklist to assign to a team member but a series of discussions the implementation team will collectively engage in and make decisions about. If you'd like to note when items have been completed, you may list the date in the space indicated for each decision.

Building Supportive Structures

It is the job of the leadership and implementation teams to develop structures that enable the implementation teams and implementers to learn, grow, and thrive. Deliberately developmental implementation focuses on meaningful leadership, adopting a flexible, motivational, and adaptive approach during the implementation process. Enabling and supporting deliberately developmental implementation means recognizing that positional authority is not always required for educators to lead and succeed in leadership roles (Hite & Donohoo, 2021). Providing supportive structures began in chapter 2 (page 41) with selecting a behavior change model, chapter 3 (page 59) with forming implementation teams, and chapters 4 (page 93) and 5 (page 119) with designing a research-based implementation plan that includes human- and learning-centered design elements. All these actions and steps build structures to support the implementation. For example, adopting a behavior change model is an enabling condition because resistance to change is inevitable and limits knowledge translation. When implementation teams use the adopted behavior change model to guide their planning and actions, it supports knowledge translation and impacts beliefs.

Implement Stage Decisions		
Decisions	**Notes**	**Date Completed**
Collectively share the compelling why throughout the organization, and develop clarity among the implementers, including the following. • Ensure building-level teams have buy-in and clarity. • Consider sharing the message together in each other's buildings; cross-pollination establishes a unified message and builds enthusiasm. • Ensure consistent messaging for the school board, community, and key stakeholders.		
Access technical assistance to ensure the implementation team has appropriate knowledge, skills, and abilities to support, engage, and train the implementers.		
Allocate funding to support implementation activities, meetings, professional learning, technical assistance, and training.		
Put the IMPACT implementation plan developed in the *Decide* stage and *Plan and Prepare* stage to work.		
Embrace flexible shared leadership, and blend technical and adaptive leadership solutions.		
Utilize the implementation strategies identified in the implementation plan, including the following. • Keep a record of all training and professional learning provided—who received it, when they received it, and how it occurred. • Regularly review progress in implementation team meetings.		
Implement agreed-on communication and feedback loops for stakeholders and implementers.		
Provide initial and follow-up training (ongoing and embedded professional learning) to implementers, including the following. • Provide opportunities for practice, reflection, and refinement. • Use learning walk implementation data to determine needs.		

Decisions	Notes	Date Completed
Engage implementers in purposeful practice, including the following. • Work toward mastery. • Engage in collectively acquiring skills. • Include reflection about skill acquisition and proficiency.		
Conduct learning walks to collect implementation-monitoring and fidelity data, including the following. • Collect data monthly in the beginning and at least three or four times a year until new practices are sustained. • Use monitoring tools cocreated by implementation teams, and perform in teams across the system. • Use the data to answer the question, "Are we doing what we said we would do?"		
Follow the professional learning plan designed in the *Plan and Prepare* stage, including the following. • Actively engage implementers in a variety of professional learning designs to support team learning and skill acquisition. • Provide peer-to-peer learning and observation opportunities.		
Regularly convene the systems- and building-level implementation teams, and utilize agreed-on agendas and protocols, including the following. • Building-level teams meet at least monthly on building in the early stages of implementation. • Systems-level team members meet every six to eight weeks and examine building-level implementation data (fidelity, outcomes, surveys, feedback, and so on) to monitor, support, remove barriers, and improve the implementation. • Engage in an iterative improvement cycle (Plan-Do-Study-Act, problem solving, and so on), identify gaps or problems, and make midcourse corrections. • Review and refine policies, procedures, staffing, and any infrastructure needs discovered during implementation.		

Figure 6.1: *Implement* stage decisions.

continued →

Decisions	Notes	Date Completed
Refine implementation team characteristics and behaviors described in chapter 3 (page 67) by engaging in rigorous and relevant team learning.		
Follow the plan to assess implementation fidelity, and bring the data to implementation team meetings, including the following. • Innovation-monitoring processes • A schedule of three times per year during the first year of implementation, two times per year following year one		
Incentivize and motivate implementation team members and implementers early and often, including the following. • Be kind to one another; this can be a challenging process. • Meet people where they are, and support them to the next level.		

*Visit **go.SolutionTree.com/schoolimprovement** for a free reproducible version of this figure.*

The Danish Clearinghouse for Educational Research studied what hinders or enables the use of research-based practices in knowledge translation. This large study looked at data from ten countries. Consider its findings:

> Finally it is interesting that the theory, the systematic review, and the experiences from the ten countries show that all six thematic areas— management and leadership, professional development, support systems, fidelity, attitudes and perceptions, and finally sustainability—are of vital importance in the implementation processes of research-based knowledge, whether this be in the form of specific interventions or a more conceptual form such as collaboration between schools. (Dyssegaard, Egelund, & Sommersel, 2017, p. 16)

Building supportive structures includes the following.

- Accessing and providing expert coaching
- Accessing and providing technical assistance from outside when warranted
- Utilizing a flexible and human-centered leadership approach

- Managing expectations and recognizing that there will be successes and setbacks

- Acknowledging resistance to change and utilizing tools (a selected behavior change model) to support staff through it

- Creating a shared understanding of the goal and the why, producing crystal clarity about what is being worked on together

- Establishing clarity on the active ingredients

- Adopting and utilizing an iterative improvement cycle (Plan-Do-Study-Act, problem solving)

- Allowing for intelligent adaptations after the active ingredients are clearly understood and securely in place (Sharples, Albers, et al., 2019)

- Securing, allocating, and funding time for teams to learn, meet, plan, and cocreate solutions to identified problems

- Aligning, adjusting, or refining schedules to support educators and implementation team meeting and planning needs

- Adopting and adhering to the use of agendas, communication protocols, and learning protocols

- Embodying and encouraging a learning and improvement mindset

- Staying unrelentingly committed to growing the implementers (Kegan & Lahey, 2016)

Applying these supportive structures allows for adaptive and technical leadership by the systems-level and building-level implementation teams during the implementation process. For the implementers and the implementation teams to gain new skills and effectively deliver the innovation, they must receive support (the Center for Implementation; Moore & Khan, n.d.). Because implementation is a process and not an isolated event, constantly assessing actions and continuously iterating and adapting to the changing implementation environment are necessary. Build supportive structures to bring out the best in the process of implementation. Utilize figure 6.1 (the *Implement* stage decisions chart, page 156) to guide teams as the system builds supportive structures.

Cultivating a Learning Culture and Using Improvement Cycles

The *Implement* stage is a time for celebration. It is a time to implement the plan (or plans) for team learning. Now is the time when all readiness steps, planning, and preparation begin to pay off. Take time to celebrate this accomplishment as you launch the *Implement* stage. Acknowledging the new stage and celebrating the progress to date as implementation teams and with staff will build enthusiasm and momentum for the next big step, getting the new practices firmly in place. Resist the temptation to overlook this vital step! Recognition enhances staff morale, improves culture, promotes team building, and keeps people going when challenging issues arise.

It is important to note that recognitions and celebrations need to be authentic (naming what milestone or skill was accomplished) and honor system and group progress (not individuals). Keep them simple and doable.

Consider the following examples we've witnessed.

- Provide root beer floats at the end of the day.

- Put together a group playlist and use it during a learning event (you would be surprised how much people love hearing their song during lunch or a break).

- End a learning session with a sentence stem such as, "I am proudest of my team for _____ because _____." Have participants share their responses.

While these actions may seem minor in terms of investment, they invariably yield both short-term and long-term benefits for individuals and teams.

The following sections offer rationale, actionable tools, and examples to enhance your team's expertise, capabilities, and mindset. These elements are crucial for those actively engaged in the innovative work. In our experience, a lack of these exact actions leads to a shortfall in change initiatives, resulting in the implementation gap.

Why Together Is Better

At its heart, human- and learning-centered design is about involving implementers throughout the course of the implementation. Practitioners must be directly engaged in the design process, relevant professional learning, and continuous and iterative improvement cycles. The benefits of employing human- and learning-centered design are well articulated in the Bellwether Education Partners report titled *Creating More Effective, Efficient, and Equitable Education Policies With Human-Centered Design* (Weeby, 2018):

> Policy practitioners can use human-centered design methods to 1) articulate more accurate definitions of problems and more relevant solutions, 2) generate a wider variety of potential solutions leading to innovation, and 3) meaningfully involve constituents in the creation of rules and laws that affect them. (p. 5)

The report goes on to state that when educational institutions effectively use human-centered design methods (we include relevant learning about the innovation to strengthen the outcomes), they can enrich and unify conventional research-based practices (Weeby, 2018).

Adopting an approach of shared learning is human and learning centered. During the *Implement* stage, we aim to get at least 50 percent of the implementers to regularly implement with integrity. To do this, learning together is key. To achieve results, educators must clearly understand the essential components required to maintain fidelity. Providing support for teachers and fostering collaborative practices are important, and these efforts may continue even after the implementation period has ended (Dyssegaard et al., 2017). Learning together is about providing every opportunity for the implementers to succeed. There's no "us versus them." Learning together means people will acquire skills together; they will skill up (build knowledge, skills, and attitudes) to scale up. Acquiring skills together allows implementers to iteratively develop mastery, safely examine encountered failures, and make adjustments.

What does it look like to acquire skills together? Table 6.2 (page 162) provides a template for guiding your team in planning skill acquisition for implementers in a human- and learning-centered manner. Use this tool with your team when planning to build the knowledge, skills, and attitudes of the people you serve.

Learning together in a psychologically safe manner is the leading variable we have seen build mastery experiences. Working toward and reaching mastery experiences is important; it is a driver of intrinsic motivation and the number-one source of efficacy (Hite & Donohoo, 2021). Engaging and involving implementers in the learning process described in table 6.2 gives them agency over their experiences and honors them as human beings.

Table 6.2: Protocols to Acquire Skills Together and Enhance Collaboration and Learning

What	How
Guide learning.	Use text-rendering protocols, select short sections related to skill acquisition, and complete in-learning events on building with staff (most important point, four As, focused reading, A–B teach, jigsaw, say something, block party, read and connect, and so on).
	Use protocols to surface problems, goal setting, and planning (fishbone diagram; force field analysis; What? So What? Now What?; if . . . then, and so on).
	Use activating protocols to involve implementers in the learning process and thinking (finding common ground; give one, get one; grounding; help wanted ads; know, want to know, learned; and so on).
	Use protocols to practice, observe, and reflect on practice (fishbowl, video of an expert, video of practitioners, video of oneself, and so on).
	Use protocols and engage in text to act as a third point to deepen conversations and promote engagement in a psychologically safe manner.
Ensure equity of voice.	The use of protocols acts as a skilled facilitator and serves to provide equity of voice. Select protocols that allow each person to contribute in order to surface the diverse perspectives in the room and create a safe space for sharing. Examples: • Ask staff to respond to questions independently on sticky notes, share the sticky notes on chart paper (no names), and then review. • Ask people to respond to questions or share in a whip (one person speaks at a time in a round-robin fashion prior to any discussion); work in pairs or triads prior to opening things up to the wider group. • Use process protocols such as chalk talk to surface thinking.
Build new skills and habits.	Protocols help build new skills and habits by: • Offering structure and consistency for focused learning, which includes initial training, highly skilled coaching, and opportunities to practice independently, with a peer, and with feedback • Encouraging a learning-focused, active, and personal approach to skill development and habit formation through collaboration and idea exchange • Promoting reflection, self-assessment, and continuous growth, while also providing the necessary time and space for individuals to work toward mastery
Surface problems.	Building- and systems-level implementation teams regularly examine implementation and fidelity data; review surveys, observation data, and artifacts; and engage in an iterative problem-solving process. Establish processes and protocols to gather feedback from the implementers (building-level implementation team meetings, surveys, and interviews).
Improve culture.	Move from work in isolation to collaboration. Work on shared goals related to a relevant why. Use protocols to engage the group, provide equity of voice, and drive a learning and improvement focus. Build in time and space for teams to learn, develop skills, exchange viewpoints, surface problems, identify solutions, address barriers, and stay the course.

What	How
Design effective professional learning for adults.	The use of protocols is important to effective professional learning design for adults, as it aligns with the seven features of effective professional development identified by the Learning Policy Institute (Darling-Hammond et al., 2017). Protocols, as structured processes or guidelines, contribute to creating meaningful and efficient learning experiences for adult participants. Here's how protocols relate to these seven features. 1. **Professional learning is content focused:** Use protocols to help center discussions on learning goals for better content understanding and relevance. 2. **Professional learning incorporates active learning:** Use protocols to foster active learning experiences that result in problem solving and discussions for effective knowledge retention and application. 3. **Professional learning supports collaboration:** Use protocols to foster teamwork, shared learning, and productive environments through group work guidelines. 4. **Professional learning uses models of effective practice:** Use protocols that incorporate evidence-based strategies to enhance professional learning's quality and impact. 5. **Professional learning provides coaching and expert support:** Use protocols to structure personalized guidance, feedback, and support. 6. **Professional learning offers feedback and reflection:** Use protocols that result in timely feedback and the opportunity to internalize new skills. 7. **Professional learning is of sustained duration:** Use protocols to support ongoing professional learning that results in deeper content exploration and ongoing growth. When designing training, workshops, and learning events, keep these seven features in mind.
Build agreements and use discussion and decision tools.	Use agendas that follow an iterative problem-solving process. Develop and use norms. Differing viewpoints, ideals, and challenging conversations are features of the *Implement* stage when deploying human- and learning-centered design. Include discussion and decision-making tools to ensure the teams remain solution focused and action oriented and do not get stalled. Dialogue and discussion are key tools for successful collaboration (Wellman & Lipton, 2017). "Data-driven dialogue and data-driven discussion . . . require the full attention of participants, careful listening, linguistic skills and the intention to separate data and facts from inference and opinions" (p. 40). What are the defining characteristics of dialogue and discussion? In *dialogue*, participants think holistically, make connections, inquire into assumptions, develop shared meaning, and seek understanding; in *discussion*, participants think analytically, make distinctions, inquire into assumptions, agree on action, and seek decisions (Wellman & Lipton, 2017).

continued ➞

What	How
Use a variety of training and learning methodologies.	Make learning events interactive, incorporate the seven features of professional learning, and include discussion, reflection, and opportunities to practice, demonstrate skills, and receive feedback.
	Provide coaching, mentoring, collaborative learning events, and structured peer-to-peer collaboration, and use exemplar videos and videos of staff and self in small- and large-group settings.
Use implementation data to identify learning needs and follow up learning events.	Perform collective and nonevaluative learning walks to gather implementation data. Gather data via surveys, observations, fidelity checklists, and interviews.
	Implementation teams participate in regularly scheduled meetings and, using an agreed-on agenda, analyze data collected to identify areas of high implementation integrity (celebrate) and areas of low implementation integrity. The teams analyze why low integrity may be happening and codesign solutions (asking, "What learning needs are not being met?") to support implementers in gaining skills and working toward mastery. Use protocols to surface data observations in a safe and objective manner (data-driven dialogue; what's the problem, what's not the problem; mapping highs and lows; consensograms; brainstorm and pass; and so on).

The table discusses the use of protocols to support acquiring skills together and planning for rich, rigorous professional learning. There are many high-quality sources of protocols to support teams as they design high-quality professional learning that utilizes adult learning principles. We recommend two books by Bruce Wellman and Laura Lipton: (1) *Groups at Work: Strategies and Structures for Professional Learning* (Lipton & Wellman, 2016) and (2) *Data-Driven Dialogue: A Facilitator's Guide to Collaborative Inquiry* (Wellman & Lipton, 2017). Additionally, the National School Reform Faculty's Harmony Education Center website (https://nsrfharmony.org) is a fantastic online resource for protocols.

While it may feel uncomfortable or new to flatten the hierarchy, focus on a narrow set of high-quality objectives, and lean into growing the implementers by acquiring skills together. Empowering collective learning is an important precondition for effective implementation. You cannot expect educators to be proficient at something they do not possess the skills to perform. For example, in our initial meetings with a school or district to implement the science of reading or new curricula, we often ask, "When was the last time your staff received training or learning in the skills you are expecting?" A long pause and quick glances around the room for an answer ensue. We then ask the follow-up question, "Was it last year?" If the answer is yes, we ask, "How often did it happen, and what methodologies and how many opportunities were provided?" Unfortunately, though, the answer to "Was it last year?" sometimes is no.

We often find that districts only provide initial training when they adopt a new reading curriculum with a couple of follow-up opportunities related to the materials. The districts also neglect to provide learning on the active ingredients of instructional routines that gain results, an essential part of teaching evidence-based reading instruction and assessment to inform the instruction. This is insufficient. How could the leadership expect the staff to perform high-quality reading instruction when they never received proper professional learning opportunities, coaching, or structures to build competence and confidence in delivering high-quality reading instruction? Simply providing materials training at the beginning of the implementation does not meet the needs of the implementers.

This is what we call a *systems failure*, not a *teacher failure*. Building cohesive teacher knowledge and skills is the system's responsibility. It is important to invest time in collaborative team learning for the implementers during the *Implement* stage. Each building-based implementation team will lead and support this work. The learning events (training) occur as large-group events, front-loading the entire district with key components, building buy-in, creating a shared understanding of the why and vision, and developing skills. Additionally, as teams determine learning needs and identify gaps in knowledge, skills, and attitudes, they will also provide site-specific or skill-specific learning opportunities.

Sample Tools

To get you started on your journey of learning together, here are some sample tools and protocols you can use in developing your team learning.

Implementation Team Meeting Agendas

Consider figure 6.2 (page 166), which contains a sample agenda teams can use for implementation team meetings.

Using protocols for team learning assists teams in building knowledge about the new instructional routines and provides a safe place for open discussions, practice, and reflection. Fostering a learning and improvement mindset and growing the implementers entail intentionally and routinely embedding learning about the innovation within the job context. This involves initiating learning protocols at the start of implementation team meetings, during staff meetings, and across training sessions and workshops. The goal and hope here is to employ intentional learning designs intended to enhance implementer skills, knowledge, and attitudes. This approach is not a one-and-done event but a sustained mindset that manifests in ongoing job-embedded learning opportunities focused on skilling staff up to scale up the evidence-based practice. Consider the following sample protocols to get started.

Implementation Team Meeting Minutes

School: Summit High School

	Date	Time (Beginning and End)	Location	Facilitator	Minute Taker	Data Analyst	Timekeeper	Administrator
Today's Meeting	November 12	2:00–3:30 p.m.	Conference room B	Dr. Helen Ramirez	Mr. Leon Yu	Ms. Anita Desai	Mr. Derek Sun	Ms. Rachel Eisner
Next Meeting	November 25	2:00–3:30 p.m.	Conference room B					

Team Members and Attendance

Place a ✓ to the left of the name if the team member is present.

☑ Dr. Helen Ramirez   ☑ Mr. Derek Sun

☑ Mr. Leon Yu   ☑ Ms. Rachel Eisner

☑ Ms. Anita Desai

Today's Agenda Items

- Examine student project submissions.
- Review PBL's impact on cross-curricular competencies.
- Discuss strategies for involving external community partners in PBL.

Agenda Items for the Next Meeting

- Present best practices for PBL assessment.
- Plan for an exhibition of student projects to the school community.

Systems Overview

Overall Status	Measures Used	Data Collection Schedule	Current Level or Rate
Meeting expectations with room for growth in student autonomy	Student project rubrics, self-assessment surveys, teacher observations	End of each grading period and upon project completion	60 percent of projects meet or exceed rubric standards (goal is 75 percent).

Problem-Solving Process

Date of initial meeting: September 1	Dates of review meetings: November 12, November 25

Brief problem description (for example, location, group identifier, brief item description):

Need to enhance critical thinking and real-world application skills in students

Precise Problem Statement *What? When? Where? Who? Why? How often?*	Goal and Timeline *What? By when?*	Solution Actions *By who? By when?*	Fidelity and Outcome Data *What? When? Who?*	IMPLEMENT SOLUTION	Did it work? Preliminary results show improvement in student engagement and project quality.
• **What?** Insufficient critical thinking and real-world application in student work • **When?** Ongoing, most noticeable at the start of the academic year • **Where?** Across all grades at Summit High School • **Who?** High school student body • **Why?** Traditional lecture-based instruction limiting student engagement • **How often?** Consistently observed in annual student performance reviews	Elevate the quality of student projects to align with PBL rubric standards by the end of the first grading period.	• **By who?** All high school teachers, PBL coordinators, and community partners • **By when?** Continuous action with periodic reviews every grading period	• **What?** Project rubrics, student and teacher surveys, community partner feedback • **When?** At the end of each project and grading period • **Who?** Teachers and PBL coordinators • **What outcome data will we collect?** Analysis of project rubric scores, student reflective journals, stakeholder feedback		**Fidelity Data:** Level of Implementation ☐ Not started ☐ Partial implementation ☐ Implemented with fidelity ☐ Stopped *Notes:* There is some inconsistency in PBL integration across different subjects. **Outcome Data (Current Levels):** Comparison to Goal ☐ Worse ☐ No change ☐ Improved but not to goal ☐ Goal met *Notes:* Student projects are showing greater depth and complexity. We need to focus on real-world relevance.

Figure 6.2: Sample implementation team meeting agenda.

Source: Adapted from Todd, Newton, Horner, Algozzine, & Algozzine, 2015. Used with permission.

Visit go.SolutionTree.com/schoolimprovement for a free reproducible version of this figure.

The Four As Protocol

The four As protocol is helpful for text-rendering activities. A team can use it to discuss a text about a new innovation or strategy and record notes in a chart. It serves as a structured method for teams to collaboratively dissect and discuss key concepts using the following categories. This variation is adapted from the National School Reform Faculty (2015).

1. **Agree:** This category is for points in the text that participants agree with. These points might include concepts that resonate with their existing beliefs or practices they find effective.

2. **Argue:** Here, participants note any disagreements with or counterpoints to the text that they have. This category encourages critical thinking and can highlight areas of potential debate or misunderstanding.

3. **Ahas:** This category captures the insights or realizations (epiphanies) that come from engaging with the text. These could be new ideas, connections to existing knowledge, or surprising elements that challenge previous assumptions.

4. **Aspire:** In this category, participants note aspirations, or actions they are inspired to take after engaging with the text. These could include changes to practice, new strategies to implement, or goals to strive for as a result of the insights gained.

Figure 6.3 shows one example of how a team may use this protocol.

Agree	Ahas
I agree that giving students a choice in their learning leads to higher engagement. When they feel in control, they're more invested.	I had an aha moment seeing that student-directed learning can be scaffolded for different age groups, adapted to their developmental stages.
I concur that student-directed learning can foster critical thinking skills as students navigate their own educational paths.	Realizing that this approach could help identify students' passions and potential career paths was enlightening.
Argue	**Aspire**
I'm skeptical about how much freedom we should give students. Without structure, some may struggle to stay on task.	I aspire to create a classroom environment where students can choose from different learning stations based on their interests.
The text doesn't address how to balance standardized curriculum requirements with student-directed projects.	One action I will take is to design a pilot project for student-directed learning in one unit of study and observe the outcomes.

Figure 6.3: Sample four As protocol.

*Visit **go.SolutionTree.com/schoolimprovement** for a free reproducible version of this figure.*

The four As protocol asks team members to read a text related to learning about the innovation, strategy, or practice being implemented. Text selection is crucial; select a text that is relevant to the shared goals, is new or reviewed, and is credible and research based.

Provide each team member a copy of the selected text for discussion and a copy of the four As chart, and set aside time for members to read the selection. Decide as a team how much time you'll devote to this protocol, usually somewhere between fifteen and thirty minutes. Keep the passage to about eight pages maximum to avoid dragging out the process.

Set a timer, read the passage, and take notes, asking participants to wait silently until the entire team has completed the task. When the time is up, partner up participants by using a numbering-off system. Partners meet to discuss their four As for a designated amount of time. Finally, come back together as a team and discuss your findings.

The Feedback Carousel

The feedback carousel is a protocol developed by the Center for Leadership and Educational Equity (n.d.b). Its purpose is to get different kinds of feedback from a large number of people in a relatively short period of time. We have found the carousel to be particularly effective for getting feedback on a plan for future work. For example, implementation teams might use the feedback carousel to gather perception data and feedback on the development of skills, attitudes toward new initiatives, and staff understanding of the new work's key components.

To set up this activity, have each participant display the significant elements of their plan on a piece of chart paper. Encourage them to use color and creativity. Next to each piece of chart paper, put up another chart paper that is divided into four parts as shown in figure 6.4.

Clarifying Questions	Probing Questions
Recommendations	Resources

Figure 6.4: Feedback carousel chart.

*Visit **go.SolutionTree.com/schoolimprovement** for a free reproducible version of this figure.*

Distribute sticky notes to all participants, set a timer, and instruct the participants to rotate through as many plans as time permits and write their feedback on a sticky note placed in the appropriate quadrant. Allow a few minutes at the end of the activity to debrief the process.

Cycle of Inquiry Protocol

The cycle of inquiry is a structured process for teams to engage in collaborative inquiry and reflection on their teaching practices, student learning, and school culture. Also developed by the Center for Leadership and Educational Equity (n.d.a), this protocol is iterative, which means that teams repeat the cycle multiple times, building on their previous learning and refining their inquiry process. The goal is to create a culture of continuous improvement of learning, where educators work collaboratively to improve their practices and enhance student learning.

Figure 6.5 illustrates the cycle of inquiry protocol.

Cycle of Inquiry

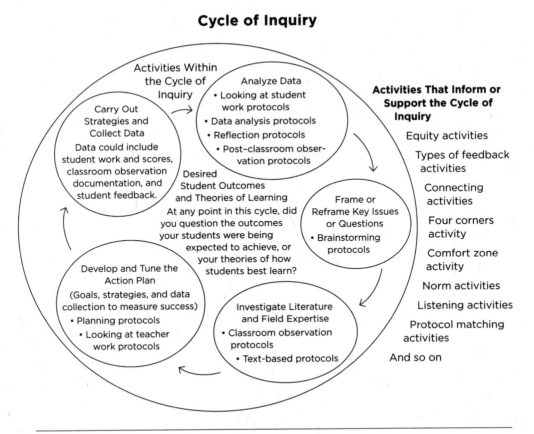

Source: Center for Leadership and Educational Equity, n.d.a.

Figure 6.5: The cycle of inquiry protocol.

The What? So What? Now What? Protocol

The What? So What? Now What? protocol, developed by educational consultant Gene Thompson-Grove (Center for Leadership and Educational Equity, n.d.c),
allows participants to connect with one another and with each other's work, while at
the same time allowing all team members to get useful feedback.

Introduce the protocol goals and steps, and then divide the team into groups of
three or four. Use the following process to undertake the cycle and complete the
protocol; note that all participants take a turn facilitating, all participants present,
and the facilitator also gives feedback.

1. Outline a challenge or success (five minutes).

    a. Participants individually outline a current challenge or success
    related to their work.

    b. Participants answer two questions: What? ("What did I do? What
    am I working on?") and So what? ("Why is this important to me?").

2. In rounds, repeat the following for each participant in the group
(approximately fifteen minutes per person).

    a. The first presenter explains what they've written to their group,
    ending with a focus question. Participants in the group take notes
    and write questions.

    b. The group asks questions, sticking to two or three only.

    c. Individuals in the group talk among themselves while the
    presenter listens in on the conversation, taking notes and
    considering new insights and possible next steps. The presenter is
    silent during this step. The group takes up each of the following
    sentence stems in some way, along with any other focused
    discussion the presenter has asked the group to have.

        i. "What I heard the presenter say was . . ."

        ii. "Why this seems important to the presenter is . . ."

        iii. "What I wonder is . . ." or "The questions this raises for
        me are . . ."

        iv. "What this means to me is . . ."

        v. "What I might suggest is . . ."

    d. The presenter reflects to the group, "Now what?"

3. Debrief.

Note an important point made by researchers Higgins and colleagues in their 2012 article "Implementation Teams: A New Lever for Organizational Change" regarding team learning. They argue that team members need to feel like they are learning and growing in order to be motivated by the implementation team's work. Otherwise, their attention may drift, and the team may become just a group of individuals who are not truly working together, which can ultimately undermine the implementation effort.

Gathering Implementation Data

The *Implement* stage is the time when the implementation teams meet regularly (at least monthly in the early stages for building-level teams) to monitor the implementation plan. They need to answer the question, "Are we doing what we said we would do?"

During this stage, implementation teams:

- Use the fidelity-monitoring forms developed in the *Plan and Prepare* stage (chapter 5, page 135)

- Review and analyze the implementation data collected and make recommendations and decisions based on the data

- Use quality iterative improvement cycles

- Respond to surfaced barriers

- Address learning gaps

- Use the completed IMPACT implementation planning template and adopted behavior change model

This work culminates in action plans to resolve the identified gaps and learning needs. Refer to the problem identification tools in chapter 4 (page 104) as needed to facilitate the process of solving problems and reviewing implementation data. Using tools such as these will allow the team to critically reflect on the data without personalizing those data. The goal is to reflect on the data by considering multiple viewpoints to understand the core issue and possible root causes (Khan & Moore, 2021).

Keep It Simple!

The primary focus of an implementation team during the *Implement* stage's team meetings is to answer these big questions.

- Is the team (are the implementers) learning and building knowledge, skills, and attitudes for the innovation?
    - › What evidence or artifacts do you have to demonstrate it? Think about materials developed for and from pieces of training, calendars of learning events, artifacts from learning events, surveys of pre-post attitudes, and so on.
- Are those knowledge, skills, and attitudes what the team needs to learn? And do they align with when the team needs to use them?
    - › How do you know? Consider what data you utilized to determine a skill gap and a demonstrated need.
    - › Is it common for implementation teams to learn ahead (frequently from outside experts) of implementers and utilize a train-the-trainer model for building knowledge, skills, and attitudes for staff?
- Is the team (are the implementers) actively involved in the learning?
    - › Are protocols to promote cognitive engagement being utilized? Are professional learning principles being utilized in designing learning events?
- Are we doing what we said we would do?
    - › Are we following the IMPACT implementation planning template? Are we using the implementation strategies?
    - › Are we collecting the fidelity data and monitoring the implementation?

If yes, we should celebrate and record successes. If no, we should use a protocol or process to discover what is getting in the way and make a midcourse correction.

The implementation team uses the following tools in the team meetings.

- Norms and agendas
- Dialogue and discussion tools
- Decision-making tools
- Learning protocols relevant to the task
- Implementation data
    - › Qualitative information: Surveys, observations, and feedback

> › Quantitative information: Artifacts, records of tasks completed, evidence of learning collected, and outcome and summative data (infrequently used in the early stages of implementation because until the innovation is firmly in place, improvement in outcome data will not be expected)

- The implementation plan
- A focus on strategies, actions, and results

Collect Implementation Data

We find that the concept of collecting implementation data is new to many organizations in the education field. Teams must collect implementation data when implementing a new program, practice, policy, or strategy (a new innovation). Note this is explicitly stated as a step in the IMPACT implementation planning template; the Monitoring Strategies column centers on data collection. It is the job of the systems-level and building-level implementation teams to monitor the implementation.

A barrier to monitoring is that collecting, reviewing, and discussing implementation and fidelity data can be uncomfortable. This does not have to be the case; teams can successfully address this barrier. The collection of implementation data is not evaluative—teams are *not* collecting teacher names or identifying markers. The data collection monitors the system and the implementation process to improve services, learning events, and training. Gathering implementation data (not teacher performance data!) is vital to solving problems and getting results from the selected innovation. Monitoring implementation fidelity helps teams understand the level of adherence to the active ingredients. This is why the IMPACT implementation framework involves the implementers' voices from the very beginning of the design process. Including implementers' voices guarantees better acceptance and understanding of the active ingredients. In fact, the implementers actively participate in formulating agreements on the active ingredients. Inclusion, in this way, helps smooth the path for monitoring implementation fidelity.

Researchers Camilla Brørup Dyssegaard, Niels Egelund, and Hanna Bjørnøy Sommersel (2017) identify the following key points for supporting fidelity.

- Using fidelity checklists
- Conducting video observations
- Providing group feedback sessions
- Raising teachers' awareness of requirements
- Offering tangible guidelines

- Tailoring program activities to staff and school settings
- Supporting teachers
- Implementing collaborative practices

Notice that all these components are embedded in the IMPACT implementation framework. So, while fidelity monitoring can sound scary or suggest blame or shame, that's not the case. The process is really about checking in to see if the team and implementers are doing what they said they would do and reacting to what they find. It's about asking, "How is it going?" and "What do you need?"

Implementation data collection focuses on collecting evidence of the percentage of implementers who implement the active ingredients as agreed upon in the implementation plan. Both qualitative and quantitative data are collected. In the early stages of implementation, teams rely more heavily on qualitative data. Remember that examining student outcome data when you are unsure whether the innovation has been successfully implemented can create confusion and contribute to implementation failure or abandonment.

Consider the following tools for collecting data.

- Cocreated monitoring tools (developed in the *Plan and Prepare* stage or along the way)
- Surveys and questionnaires
- Interviews
- Observations
- Examination of artifacts
- Audits of records, notes, and documents that are evidence of implementation

Collect implementation data monthly early on in the implementation. This data collection occurs systemwide, not teacher by teacher or school by school. The implementation teams use the data to determine whether the innovation is taking hold. Is it persistently and pervasively in place across the system? Teams review the collected data utilizing the adopted iterative improvement cycle and other protocols to ensure that feelings, emotions, and perceptions do not cloud the interpretation of the data. When creating tools, make sure they monitor the active ingredients and the core components of the innovation.

Let's look at an example. Figure 6.6 (page 176) contains a sample of an observation data collection tool designed by a school district implementing multitiered systems of supports. One strategy the district selected was to improve core instruction in reading. The district adopted daily differentiated small-group instruction during the core reading block to do so. After the district provided initial and ongoing training, it was time to monitor the practice to determine uptake and further training and learning needs. Figure 6.6 is the implementation-monitoring tool the implementation teams codesigned based on the active ingredients of the practice within grades K–2 and grades 3–5.

Elementary Small-Group Differentiated Instruction Form for Phonics Learning Walks

Date:	Observer:	K–2 or 3–5 (circle which grades observed)		
Group size:	Lesson objective:			
Classroom Routines and Procedures		**Yes**	**No**	**Questions for Discussion**
Less than one minute of transition time to or from group • Each observer should time the transition from start to finish, including any instructions given. • The entire transition time is recorded, even if there are directions for those not in the group.		☐	☐	
100 percent small-group student participation the majority of the time		☐	☐	
*Opportunities to respond (Tally below; see the next page for more guidance.) Total: _____				
Materials		**Yes**	**No**	**Questions for Discussion**
Materials prepared prior to the beginning of the Tier 2 lesson (List the ones used.)		☐	☐	
Evidence-based materials (List the ones used.)		☐	☐	
Materials at students' instructional level—not too easy, not too hard (List the ones used.)		☐	☐	

Figure 6.6: Sample implementation-monitoring tool.

Instructional Focus That Follows a Clear Evidence-Based Sequence (Select one from the following.)	Yes	No	Questions for Discussion
• Comprehension (Write notes on the back.)	☐	☐	
• Phonemic awareness	☐	☐	

• Phonics (Check for the following.)
 	
  – Phonemic awareness or high-frequency words routine followed
 	
  – Intro sound and blending—skill explicitly stated and taught or reviewed
 	
  – Decodable text routine followed
 	
  – Writing on connected text (optional)
	☐	☐	

• Other: _____	☐	☐	
Other Areas Working Toward	**Yes**	**No**	**Questions for Discussion**
Meaningful standards-based work independent of the teacher (partner, individual, or small group)	☐	☐	
Comprehension notes:			

Opportunities-to-Respond Agreements:

- Every time a teacher cues for a response is an opportunity to respond.
- Record *C* for "choral" and *I* for "independent."
- Sound/blend/word counts as three opportunities to respond.
- Letter/sound/card counts as one opportunity to respond.
- Grades K–2 (likely age) read a sentence to themselves, then chorally count as one opportunity to respond.
- Grades 3–5 (likely age) read a paragraph to themselves, then chorally count as one opportunity to respond.

Types of Responses:

Verbal

- Choral response
- Partner response
- Team response
- Individual response
- Discussion

Written

- Graphic organizers
- Whiteboards
- Response cards or response sheets
- Writing frames

Action

- Acting or simulations
- Gestures
- Facial expressions
- Hand signals

Reading

- Whisper (silent) reading
- Echo reading
- Choral reading
- Cloze reading
- Partner reading

Source: Klamath Falls City School District, Oregon. Used with permission.

*Visit **go.SolutionTree.com/schoolimprovement** for a free reproducible version of this figure.*

The first time the implementation teams deployed their implementation-monitoring tool, they realized they needed to calibrate a couple of areas and refine the form. They needed to clarify what counted as an opportunity to respond and specify what 100 percent engagement in small-group instruction looked and sounded like. At the following meeting, they made the necessary adjustments to the specified areas and improved the form's design for better functionality. This is the refined version of the form. The next time they went out and gathered data, they were aligned. The point is to develop the tool, get it into action, and improve it as the team deems necessary.

Teams collect implementation data across all campuses that are implementing the innovation. To alleviate anxiety for staff and develop clarity across all buildings, implementation teams must communicate to staff about the purpose of data collection. Before collecting data, communicate why the data are being collected, how they will be collected, and what will be done with them. Be *transparent, inclusive,* and *planful* when setting out to collect implementation data. Inform implementers that the activity will occur; explicitly tell them that it is geared toward systems evaluation, not teacher evaluation; and never collect teacher names on forms.

Implementation team members may be familiar with instructional rounds and walkthroughs, but these are not the same as implementation learning walks. These learning walks focus solely on gathering data to improve implementation. Teams conduct them across the system, not to gather teacher-specific information (these are not coaching sessions for staff members), but to collect fidelity data to inform the quality of implementation. Prior to performing learning walks, implementation teams develop clarity about the walks' purpose, calibrate the walks, and create agreements on how to conduct the process, deciding what behaviors and routines they will analyze. They can and should provide systems-level feedback while avoiding individual teacher feedback.

Table 6.3 contains a chart clarifying what implementation learning walks are and are not. Share it with implementers prior to coperforming these learning walks.

Table 6.3: Characteristics of Implementation Learning Walks Chart

Implementation Learning Walks Are:	Implementation Learning Walks Are Not:
Monitoring implementation	Walkthroughs
Focused on active ingredients of agreed-on implementation activities	Peer observations
Collecting systemwide implementation data	Teacher-by-teacher or school-by-school data collection
Collecting data to inform the implementation	Evaluations
Focused on learning and improvement for the system	Peer feedback or coaching
Used to design professional learning for adults to improve skill acquisition and competencies	Random acts of training in reaction to individual findings
Used to identify systemwide skill and knowledge gaps and plan learning events to address them across the system	Observations used as a reactive strategy, such as to target monitoring of specific teachers because there is a concern
Conducted by implementation teams (which include implementers)	Composed of only leadership (the principal, superintendent, district staff, and so on)

The building-level implementation team and principal host a staff meeting, share a copy of the chart in table 6.3, and answer any questions staff may have. They describe why they are conducting the learning walks (for systemwide implementation data, not teacher evaluation), when the learning walks will happen, and how they will occur. After conducting the learning walks and analyzing the data, teams develop concrete action plans to address any gaps observed in the learning walks. For example, the teams monitoring the implementation of elementary small-group differentiated instruction for phonics (figure 6.6, page 176) observed that only 55 percent of staff were accurately utilizing opportunities to respond. To address this identified gap, the teams agreed on three action items: (1) provide refresher trainings at each school, (2) provide opportunities for staff to request that a coach support them in the strategy, (3) provide time for peers to observe each other and provide feedback. Additionally, the implementation teams agreed on a completion date and set a time to conduct cross-campus learning walks to determine whether at least 80 percent of the staff were utilizing the opportunities to respond to the strategy with fidelity.

To prepare for implementation learning walks, implementation teams *collectively* do the following.

- Design and agree on a fidelity-monitoring tool (tied to implementation planning template goals).

- Provide training and calibration for utilizing the agreed-on tool (use table 6.3 in training).

- Emphasize a learning and improvement mindset.

- Use inclusive language, such as *ours* (not *mine*, *yours*, or *theirs*).

- Suspend a judgmental mindset, and instead ask, "What can *we* do better?" "How can *we* help?" and "What do implementers need?"

- Schedule the implementation learning walks to occur regularly, at least quarterly. Monthly is good in the early stages. Ensure these are added to all calendars for full attendance, and provide staff substitutes as needed.

- Provide supplies such as clipboards, multiple copies of the form for each participant, and space to meet and debrief before and after conducting the walk.

- Select a protocol to use to examine the data, and have the implementation plan available for all participants.

Harnessing Data for Strategic Action

Once the teams have collected implementation fidelity data, it is time to use the data to create actions. Design a process to review the learning walk data collected. Use what you have learned in previous chapters about learning designs, protocol selection, team learning, and functioning.

After the implementation learning walks, teams *collectively*:

- Review norms and any tools selected to facilitate the meeting

- Utilize a selected protocol to examine the collected data

> Provide time for each participant to individually review their data, a partner's data, or the entire team's data. (Teams do occasionally copy data collected so that all team members can see all the forms, but this generally proves cumbersome in relatively large systems.)

> Select a protocol that supports reviewing overall findings and does dive into individual issues.

> Select a protocol that supports and objectively discusses the findings.

- Go back to the implementation plan and record the next steps

- Complete an action plan (This occurs after collectively reviewing data with a protocol.)

Figure 6.7 (page 182) contains a sample action plan a team created after completing its learning walks. Note this sample comes from the same district that designed the sample monitoring tool in figure 6.6 (page 176).

In summary, at this point, teams have communicated why data are being collected, coperformed learning walks, completed the data review process with agreed-on protocols and processes to subjectively unpack the data, and created an action plan. Next, they should include the action plan in their IMPACT implementation planning template. It's essential that they periodically return to the planning template and ensure it's up to date with the tasks they have completed. This will allow teams to keep a clear record of their work and enable them to use it for future planning. They should ensure the appropriate team members have shared access to this accurate record of adaptation, goal attainment, or revision. Full and effective implementation takes two to four years, so accurate recordkeeping is critical. Team membership may shift, and leaders may change, but with this shared meaningful leadership model and a strongly articulated and widely understood plan, the work lives on.

Conclusion

During the *Implement* stage, teams focus on growing the implementers; building supportive structures; learning together to build knowledge, skills, and attitudes; gathering implementation data; and harnessing the data to take action. To do these things, implementation teams meet regularly and use agendas, tools, and protocols to create and support the scaling of the implementation plan. They use their IMPACT implementation planning template and selected behavior change model to guide their work. Also during this stage, teams perform learning walks to gather implementation data. They actively engage in iterative improvement cycles to

Implementation Plan Goal	Celebrations	Evidence of Progress	Barriers	Opportunities for Growth	Action Plan
By June of next year, 80 percent of Klamath Falls City Schools' K–5 teachers will implement small-group differentiated instruction within the classroom to improve student success as measured by classroom observations and walkthroughs.	Modeling lessons and recording lessons	Trainings scheduled (We have slide presentations to show this.)	Time to plan	Involvement of teachers as leaders	Maintain progress toward agreed-on goals and actions to achieve those goals to include rehearsals, modeling, and practice.
	Teaching EBP	Modeled lesson scheduled and taught by coaches in other teachers' classrooms	Tier 1 and Tier 2 confusion about where those groups take place	Climate and culture	Rationale: Impact culture and climate around adopting MTSS and the PLC process.
	Planning differentiation	MTSS implementation school site meetings scheduled for the whole year	Time to find and prep materials	Teachers modeling Tier 2 phonics instruction	Improve teacher skills and strategies with EBP, which will generalize into other areas of instructional provision.
	Teaching differentiation based on data	Assigned team roles	Time allotted in the classroom for differentiated instruction over 90 minutes	Learning walks for teachers in successful classrooms implementing strategies	
	Staff asking targeted questions about Tier 2 strategies	Small-group lesson plans	Classroom management	Classroom management	
	Curiosity from teachers	Diagnostic data for all students to assist in differentiation for all grade levels	Not knowing what students should do during independent work that is meaningful	English language arts adoption	

Figure 6.7: Sample implementation action plan for use after learning walks.

Implementation Plan Goal	Celebrations	Evidence of Progress	Barriers	Opportunities for Growth	Action Plan
	Several teachers embracing the Tier 2 instructional strategies and executing them with fidelity	Established norms for meetings	Resisters who don't want to change	Scheduling (120 minutes for English language arts possibly?)	
	Tier 2 instructional guide	Tier 2 instructional phonics guide	Current reading adoption that is terrible and not readily accessible to 70 percent of students	Attendance	
	Teachers using materials presented during presentations	Observations and walkthroughs	Monitoring tool	Walkthroughs for data collection	
	All schools using the same information and presentations	Videos of instruction and modeling	Substitutes	Effective Tier 1	
	Teachers having fifteen exposures to new info	Information regarding MTSS and PLC work with stakeholders (board meeting, building rollout)	Resistance to the monitoring tool	More community involvement	

Source: Klamath Falls City School District, Oregon. Used with permission.

*Visit **go.SolutionTree.com/schoolimprovement** for a free reproducible version of this figure.*

monitor the implementation plan's progress and determine implementers' learning needs and goal attainment. The implementation teams and implementers collectively practice, reflect, and work toward mastery of the new skills necessary to implement the new work.

Remember to use the *Implement* stage's key activities and objectives on page 154 to guide your work during this stage. Review them with implementation teams, key stakeholders, and staff impacted by the change. Be transparent, inclusive, and planful by communicating frequently and clearly. Select a text-rendering protocol such as the four As to collectively build shared understanding of the stage.

Implement Stage IMPACT Implementation Planning Template

Complete the appropriate sections of the template with your team, recording your decisions in the space provided.

Inclusion | Meaningful Leadership | Professional Learning | Assess and Adjust | Collective Efficacy | Team

Implementation Planning Template

Implementation Team Members: ☐ System ☐ School

Goal: Where are we going? (State the goal in SMART format.)

Stage	Problem	Evidence-Based Solutions	Implementation Strategies	Monitoring Strategies
Decide	Name the problem and why this problem needs to be solved.	Name the proposed solution (EBP).		
Plan and Prepare		Identify the active ingredients of the EBP. What is the EBP and its associated active ingredients?	How will we skill up to scale up? List implementation strategies here.	Are we doing what we said we would do? Identify the monitoring tools.
Implement		What intelligent adaptations to the EBP are needed based on culture, climate, and context?	Adapt existing implementation strategies or add new ones here.	Adapt existing monitoring tools or add new ones here.
Spread and Sustain		Identify resources needed to sustain implementation of the innovation.	Identify implementation strategies to support, spread, and sustain effective implementation.	Identify ongoing monitoring tools to inform implementation integrity.

Source: © 2022 by Jenice Pizzuto and Steven Carney.

Implement With IMPACT © 2024 Solution Tree Press • SolutionTree.com
Visit **go.SolutionTree.com/schoolimprovement** to download this free reproducible.

The *Implement* Stage Learning Journey Map

Use the following two questions to prompt active discussion and thoughtful responses, helping your team assess current practices and plan for future development. This is an opportunity for collective reflection and strategic action.

Together, review the concepts and practices from chapter 6 that your organization has already implemented. Discuss the effectiveness of your leadership and the progress of your implementation efforts. Use the questions to guide a rich conversation, and document your team's insights, commitments, and objectives in the learning journey map.

1. What concepts and practices from chapter 6 does our district or school currently have in place (with varying degrees of implementation)?

2. What observations and insights are we making about our leadership, leadership team, or organizational implementation efforts?

Team Takeaways	Team Commitment	Team Practice	Team Reflection	Team Goals
New learning, insights, and notices	Concepts, ideas, and practices we *commit to developing*	Strategies, processes, and tools we plan to *learn and practice*	Strategies, processes, tools, concepts, ideas, and so on we want to *go deeper into and share early successes on*	Strategies, processes, tools, concepts, ideas, and so on we want to *fully operationalize* through a commitment of time, resources, and policy

chapter 7

THE *SPREAD AND SUSTAIN* STAGE

However beautiful the strategy, you should occasionally look at the results.

—Winston Churchill

Understanding the natural progression from the *Implement* stage to the *Spread and Sustain* stage represents a critical shift from active deployment to long-term integration. It's a transformative phase where the focus moves from the *how-to* of implementation to the *how-to-keep* of sustainment. This stage is the bridge between the initial enthusiasm for change and the enduring adoption that characterizes truly successful implementation of initiatives.

After the groundwork laid in the *Implement* stage, the *Spread and Sustain* stage is where the fruits of labor begin to show. It's where educators' and administrators' collective efforts are measured not just by the implementation of strategies but by their lasting impact. This stage involves embedding new practices into the fabric of the school's culture so that they remain effective long after the initial push for change has passed.

This chapter explores how to maintain the momentum generated in the *Implement* stage and expand the reach of successful practices. We'll discuss strategies for reinforcing the changes made and ensuring they become permanent fixtures in every student's educational experience. The true victory lies not in the planning, nor the initial triumph, but in the enduring legacy of our strategies. Together, let's embark on a journey to ensure that the strategies we spread are not only adopted but also sustained and celebrated.

In this chapter, we examine key activities and objectives of the *Spread and Sustain* stage in order to navigate from implementation to sustainment. To maximize spread and sustainment, teams must cultivate partnerships that provide access to a wide range of resources, expertise, and perspectives. Finally, it's time to celebrate and reward implementation success!

Sustaining Success

The following story of Maplewood High School, guided by the visionary Principal Chen, serves as an archetype of the educational quest for effective implementation and socially significant results. Although the names and setting in this narrative are fictional, the challenges and triumphs echo the shared experiences and genuine journeys of schools that have championed transformative change.

At Maplewood High School (a fictitious school), Principal Chen (a fictitious principal) and several teachers and administrators were excited to implement competency-based learning (CBL), an evidence-based approach to learning that focuses on student mastery of skills and knowledge. As part of the *Plan and Prepare* stage, they established a CBL implementation team, which was responsible for overseeing implementation across the school and ensuring ongoing support for teachers. The team also developed a comprehensive implementation plan that included strategies for addressing potential challenges and ensuring the innovation's success.

As implementation began, the CBL implementation team encountered a lack of teacher buy-in and a need for ongoing support and training. To address these challenges, they focused on providing ongoing professional development opportunities for teachers, such as workshops on CBL pedagogy and curriculum development. They also offered coaching and mentoring to support the teachers' implementation of CBL, pairing new CBL teachers with experienced ones who could guide them. In addition, the team developed a library of resources and support materials to aid these efforts, including a CBL curriculum guide and a repository of CBL projects and assessments.

As implementation progressed, the team remained committed to monitoring implementation fidelity and student outcomes, using data to inform decision making and adjusting implementation as needed. They monitored fidelity by conducting learning walks that provided the system data, feedback, and support to improve their implementation. They also collected data on student outcomes, such as student mastery of learning objectives and overall student engagement, to inform ongoing improvements to the implementation.

As Maplewood High School reached a high degree of implementation fidelity and saw consistent improvements in student outcomes, the team shifted their focus to sustainability planning and infrastructure. They developed a comprehensive sustainability plan called "Maplewood CBL Strong," which included strategies for continuing to provide training and support for teachers, such as ongoing professional development opportunities and the establishment of a CBL mentorship program. The school also built partnerships and collaborations to promote the spread and sustainability of CBL; this included partnering with local universities to provide resources and support for CBL implementation.

To establish a strong foundation of planning and infrastructure, the team members further refined the CBL implementation team structure to support ongoing implementation and sustainability efforts. They established decision-making, communication, and resource allocation systems, such as regular CBL team meetings and a CBL resource center. Additionally, the team secured funding and other resources to support ongoing implementation and sustainability efforts, pursuing grant opportunities and engaging with community stakeholders to build support for CBL implementation.

To ensure the long-term success of the evidence-based innovation, the team conducted ongoing evaluations of sustainability efforts to make adjustments and improvements as needed. For example, they solicited teacher feedback on the effectiveness of professional learning offerings and adjusted the CBL curriculum guide to reflect evidence-informed practices. They also continued to monitor implementation fidelity and student outcomes to ensure that the innovation remained a priority for the school system.

Through their efforts, Principal Chen and the CBL implementation team successfully implemented and sustained CBL, improving student learning and engagement and promoting positive outcomes for all stakeholders. By developing and executing a comprehensive implementation and sustainability plan that incorporated evidence-informed practices and strategies from implementation science, the team overcame challenges and ensured the evidence-based innovation's long-term success.

Looking back, the team members realized that the truth they stumbled over was the importance of building a strong implementation team and using implementation science strategies to ensure the success of evidence-based innovations. They achieved deliberately developmental implementation, incorporating IMPACT's human- and learning-centered design components to support ongoing adult learning and improvement. Maplewood's sustainability plan built on this foundation, establishing a comprehensive system of ongoing support, evaluation, and adjustment to ensure long-term success. As they shared their story with others, the principal and the implementation team emphasized the importance of being deliberate, reflective, and committed to ongoing improvement in implementing evidence-based innovations in education.

Starting at the Beginning

Let's go back to the beginning. Why focus on implementing evidence-based innovations in education? The answer is simple: educators want to get results and positively impact students, staff, and communities. Every leader wants to know how they can efficiently and effectively achieve success. Experience has taught us that planning for sustainability from the very beginning is key. Schools cannot just launch a new innovation and hope for the best—they must continuously nurture the implementation effort and solve problems along the way.

In fact, the keys to successful sustainability lie in the early planning of the innovation. As Aaron Lyon (2007) writes, "In the education system, where resources and time are limited, strategic implementation can often be the difference between programs that fail and programs that create sustainable change" (p. 6). That's why Lyon advocates for focusing on implementation science and frameworks to implement evidence-based practices sustainably.

The education sector is facing an emergency. Only one in three efforts to install new programs succeeds, and that's just not good enough (Damschroder et al., 2009). We need to pay attention to this emergency, as school systems' efforts to ensure evidence-based practices get the intended results have profound implications for the students, staff, and communities they serve. When reform efforts fail, a lot is at stake—lost revenue, wasted time, and erosion of trust from all constituents. That's why it's crucial to shine a light on building implementation literacy in education and prioritize sustainability from the very beginning. The Education Endowment Foundation in the United Kingdom emphasizes this point:

> Once a new programme or practice is integrated into the normal routines of a school, there is a risk of assuming that the implementation process requires no further leadership support; however, to ensure that the changes brought to a school can be sustained, school leaders should continuously acknowledge, support, and reward its use. (Sharples, Albers, et al., 2019, p. 39)

During the *Decide* and *Plan and Prepare* stages, teams lay the groundwork for sustaining a new innovation as they select evidence-based practices, form implementation groups across various levels, and meticulously plan the implementation process. Achieving sustainability in evidence-based innovations is more than just the next step after the *Implement* stage. In 2019, researchers Bjarne Strøm, Janne K. Vekenshtein, Ingvild S. Paulsen, and Anne M. S. Gjerdalen conducted a comprehensive review and analysis that determined achieving sustainability for an innovation requires a strategic focus on important goals, such as effective leadership, comprehensive training and professional development for educators, the establishment of a shared language, ongoing planning, regular communication, continuous evaluation and assessment, enduring stakeholder engagement, and consideration of environmental and contextual factors. In other words, teams must intentionally ensure ongoing communication, continued fidelity, and sustained engagement from the beginning of the implementation process.

Table 7.1 (page 192) introduces the *Spread and Sustain* stage's key activities and objectives through the IMPACT lens. You and your team will find this tool valuable to prepare for the stage. It describes what outcomes result from the major activities that take place. Use this overview to help key stakeholders or staff understand the purpose of the stage and build deliberately developmental implementation. Although this table covers the key activities to include in an IMPACT implementation plan, the table is not comprehensive. There are other activities involved in this stage, as described throughout the chapter. Review the activities in the table and check your plan to ensure you have built-in protocols, time, and resources to meet each objective.

Consider the following rationale for including IMPACT in your *Spread and Sustain* stage.

- Inclusion ensures that stakeholders are actively involved in the innovation process and have a voice in shaping its direction. This helps build trust and engagement among stakeholders, which are essential for sustaining any innovation over the long term.

- Meaningful leadership is critical for sustainability because it ensures leaders have the skills and knowledge necessary to support ongoing innovation efforts. By maintaining infrastructures and sustaining engagement with stakeholders, leaders can ensure that the innovation aligns with the organization's goals and that all stakeholders remain committed to its success.

- Professional learning is essential for sustainability because it enables stakeholders to continuously learn and adapt to changing circumstances.

Table 7.1: *Spread and Sustain* Stage Key Activities and Objectives

IMPACT	Key Activities	Key Objectives
Inclusion	Include stakeholders in feedback loops, focus on purposeful practice, and ensure ongoing communication and collaboration among stakeholders.	Increase stakeholder ownership and commitment; improve communication and collaboration between stakeholders; improve innovation outcomes through stakeholder feedback and engagement.
Meaningful Leadership	Maintain infrastructures that provide time and processes designed to support practice, reflection, meaning making, and understanding of any adaptations.	Sustain stakeholder engagement and commitment; improve understanding and reflection among stakeholders; improve innovation outcomes through effective leadership and support.
Professional Learning	Continue ongoing collaborative professional learning and data-informed learning designs; develop professional learning for adaptations and new implementers.	Have continuous professional learning for stakeholders; improve outcomes for students; sustain stakeholder engagement and commitment through ongoing learning and growth opportunities.
Assess and Adjust	Collect and use data to support continued fidelity monitoring and improvement of the innovation's outcomes.	Improve innovation fidelity over time; make evidence-based decisions; improve innovation outcomes through ongoing monitoring and assessment.
Collective Efficacy	Celebrate mastery moments and met milestones, and recognize stakeholders' contributions to the innovation's success.	Sustain engagement and commitment over the long term; improve stakeholder motivation and commitment; increase innovation sustainability through sustained stakeholder engagement; increase stakeholder ownership and shared responsibility for the innovation's success.
Team	Use improvement cycles, develop and test adaptations and enhancements, and sustain stakeholder engagement and ongoing communication.	Ensure effective teamwork and collaboration among stakeholders; improve innovation outcomes through effective improvement cycles and adaptations; sustain stakeholder engagement and commitment through ongoing communication and collaboration.

Visit **go.SolutionTree.com/schoolimprovement** *for a free reproducible version of this table.*

Ongoing professional learning ensures that stakeholders have the skills and knowledge necessary to make the most of the innovation and adapt it to meet evolving needs.

- Assess and adjust is important for sustainability because it enables stakeholders to monitor progress, identify areas for improvement, and make necessary adjustments to ensure ongoing success. By collecting and using data to inform decision making, stakeholders can ensure that the innovation is meeting its intended objectives and making a positive impact.

- Collective efficacy is critical for sustainability because it celebrates the innovation's successes and recognizes all stakeholders' contributions. By celebrating mastery moments and met milestones, stakeholders are more likely to remain engaged and committed to the innovation over the long term.

- An effective implementation team is essential for sustainability because it enables stakeholders to effectively work together to achieve the innovation's intended outcomes. By using improvement cycles, developing and testing adaptations and enhancements, and sustaining engagement and ongoing communication, the implementation team can ensure that the innovation remains relevant and effective over time.

Navigating the Implementation to Sustainment

Knowing when to shift focus from the *Implement* stage to the *Spread and Sustain* stage is crucial for ensuring the success of new programs or initiatives. How will teams know when they've entered the *Spread and Sustain* stage of implementing a new practice? Figure 7.1 (page 194) provides examples of indicators that can help you determine when it's time to turn your attention to sustaining a program.

As you review the indicators in figure 7.1, use the Evidence column to document specific instances, observations, or data points that substantiate the presence of each indicator within your organization. This column is not merely for checking off indicators that are met; rather, it is a space to take detailed notes that illustrate how the indicators manifest in the day-to-day operations of your school or district. Consider the following forms of evidence you might look for and document.

- **Qualitative evidence:** Note any anecdotes, quotes, or narratives that capture the spirit and reality of the indicator. For example, if the innovation is "business as usual," describe a scenario where this was evident without prompting or special attention.

- **Quantitative evidence:** Include relevant metrics or statistics that support the indicator's status. If you have a high level of implementation integrity, provide the percentage of implementers using the innovation effectively, or reference specific data that reflect this.

Indicator	Description	Evidence
The innovation is business as usual.	The evidence-based innovation is seen no longer as new or extra but as standard practice.	
Evidence-based practices are integrated into the culture.	The evidence-based practices are embedded into the organization's culture, and the majority of the staff are invested in continuing the practices and maintaining their integrity.	
There is a high level of implementation integrity.	The implementation is of high integrity, with at least 50 percent (and a target of 80 percent) of implementers using the innovation well and right.	
Implementation data are regularly collected.	Implementation data are routinely collected and show high integrity to the innovation.	
Successful outcome data are gathered and shared.	Successful outcomes are consistently achieved and shared throughout the organization.	
The organizational system supports and sustains effective implementation practices.	The organization has created a system that supports and sustains effective implementation practices; this includes coaching, professional learning, and training supports.	
Monitoring and support are ongoing.	The organization regularly monitors and supports the ongoing use of the innovation; this includes being aware of changes in the implementation context and having contingency plans in case of interruptions.	
Stakeholders, champions, and leaders are involved.	Stakeholders, champions, and leaders continue to participate in the process and promote the effective use of the evidence-based innovation.	

Figure 7.1: Indicators for shifting your focus to sustainment.

Visit go.SolutionTree.com/schoolimprovement for a free reproducible version of this figure.

- **Documentary evidence:** Reference any documents, meeting minutes, or official records that reflect the practice's integration into the organizational culture or the regular collection of implementation data.

- **Visual evidence:** If applicable, you can also include or reference photographs, screenshots, or other visual aids that capture evidence of the indicators.

By filling out the Evidence column with this level of detail, you create a rich, multidimensional picture of how the innovation is functioning within your organization. This serves not only as a record of progress but also as a resource for identifying areas of strength and opportunities for further development.

We implement the threshold of "50 percent of implementers regularly employ the new practice" to assist schools and districts in assessing whether their programs have attained a level of stability indicative of readiness for sustainment (Fixsen et al., 2019). This information can help the schools and districts make informed decisions about which programs to focus on sustaining and how to allocate resources to support the programs' long-term success.

In other words, you have reached the *Spread and Sustain* stage when all the changes associated with your innovation—including changes in instruction, assessment, and program support—are well underway and expectations are clearly documented. Additionally, at least 50 percent of the staff using the innovation should be doing so with high integrity.

Consider the example of an elementary school implementing a new literacy program. To progress to the *Spread and Sustain* stage, at least half of the primary teachers should be using the new program and implementing it as intended. This means they fully integrate the program's skills, strategies, and materials into their daily routines. Furthermore, expectations for the program's use are explicitly communicated to and understood by all staff to ensure widespread adoption and fidelity to the program's core components.

In the journey of implementing evidence-based innovations, reaching the 50 percent mark of implementers regularly implementing the new practice with integrity marks a significant turning point. This milestone indicates that the innovation is no longer in its nascent stages but is becoming a standard part of practice. However, it's not the end goal. To move beyond this initial acceptance and integration to a more robust and widespread adoption, it's important to continue supporting implementers and monitoring implementation fidelity over time.

To truly embed an innovation in the fabric of an educational entity, a higher threshold of 80 percent is often set. This ambitious yet attainable goal ensures that the vast majority of staff are not just using the innovation but doing so effectively and consistently. Achieving 80 percent implementation with fidelity signifies a deeper level of institutionalization where the innovation is part of the regular functioning of the entity and is delivering on its promise of improved outcomes on a larger scale.

Reaching this 80 percent marker is indicative of a mature stage of implementation where the innovation has been thoroughly tested, refined, and proven to work within the specific context of the school or district. It also suggests that the necessary supports, such as professional development, coaching, and resources, are in place to sustain the innovation over time. At this level, the innovation is likely to have a significant and lasting impact on the educational process and student achievement, reflecting a true transformation in practice.

To progress from the 50 percent point to the 80 percent point requires ongoing professional development and support for stakeholders, strategies for monitoring and evaluation, and a plan for ongoing communication and collaboration among stakeholders. Additionally, sustainability requires a commitment to continuous improvement. The team should regularly review the implementation and sustainability plans, updating them to reflect organizational changes, new research on innovation, and stakeholder feedback. This may include incorporating new strategies and best practices, adjusting training and support materials, and developing new partnerships and collaborations.

Throughout the *Spread and Sustain* stage, keep the IMPACT model in mind as you make decisions and plan professional learning events. Figure 7.2 lists examples of decisions to be made at this stage and includes space your team can use to take notes. It's important to note that this is *not* a checklist to assign to a team member but a series of discussions the implementation team will collectively engage in and make decisions about. If you'd like to note when items have been completed, you may list the date in the space indicated for each decision.

Spread and Sustain Stage Decisions		
Decisions	**Notes**	**Date Completed**
Resource allocation: How can we allocate resources to sustain implementation of the innovation? This may include decisions about funding, staffing, and other resources needed to support ongoing implementation.		
Monitoring and assessment: How can we monitor and assess the ongoing implementation of the innovation to ensure that it continues to be implemented with fidelity and achieves the desired outcomes?		
Professional learning: What ongoing professional learning is needed to support teachers and other stakeholders in implementing the innovation with fidelity?		
Partnerships and collaborations: How can we build and sustain partnerships and collaborations with other stakeholders to promote the spread and sustainability of the innovation?		

Figure 7.2: *Spread and Sustain* stage decisions.

*Visit **go.SolutionTree.com/schoolimprovement** for a free reproducible version of this figure.*

Collect Tools for Sustaining Educational Innovations

To ensure the sustainability of evidence-based innovations in education, it is critical to develop and maintain tools and protocols that support ongoing success. Implementation teams and leadership should collaboratively work to design processes, protocols, and routines that they can institutionalize throughout the organization. These processes may include ongoing training, coaching, leadership, and data monitoring, which should be continuously maintained and built on over time.

To facilitate onboarding for new staff members, you must document processes that support the acquisition of knowledge, skills, and behaviors necessary to successfully use the innovation. These processes may include the following.

- Develop new job descriptions to ensure that new staff members have a clear understanding of their roles and responsibilities in implementing the innovation.

- Create learning protocols and resources to support new staff members in building the knowledge, skills, and behaviors necessary to successfully use the innovation.

- Develop standards of practice for the innovation to ensure that all staff members have a common understanding of best practices and expectations for implementation.

- Evaluate implementation team meeting structures, resources, tools, and expectations to ensure that new staff members are seamlessly integrated into the implementation team.

- Create innovation-specific documents and agreements to ensure that all staff members clearly understand how they should use the innovation and what outcomes they should expect.

- Develop professional learning plans for onboarding and maintaining expertise in the innovation to ensure that new staff members have access to ongoing training and support.

By building a robust repository of resources and tools that are easily accessible to appropriate staff members, leadership teams can ensure that they allocate all relevant training and resources to sustain the innovation. Developing a plan and process to ensure ongoing access to these resources and tools is essential for the innovation's continued success.

In addition, developing and maintaining these tools and protocols can support the scaling and spread of evidence-based innovations to other schools and districts. By sharing evidence-informed practices and supporting the development of a community of practice, schools and districts can collaborate and build on the successes of others to improve student outcomes across a broad range of settings.

Allocate Resources for Lasting Innovation

Resource allocation is a critical component of sustainability planning for evidence-based innovations in education. Schools must carefully plan for the resources necessary to implement and sustain an evidence-based innovation over time, whether they be funding, staffing, technology, or physical resources. Failure to do so can lead to inconsistent implementation, limited professional development and support opportunities, and a lack of sustainability in innovation.

In schools that do not plan for resource allocation, innovation implementation tends to be inconsistent and disorganized; innovations may struggle to gain a foothold or last over time, leading to confusion in the classroom and missed opportunities for students. In contrast, schools that plan for resource allocation tend to have more effective and consistent implementation of educational innovations. By dedicating sufficient resources to their innovations, schools can provide the necessary support and training to teachers, leading to better implementation and student learning outcomes.

Figure 7.3 (page 200) provides a chart teams can use to identify available resources for implementing and sustaining an evidence-based innovation, organized by category. By following these strategies and recording the identified resources in the blank cells, schools and districts can effectively allocate resources to support the implementation and sustainability of evidence-based educational innovations.

Figure 7.3 can serve as a recording sheet for schools and districts to keep track of the resources identified for each category.

Schools that plan for resource allocation can scale the innovation, therefore reaching many students and promoting equity and access. In contrast, schools that don't plan for resource allocation may have limited scope and impact, missing out on the potential to benefit more students.

Use Strategies and Recommendations for Scaling

As schools and districts move from the initial implementation of an innovation to broader application, the process of scaling becomes critical. Scaling is not merely an expansion in numbers—it's a strategic process that ensures the integrity of the innovation is maintained while reaching a larger audience. This transition requires thoughtful planning, deep understanding of the contextual variables, and a commitment to maintain the quality of the program. Consider the following strategies and recommendations for scaling evidence-based innovations to ensure they deliver their intended benefits across a wider educational landscape.

- **Embrace a phased approach:** Scaling should be not a leap but a series of calculated steps. Begin with a pilot phase, assess its outcomes, and refine the approach. Once the pilot demonstrates success, expand incrementally to additional classrooms, grades, or schools. This phased approach allows for learning and adaptation, ensuring that the innovation is robust and adaptable to different contexts.

- **Strengthen the infrastructure:** As you scale, it's essential to reinforce the infrastructure that supports the innovation. This includes enhancing professional development, expanding coaching models, and ensuring that administrative systems are equipped to handle the increased scope. For instance, if a new literacy program is scaling up, ensure that there

Resource	Conduct a Resource Inventory	Seek External Funding	Repurpose Existing Resources	Leverage Partnerships	Prioritize Resources	Identify Resources
Staff time	Identify available staff time to support the innovation.	Seek external funding to hire additional staff if needed.	Repurpose staff time from other areas to support the innovation.	Partner with a community organization to provide volunteers to support the innovation.	Prioritize staff time to ensure that it is being used effectively to support the innovation.	
Funding	Identify existing funding sources that can be used to support the innovation.	Seek grants or other external funding to support the innovation.	Repurpose existing funding to support the innovation.	Partner with a business or philanthropic organization to provide funding.	Prioritize funding to ensure that it is being used effectively to support the innovation.	
Technology	Conduct an inventory of existing technology resources that can be used to support the innovation.	Seek funding to purchase additional technology resources if needed.	Repurpose existing technology resources to support the innovation.	Partner with a technology company to provide technology resources.	Prioritize technology resources to ensure that they are being used effectively to support the innovation.	
Physical resources	Identify existing physical resources that can be used to support the innovation.	Seek funding to purchase additional physical resources if needed.	Repurpose existing physical resources to support the innovation.	Partner with a community organization to provide physical resources.	Prioritize physical resources to ensure that they are being used effectively to support the innovation.	

Figure 7.3: Chart for identifying available resources for implementing and sustaining innovations.

Visit go.SolutionTree.com/schoolimprovement for a free reproducible version of this figure.

are enough trained literacy coaches and that the curriculum materials are readily available and adaptable for diverse student populations.

- **Cultivate leadership and build capacity:** Identify and train leaders at all levels who are committed to the innovation. These leaders will act as champions, promoting the innovation and supporting their peers through change. Building capacity also involves ensuring that staff at all levels have the necessary skills and resources to effectively implement the innovation.

- **Engage stakeholders:** Scaling is a collaborative effort. Engage with all stakeholders, including students, families, educators, and community partners, to build a shared vision for the innovation. Their input and buy-in are crucial for the innovation to take root and flourish.

- **Monitor and evaluate outcomes and fidelity:** Use data to drive the scaling process. Regularly collect and analyze data not only on student outcomes but also on implementation fidelity. This will inform continuous improvement and ensure that the innovation is having the desired impact.

- **Adapt and customize the innovation:** Recognize that one size does not fit all. As the innovation reaches new settings, be prepared to adapt it to meet local needs while maintaining fidelity to the core components that make it effective.

- **Ensure sustainability:** Consider the long-term financial and resource implications of scaling. Develop a sustainability plan that includes diverse funding streams, in-kind support, and policy advocacy to embed the innovation within the system.

By following these strategies, educational leaders can scale innovations in a way that is thoughtful, equitable, and sustainable, ultimately leading to significant improvements in educational outcomes.

Monitor and Assess for Long-Term Success

Remember that monitoring and assessing are essential components of effectively implementing your innovation and ensuring its long-term success. This continues to be true at the *Spread and Sustain* stage. Collecting data on the implementation process and the innovation's outcomes makes it possible to identify improvement areas and make necessary adjustments to ensure the innovation is sustainable. Scaling an innovation requires careful planning and monitoring. By tracking progress and outcomes at a larger scale, you can identify potential barriers and make necessary adaptations to overcome them. This helps ensure that the innovation is implemented with the same level of fidelity as the initial implementation, even in a larger context.

Moreover, monitoring and assessing help ensure the innovation remains relevant over time. Collecting data on the ongoing implementation and outcomes makes it possible to identify areas where the innovation might be struggling to maintain its effectiveness or where additional support is needed. By collecting data and making necessary adaptations, you can ensure the innovation's long-term success and its continued impact on the intended beneficiaries.

Foster Ongoing Professional Learning

Once an innovation is fully implemented, professional learning remains critical to its ongoing sustainment (Fullan, 2016). That is because the needs of stakeholders and the context in which the innovation operates constantly evolve, and professional learning provides the opportunity to keep pace with these changes. Professional learning can reinforce and refine the skills and knowledge that implementers gain during the implementation process. This professional learning can include any updates or changes to the innovation or its implementation, evidence-informed practices for sustaining the innovation's success, and ongoing support to ensure that stakeholders remain competent and confident in their use of the innovation.

Professional learning can also support ongoing adaptation of the innovation for changing contexts and stakeholder needs. As stakeholders gain experience with the innovation, they may identify areas where it can be modified to better meet their needs. Professional learning can provide the opportunity to explore and develop these adaptations in a structured way, ensuring that they align with the innovation's original goals and intended outcomes.

In addition, ongoing professional learning can foster a culture of continuous improvement and innovation. When you encourage stakeholders to reflect on their practice and to engage in ongoing learning, the innovation can continue to evolve and improve over time, leading to even more significant impact and success.

During the *Spread and Sustain* stage, implementation teams need to consider the ongoing needs of implementers. As the innovation becomes embedded in the organization or community, the needs and priorities of implementers may change, and new challenges may arise. Teams must ask the right questions and listen carefully to the answers to support ongoing implementation and sustainability efforts. By doing so, implementation teams can gain valuable insights into the evolving needs of implementers and develop strategies and activities to support ongoing learning, improvement, and success.

Table 7.2 serves as a dynamic tool for implementation leaders to gauge the ongoing needs and challenges implementers face. This tool is designed to be interactive, encouraging leaders to engage with implementers through discussions, surveys, or reflective sessions. By involving implementers in answering these questions, leaders can obtain direct insights into the practicalities and impacts of the innovation on the ground. This collaborative approach not only informs the support and resources required but also fosters a sense of ownership among implementers, ensuring that the innovation is sustained through collective efforts and a shared commitment. Leaders should use the responses to these questions to tailor support, provide necessary resources, and adapt strategies to meet the evolving needs of implementers.

Table 7.2: Ten Questions for Understanding Needs During the Sustainability Stage

1. What impact has the innovation had on implementers so far?
2. What are the strengths and weaknesses of the innovation as it has been implemented thus far?
3. What challenges have implementers faced in implementing and sustaining the innovation, and how have they overcome these challenges?
4. What changes have occurred in the needs and priorities of implementers since implementation of the innovation began?
5. What ongoing support do implementers need to continue implementing and sustaining the innovation?
6. What new skills or knowledge do implementers need to continue implementing and sustaining the innovation?
7. What additional infrastructure or resources are needed to support the ongoing implementation and sustainability of the innovation?
8. How can implementers continue to collaborate and share their experiences to support ongoing learning and improvement?
9. What barriers or challenges might arise in the future, and how can they be anticipated and addressed in advance?
10. How can implementers be engaged and empowered to take ownership of the ongoing implementation and sustainability efforts?

*Visit **go.SolutionTree.com/schoolimprovement** for a free reproducible version of this table.*

Cultivating Partnerships for Spread and Sustainment

Cultivating partnerships and collaborations serves as a superpower to maximize the *Spread and Sustain* stage. Partnerships and collaborations help in spreading and sustaining innovative practices and programs, as they provide access to a broader range of resources, expertise, and perspectives. Schools can overcome shifts in staffing and resources by creating and maintaining partnerships and collaborations.

Partnerships between schools and universities or community organizations can be particularly effective in promoting the spread and sustainment of evidence-based practices and programs. For example, a school district and a university may collaborate to implement a literacy program for struggling readers. Through this partnership, the university can provide training and support for teachers to implement evidence-based practices, while the school district can provide resources and infrastructure to support the program's implementation in the classroom. Similarly, a school and a community organization may collaborate to implement a mentoring program for students who have historically been underserved. Through this partnership, the community organization can provide resources and support for volunteer mentors, while the school can provide space and infrastructure to support the program's implementation.

Partnerships with other schools or districts can also effectively promote the scaling and sustainability of evidence-based practices and programs. For example, a school district that has successfully implemented an evidence-based practice or program may collaborate with other districts to share its experiences and provide implementation support. Similarly, individual schools that have successfully implemented an evidence-based practice or program may collaborate with other schools in their district or other districts to share their experiences and provide implementation support.

These partnerships and collaborations are helpful for both spreading and sustaining the innovative practices and programs. By working together, stakeholders can leverage their collective resources and expertise to address challenges and overcome barriers, foster ownership and commitment among stakeholders, and facilitate ongoing learning and improvement. This helps ensure that the innovative practices and programs remain relevant and sustainable over time, resulting in positive outcomes for the individuals or groups served by the innovation.

Effective implementation efforts cannot be attributed to a single person or group. Utilize resources (human, capital, and relational) to branch out to build and sustain partnerships within and outside the organization, establish a supportive system for the initial implementation, and facilitate the spread and sustainability of the implementation.

Celebrating and Rewarding Implementation Success

Celebrating and rewarding implementation successes along the way is a crucial implementation component and should be woven into the *Spread and Sustain* stage.

By recognizing and celebrating small and big wins, schools and districts can establish a positive implementation culture leading to sustained success. This culture of celebration can also help build momentum for continuous improvement and motivate the implementation team to stay focused on the shared goals.

The Glows and Grows protocol, as shown in figure 7.4, offers a structured approach for teams to reflect on successes and areas for growth. This protocol not only celebrates achievements but also fosters a culture of continuous improvement—key for sustaining educational innovations. It's grounded in formative assessment and reflective practice principles, supporting a cycle of ongoing development. Figure 7.4 illustrates how a collaborative team might complete the protocol.

Glows (Areas of Success)	Grows (Areas That Need Improvement)	Next Steps
Increased collaboration and collective responsibility among teachers in improving student learning outcomes	Limited engagement and participation from all teachers	Develop a shared understanding of the purpose and benefits of collaborative teams and the roles and responsibilities of all participants.
Use of data to inform instruction and decision making	Limited understanding of how to use data effectively and efficiently	Provide additional training and resources for using data to inform instruction and decision making.
Increased focus on student learning and achievement	Limited followthrough on action items and next steps from meetings	Develop a system for tracking and following up on action items and next steps from team meetings.
Positive feedback from teachers on the effectiveness of collaborative teams	Limited support and buy-in from school leadership	Develop a plan for presenting the effectiveness of collaborative teams to school leadership and gaining their support.
Improved communication and alignment with school goals and priorities	Limited time and resources for ongoing collaborative team meetings and activities	Develop a plan for prioritizing and scheduling regular collaborative team meetings and activities, and securing additional resources and time as needed.

Figure 7.4: Sample Glows and Grows protocol.

*Visit **go.SolutionTree.com/schoolimprovement** for a free reproducible version of this figure.*

Tools like this protocol can help maintain momentum and build a learning and action focus, leading to targeted action and continuous improvement. By identifying areas of success and areas that need improvement, the implementation team can make necessary adjustments to improve the implementation process and sustain the innovation over time.

Start with and exhaust the Glows column before moving on to the Grows column. Human nature tends to make people using the protocol want to leap into problem and solution identification, so they miss out on the critical opportunities to celebrate successes organically. Pause and push the team to focus on what is going well. You will not regret it!

It is important to continue celebrating and rewarding implementation successes even after achieving high implementation fidelity, as this can contribute to the sustainability of the evidence-based innovation. By maintaining a positive implementation culture, schools and districts can ensure that the innovation remains relevant and effective over time. Moreover, continuing to celebrate implementation successes, even after achieving high implementation fidelity, can inspire others to adopt the practices or programs. Celebrating and rewarding implementation successes is a powerful way to establish a positive implementation culture and build momentum for continuous improvement and innovation.

Conclusion

At this stage of innovation implementation, it's important to keep monitoring and supporting the ongoing use of the innovation. Once you've got about 50 percent of implementers using the innovation well and right, it's time to shift your focus toward ensuring that the enabling factors that got you there remain present. You'll want to keep an eye out for changes in the implementation context and be aware of shifts and context changes as you work toward getting at least 80 percent of the implementers using the innovation well and right.

Don't let up on the coaching, professional learning, or training supports just yet. Be cautious about removing these supports, and have a contingency plan in case of implementation interruptions. And when you do reach the point where the innovation is seen as business as usual rather than new or extra, and you reap the socially significant outcomes for which it was selected, celebrate it! Involve stakeholders, champions, and leaders to continue participating in the process and promote the effective use of evidence-based innovation from this point forward.

At this stage, the implementation team members should have supporters who have expanded vertically and horizontally through the various stages of implementation. This is the tipping point—the innovation becomes how you do the work, and all staff are invested in its continuation and integrity. You'll reach sustainability in evidence-based innovations by utilizing the implementation literacy and deliberately developmental implementation built throughout the organization and creating an organizational system that supports and sustains effective implementation practices. This sustainable effort transforms the organizational culture and readies the organization to implement new innovations using the developed skills and knowledge.

Remember to use the *Spread and Sustain* stage's key activities and objectives on page 192 to guide your work during this stage. Review the key activities and objectives with implementation teams, key stakeholders, and staff impacted by the change.

Spread and Sustain Stage IMPACT Implementation Planning Template

Complete the appropriate sections of the template with your team, recording your decisions in the space provided.

Inclusion | Meaningful Leadership | Professional Learning | Assess and Adjust | Collective Efficacy | Team

Implementation Planning Template

Implementation Team Members: ☐ System   ☐ School

Goal: Where are we going? (State the goal in SMART format.)

Stage	Problem	Evidence-Based Solutions	Implementation Strategies	Monitoring Strategies
Decide	Name the problem and why this problem needs to be solved.	Name the proposed solution (EBP).		
Plan and Prepare		Identify the active ingredients of the EBP. What is the EBP and its associated active ingredients?	How will we skill up to scale up? List implementation strategies here.	Are we doing what we said we would do? Identify the monitoring tools.
Implement		What intelligent adaptations to the EBP are needed based on culture, climate, and context?	Adapt existing implementation strategies or add new ones here.	Adapt existing monitoring tools or add new ones here.
Spread and Sustain		Identify resources needed to sustain implementation of the innovation.	Identify implementation strategies to support, spread, and sustain effective implementation.	Identify ongoing monitoring tools to inform implementation integrity.

Source: © 2022 by Jenice Pizzuto and Steven Carney.

The *Spread and Sustain* Learning Journey Map

Use the following two questions to prompt active discussion and thoughtful responses, helping your team assess current practices and plan for future development. This is an opportunity for collective reflection and strategic action.

Together, review the concepts and practices from chapter 7 that your organization has already implemented. Discuss the effectiveness of your leadership and the progress of your implementation efforts. Use the questions to guide a rich conversation, and document your team's insights, commitments, and objectives in the learning journey map.

1. What concepts and practices from chapter 7 does our district or school currently have in place (with varying degrees of implementation)?

2. What observations and insights are we making about our leadership, leadership team, or organizational implementation efforts?

Team Takeaways *New* learning, insights, and notices	Team Commitment Concepts, ideas, and practices we *commit to developing*	Team Practice Strategies, processes, and tools we plan to *learn and practice*	Team Reflection Strategies, processes, tools, concepts, ideas, and so on we want to *go deeper into and share early successes on*	Team Goals Strategies, processes, tools, concepts, ideas, and so on we want to *fully operationalize* through a commitment of time, resources, and policy

Epilogue

*Without change, there can't be improvement. Without
improvement, equity in education will not be achieved.*

—Stefani Hite and Jenni Donohoo

We are genuinely delighted that you have reached the end of this book! Your persistence is a testament to your dedication to building implementation literacy. We hope as you journeyed through these pages, you encountered numerous "tripping over the truth" moments—those instances when insights suddenly spark a deeper understanding for you or others. Chip Heath and Dan Heath (2017) identify three key elements for tripping over the truth: (1) a clear insight, (2) compressed in time, and (3) discovered by the audience itself. They emphasize that these moments do not occur spontaneously; rather, we must create opportunities for our audience to uncover truths (Heath & Heath, 2017).

Throughout this book, we presented the concepts of utilizing human- and learning-centered design and building deliberately developmental implementation. We hope that these concepts allowed you to trip over the truth that good implementation involves including implementers in the design process; utilizing a team; investing time; requiring support (both human and capital); and developing implementers' knowledge, skills, and attitudes. Ultimately, our goal is for you and your team to build implementation literacy, giving your educational organization the tools and resources needed to halt the frustrating cycle of adopting and abandoning initiatives and bridge the gap between knowing what to do and actually doing it.

This book aims to distill the complexities of implementation, implementation science, and change into manageable chunks, empowering educators to apply research and make a positive, powerful impact on their organizations. By putting these resources and tools into the hands of educators, we want to transform the hope for change into tangible, successful action. As you embark on transforming your organization through effective implementation, remember that this book is only the beginning. The insights and principles you have gleaned from these pages will serve as your compass, guiding you toward a future where your organization thrives and reaps the benefits of successful implementation.

As you stand at the threshold of a new era in your educational organization, take a moment to reflect on the journey that has brought you here. Through each chapter of this book, you have acquired valuable insights, strategies, and tools to navigate the complexities of deliberately developmental implementation. With these newfound skills and knowledge, you are now well equipped to lead your team and create meaningful, sustainable change within your organization.

The journey doesn't end here. This book represents a launchpad from which you and your team will soar to new heights. It is now up to you to take these learnings and put them into action, transforming your organization and positively impacting the lives of your students.

As you close this book, we urge you to take the following steps.

1. Share your learnings with your team, fostering a shared understanding of deliberately developmental implementation and its critical elements.

2. Embrace the power of a learning and improvement mindset, cultivating a culture of collaboration, trust, and open communication within your team.

3. Develop a shared vision and set clear, achievable goals that align with your organization's mission and values.

4. Be resilient in the face of challenges, supporting one another as you navigate the inevitable obstacles that arise during implementation.

5. Continuously learn and adapt, utilizing feedback and data to inform your decisions and drive improvements.

Above all, remember that you are not alone on this journey. You are part of a community of dedicated educators and leaders, each striving to create a better future for your students. As you embark on this exciting new chapter, know that the power to make a difference lies within you and your team—and that together, you can achieve incredible things.

References and Resources

Aarons, G. A., Hurlburt, M., & Horwitz, S. M. (2011). Advancing a conceptual model of evidence-based practice implementation in public service sectors. *Administration and Policy in Mental Health*, *38*(1), 4–23. https://doi.org/10.1007/s10488-010-0327-7

Active Implementation Research Network. (n.d.). *Implementation teams.* Accessed at www .activeimplementation.org/frameworks/implementation-teams on December 14, 2022.

Albers, B., Shlonsky, A., & Mildon, R. (Eds.). (2020). *Implementation science 3.0.* Cham, Switzerland: Springer.

Archer, A. L., & Hughes, C. A. (2011). *Explicit instruction: Effective and efficient teaching.* New York: Guilford Press.

Bandura, A. (1997). *Self-efficacy: The exercise of control.* New York: Freeman.

Barwick, M. A., Peters, J., Boydell, K. M., Jordan, M., & Curry, J. (2021). Implementation science: Maximizing the potential of implementation science within mental health research. *Canadian Journal of Psychiatry*, *66*(2), 97–102.

BrainyQuote. (n.d.). *Vince Lombardi quotes.* Accessed at www.brainyquote.com/quotes /vince_lombardi_386290 on January 2, 2024.

Briselli, J., & Bucher, A. (2021, August 23). COM-B + experience mapping: A design thinking love story [Blog post]. *Bootcamp.* Accessed at https://bootcamp.uxdesign .cc/com-b-experience-mapping-a-design-thinking-love-story-f09e3403495#2559 on February 1, 2023.

Bryk, A. S., Gomez, L. M., Grunow, A., & LeMahieu, P. G. (2015). *Learning to improve: How America's schools can get better at getting better.* Cambridge, MA: Harvard Education Press.

Center for Leadership and Educational Equity. (n.d.a). *Cycle of inquiry.* Accessed at www .schoolreforminitiative.org/download/cycle-of-inquiry on March 3, 2023.

Center for Leadership and Educational Equity. (n.d.b). *Feedback carousel.* Accessed at www .schoolreforminitiative.org/download/the-feedback-carousel on December 5, 2023.

Center for Leadership and Educational Equity. (n.d.c). *What? So what? Now what?* Accessed at www.schoolreforminitiative.org/download/what-so-what-now-what on March 3, 2023.

Centers for Disease Control and Prevention. (2023). *Hand hygiene in healthcare settings.* Accessed at www.cdc.gov/handhygiene/index.html on December 7, 2022.

Chevallier, A. (2016). *Strategic thinking in complex problem solving.* New York: Oxford University Press.

Collins, K. (2019). In J. Sharples, B. Albers, S. Fraser, & S. Kime, *Putting evidence to work: A school's guide to implementation* (p. 2). London: Education Endowment Foundation. Accessed at https://educationendowmentfoundation.org.uk/education -evidence/guidance-reports/implementation on August 11, 2023.

Colorado Department of Education. (n.d.). *Implementation guide: Planning for improvement strategy implementation.* Accessed at www.cde.state.co.us/uip/implementation-guide on February 23, 2022.

Conzemius, A. E., & O'Neill, J. (2014). *The handbook for SMART school teams: Revitalizing best practices for collaboratio*n (2nd ed.). Bloomington, IN: Solution Tree Press.

Damschroder, L. J., Aron, D. C., Keith, R. E., Kirsh, S. R., Alexander, J. A., & Lowery, J. C. (2009). Fostering implementation of health services research findings into practice: A consolidated framework for advancing implementation science. *Implementation Science, 4*(50).

Damschroder, L. J., Lowery, J. C., & Jagger, C. (2020). Implementation of clinical quality improvement for pressure injury prevention in a hospital setting. *JAMA Network Open, 3*(9).

Darling-Hammond, L., Hyler, M. E., & Gardner, M. (2017). *Effective teacher professional development.* Palo Alto, CA: Learning Policy Institute.

Dawn Chorus Group. (n.d.). *Brief readiness thinking tool.* Lancaster, PA: Author. Accessed at https://dawnchorusgroup.com/the-brief-readiness-thinking-tool on December 5, 2023.

The Decision Lab. (n.d.). *The COM-B model for behavior change.* Accessed at https:// thedecisionlab.com/reference-guide/organizational-behavior/the-com-b-model-for -behavior-change on January 30, 2023.

Donohoo, J., Hattie, J. A. C., & Eells, R. (2018). The power of collective efficacy. *Educational Leadership, 75*(6). Accessed at www.ascd.org/el/articles/the-power-of -collective-efficacy on August 11, 2023.

Donohoo, J., & Katz, S. (2020). *Quality implementation: Leveraging collective efficacy to make "what works" actually work.* Thousand Oaks, CA: Corwin.

Doran, G. T. (1981). There's a S.M.A.R.T. way to write management's goals and objectives. *Management Review, 70*(11), 35–36.

Dorn, E., Hancock, B., Sarakatsannis, J., & Viruleg, H. (2020, June). *COVID-19 and student learning in the United States: The hurt could last a lifetime.* Accessed at www.mckinsey.com/industries/education/our-insights/covid-19-and-student-learning-in-the-united-states-the-hurt-could-last-a-lifetime# on December 1, 2023.

DuFour, R., DuFour, R., Eaker, R., Many, T. W., & Mattos, M. (2016). *Learning by doing: A handbook for Professional Learning Communities at Work* (3rd ed.). Bloomington, IN: Solution Tree Press.

Dyssegaard, C. B., Egelund, N., & Sommersel, H. B. (2017). *A systematic review of what enables or hinders the use of research-based knowledge in primary and lower secondary school.* Copenhagen: Danish Clearinghouse for Educational Research, Department of Education, Aarhus University.

Education Development Center. (2015). Implementing evidence-based programs: The importance of identifying and understanding active ingredients. *Journal of Children's Services, 10*(3), 241–254.

Education Endowment Foundation. (2021). *Putting evidence to work: A school's guide to implementation—Implementation theme, active ingredients.* London: Author. Accessed at https://d2tic4wvo1iusb.cloudfront.net/production/eef-guidance-reports/implementation/EEF-Active-Ingredients-Summary.pdf?v=1701785948 on April 1, 2023.

Fisher, D., Frey, N., & Hattie, J. (2016). *Visible learning for literacy, grades K–12: Implementing the practices that work best to accelerate student learning.* Thousand Oaks, CA: Corwin Press.

Fixsen, D. L., Blase, K. A., Duda, M. A., Naoom, S. F., & Van Dyke, M. (2010). Implementation of evidence-based treatments for children and adolescents: Research findings and their implications for the future. In J. R. Weisz & A. E. Kazdin (Eds.), *Evidence-based psychotherapies for children and adolescents* (2nd ed., pp. 435–450). New York: Guilford Press.

Fixsen, D., Blase, K. A., Horner, R., & Sugai, G. (2009, February). *Scaling-up evidence-based practices in education* (Scaling-Up Brief No. 1). Chapel Hill, NC: Frank Porter Graham Child Development Institute, University of North Carolina at Chapel Hill.

Fixsen, D. L., Blase, K. A., & Van Dyke, M. K. (2019). *Implementation practice and science.* Chapel Hill, NC: Active Implementation Research Network.

Fletcher, A. (2002). *Firestarter youth power curriculum: Participant guidebook.* Olympia, WA: Freechild Project.

Fullan, M. (2006). *Turnaround leadership.* San Francisco: Jossey-Bass.

Fullan, M. (2016). *The new meaning of educational change* (5th ed.). New York: Teachers College Press.

Fullan, M., & Gallagher, M. J. (2020). *The devil is in the details: System solutions for equity, excellence, and student well-being.* Thousand Oaks, CA: Corwin.

Garmston, R., & Wellman, B. (n.d.). *The seven norms of collaborative work.* Accessed at http://theadaptiveschool.weebly.com/7-norms-of-collaborative-work.html on January 1, 2023.

Glasgow, R. E., Eckstein, E. T., & ElZarrad, M. K. (2013). Implementation science perspectives and opportunities for HIV/AIDS research integrating science, practice, and policy. *JAIDS: Journal of Acquired Immune Deficiency Syndromes*, *63*, 26–31. https://doi.org/10.1097/qai.0b013e3182920286

Grant, A. (2021). *Think again: The power of knowing what you don't know*. New York: Viking.

Hall, B. (2021). *Powerful guiding coalitions: How to build and sustain the leadership team in your PLC at Work*. Bloomington, IN: Solution Tree Press.

Hansen, M., Levesque, E., Valant, J., & Quintero, D. (2018). *The 2018 Brown Center report on American education: How well are American students learning?* Washington, DC: Brookings Institution.

Heath, C., & Heath, D. (2017). *The power of moments: Why certain experiences have extraordinary impact*. New York: Simon & Schuster.

Heath, D. (2020). *Upstream: The quest to solve problems before they happen*. New York: Avid Reader Press.

Higgins, M. C., Weiner, J., & Young, L. (2012). Implementation teams: A new lever for organizational change. *Journal of Organizational Behavior*, *33*(3), 366–388.

Hite, S. A., & Donohoo, J. (2021). *Leading collective efficacy: Powerful stories of achievement and equity*. Thousand Oaks, CA: Corwin Press.

Hord, S. M. (2009). Professional learning communities: Educators work together toward a shared purpose. *Journal of Staff Development*, *30*(1), 40–43.

IDEO. (2015). *The field guide to human-centered design: Design kit*. San Francisco: Author.

IRIS Center. (2023a). *Evidence-based practices (part 1): Identifying and selecting a practice or program* [Module]. Accessed at https://iris.peabody.vanderbilt.edu/module/ebp_01/#content on September 22, 2023.

IRIS Center. (2023b). *Evidence-based practices (part 2): Implementing a practice or program with fidelity* [Module]. Accessed at https://iris.peabody.vanderbilt.edu/module/ebp_02/#content on February 20, 2023.

Ishikawa, K. (1990). *Introduction to quality control* (3rd ed.). Tokyo: 3A.

Jeary, T. (2011). *Strategic acceleration: Succeed at the speed of life*. New York: Vanguard Press.

Johns Hopkins Medicine. (n.d.). *Hand hygiene*. Accessed at www.hopkinsmedicine.org/patient_safety/infection_prevention/hand_hygiene.html on December 7, 2022.

Jourdain, K., & Nagel, J. (2019). *Building trust and relationship at the speed of change*. Apple Valley, MN: Worldview Intelligence.

Joyce, B., & Showers, B. (2002). *Student achievement through staff development* (3rd ed.). Alexandria, VA: ASCD.

Kegan, R. & Lahey, L. L. (2009). *Immunity to Change: How to Overcome It and Unlock the Potential in Yourself and Your Organization*. Boston: Harvard Business Review Press.

Kegan, R., & Lahey, L. L. (2016). *An everyone culture: Becoming a deliberately developmental organization.* Boston: Harvard Business Review Press.

Khan, S., & Moore, J. E. (2021, June 29). *Core competencies for implementation practice.* Accessed at https://i2insights.org/2021/06/29/implementation-competencies on April 19, 2023.

Knoster, T., Villa, R. A., & Thousand, J. S. (2000). A framework for thinking about systems change. In R. A. Villa & J. S. Thousand (Eds.), *Restructuring for caring and effective education: Piecing the puzzle together* (2nd ed., pp. 93–128). Baltimore: Brookes.

Leeman, J., Rohweder, C., Lee, M., Brenner, A., Dwyer, A., Ko, L. K., et al. (2021). Aligning implementation science with improvement practice: A call to action. *Implementation Science Communications, 2*(99).

Lencioni, P. (2016). *The ideal team player: How to recognize and cultivate the three essential virtues—A leadership fable.* Hoboken, NJ: Jossey-Bass.

Levin, S., & Bradley, K. (2019). *Understanding and addressing principal turnover: A review of the research.* Reston, VA: National Association of Secondary School Principals.

Lipton, L., & Wellman, B. (2016). *Groups at work: Strategies and structures for professional learning.* Cheltenham, Victoria, Australia: Hawker Brownlow.

Lyon, A. R. (2007). *Implementation science and practice in the education sector.* Accessed at https://education.uw.edu/sites/default/files/Implementation%20Science%20Issue%20Brief%20072617.pdf on December 15, 2022.

Lyon, A. R. (2017). Strategic implementation and scaling-up of evidence-based practices in education: A review and synthesis. *Educational Psychology Review, 29*(1), 153–168.

Lyon, A. R., Corbin, C. M., Brown, E. C., Ehrhart, M. G., Locke, J., Davis, C., et al. (2022). Leading the charge in the education sector: Development and validation of the School Implementation Leadership Scale (SILS). *Implementation Science, 17*(48).

Mattos, M., DuFour, R., DuFour, R., Eaker, R., & Many, T. W. (2016). *Concise answers to frequently asked questions about Professional Learning Communities at Work.* Bloomington, IN: Solution Tree Press.

Metz, A., Albers, B., Burke, K., Bartley, L., Louison, L., Ward, C., et al. (2021). Implementation practice in human service systems: Understanding the principles and competencies of professionals who support implementation. *Human Service Organizations: Management, Leadership and Governance, 45*(3), 238–259. https://doi.org/10.1080/23303131.2021.1895401

Meyers, D. C., Durlak, J. A., & Wandersman, A. (2012). The quality implementation framework: A synthesis of critical steps in the implementation process. *American Journal of Community Psychology, 50*(3–4), 462–480. https://doi.org/10.1007/s10464-012-9522-x

Michie, S., van Stralen, M. M., & West, R. (2011). The behaviour change wheel: A new method for characterising and designing behaviour change interventions. *Implementation Science, 6*, Article 42.

Moore, J. E., & Khan, S. (n.d.). *Implementation, spread, and scale course workbook* [Modules 1–4]. Accessed at https://thecenterforimplementation.com/spread-and-scale on September 1, 2021.

National Implementation Research Network. (2015). *Implementation teams overview* [Module 3]. Accessed at https://implementation.fpg.unc.edu/wp-content/uploads /Implementation-Teams-Overview.docx.pdf on December 1, 2023.

National School Reform Faculty. (2015). *Four A's text protocol.* Accessed at www.nsrf harmony.org/wp-content/uploads/2017/10/FourAsTextProtocol-N.pdf on November 8, 2023.

PBLWorks. (2021). *What is PBL?* Accessed at www.pblworks.org/what-is-pbl on August 11, 2023.

Penuel, W. R., & Gallagher, D. J. (2017). *Creating research-practice partnerships in education.* Cambridge, MA: Harvard Education Press.

Pfeffer, J., & Sutton, R. I. (2008). *The knowing-doing gap: How smart companies turn knowledge into action.* Harvard Business School Press.

Powell, B. J., Waltz, T. J., Chinman, M. J., Damschroder, L. J., Smith, J. L., Matthieu, M. M., et al. (2015). A refined compilation of implementation strategies: Results from the Expert Recommendations for Implementing Change (ERIC) project. *Implementation Science, 10*(21).

Proctor, E. K., Powell, B. J., & McMillen, J. C. (2013). Implementation strategies: Recommendations for specifying and reporting. *Implementation Science, 8*(139). https://doi.org/10.1186/1748-5908-8-139

Sharples, J., Albers, B., Fraser, S., & Kime, S. (2019). *Putting evidence to work: A school's guide to implementation.* London: Education Endowment Foundation. Accessed at https://educationendowmentfoundation.org.uk/education-evidence/guidance-reports /implementation on August 11, 2023.

Sharples, J., Webster-Wright, A., Reynolds, D., & Williams, D. (2019). Successful implementation of educational innovation: Lessons for leaders. *Management in Education, 33*(4), 149–156.

Sinek, S. (2009, September). *How great leaders inspire action* [Video file]. TED Conferences. Accessed at www.ted.com/talks/simon_sinek_how_great_leaders _inspire_action?language=en on November 7, 2023.

Solution Tree. (n.d.). *Why PLC at Work?* Accessed at www.solutiontree.com/plc-at-work /why-plc-at-work on September 21, 2023.

Strøm, B., Vekenshtein, J. K., Paulsen, I. S., & Gjerdalen, A. M. S. (2019). Achieving sustainability in education innovations: A comprehensive review and analysis of the literature. *Educational Research Review, 26*, 35–49.

Taylor, M. J., McNicholas, C., Nicolay, C., Darzi, A., Bell, D., & Reed, J. E. (2014). Systematic review of the application of the plan–do–study–act method to improve quality in healthcare. *BMJ Quality and Safety, 23*, 290–298. Accessed at https:// qualitysafety.bmj.com/content/qhc/23/4/290.full.pdf on October 6, 2023.

Todd, A. W., Newton, J. S., Horner, R., Algozzine, B., & Algozzine, K. M. (2015). TIPS 2 Meeting Minutes Form. Eugene, OR: University of Oregon, Educational and Community Supports. Accessed at www.pbis.org/resource/tips-meeting-minutes -template on March 11, 2024.

University of Washington. (n.d.). *What is implementation science?* Accessed at https:// impsciuw.org/implementation-science/learn/implementation-science-overview on October 4, 2022.

Visible Learning. (2018, March 7). *Collective teacher efficacy (CTE) according to John Hattie.* Accessed at https://visible-learning.org/2018/03/collective-teacher-efficacy -hattie on November 6, 2023.

Waltz, T. J., Powell, B. J., Chinman, M. J., Smith, J. L., Matthieu, M. M., Proctor, E. K., et al. (2014). Expert Recommendations for Implementing Change (ERIC): Protocol for a mixed methods study. *Implementation Science, 9*(39).

Weeby, J. (2018). *Creating more effective, efficient, and equitable education policies with human-centered design.* Sudbury, MA: Bellwether Education Partners. Accessed at https://bellwether.org/wp-content/uploads/2018/02/Bellwether_HumanCenterDesign _DYD_Final.pdf on March 8, 2023.

Wellman, B., & Lipton, L. (2017). *Data-driven dialogue: A facilitator's guide to collaborative inquiry.* Charlotte, VT: MiraVia.

Williams, G. R. (2015). *What does it really cost when we don't pay attention to implementation? Invited commentary.* Tampa Bay, FL: Implementation Scientists.

Wiseman, L. (2010). *Multipliers: How the best leaders make everyone smarter.* New York: HarperBusiness.

Index

A

Active Implementation Research
  Network, 66

agendas, 165, 166–167

assessments and adjustments. *See also*
  IMPACT implementation
  framework

  human- and learning-centered design
    elements and, 32–33

  Implement stage and, 154

  monitoring and assessing for long-term
    success, 201–202

  Plan and Prepare stage and, 121

  Spread and Sustain stage and, 192

  supporting people through change
    and, 51

B

Bandura, A., 33

Bellwether Education Partners, 160–161

Blase, K., 22, 104

Bryk, A., 105

building teams and configurations. *See also*
  implementation teams

  about, 68, 70–71

  ideal implementation team
    configurations, 71–73

roles and expectations, 76–79

team availability and commitment, 74

team communication, 79–82

team composition, 73–74

time for implementation teamwork,
  74–76

building-level implementation teams,
  70, 71–72. *See also* implementation
  teams

C

celebrating and rewarding implementation
  success, 204–206

change

  about, 41–42, 45

  conclusion, 56

  embracing the need for, 45–47

  Expert Recommendations for
    Implementing Change, 128–133

  IMPACT implementation strategies for,
    48–50

  naming the problem/need for change
    (the why), 104–109

  navigating the difficulty of, 47–48,
    50–51

  organizational readiness for, 46, 95,
    113, 114–116

reproducibles for, 57–58

supporting people through, 51–55

vignette for, 42–45

collaboration, protocols to acquire skills together and enhance, 162–164

collective efficacy. *See also* IMPACT implementation framework

human- and learning-centered design elements and, 33–34

Implement stage and, 154

Plan and Prepare stage and, 121

Spread and Sustain stage and, 192, 193

supporting people through change and, 51

Collins, K., 21

Colorado Department of Education, 65

COM-B model of behavioral change, 53–55

communication

IMPACT implementation team communication map, 79

sample implementation team communication plan, 81–82

staff communication plans, 131–133

team communication, 79–80

consensus-building tools, 77–78

Creating More Effective, Efficient, and Equitable Education Policies with Human-Centered Design (Bellwether Education Partners), 160–161

cultivating a learning culture and using improvement cycles

about, 160

sample tools for, 165–172

why together is better, 160–165

culture

knowing-doing gap and, 4

protocols to acquire skills together and enhance collaboration and, 162

shifting the culture, 2–3

cycle of inquiry protocol, 170

D

Danish Clearinghouse for Educational Research, 158

Darling-Hammond, L., 31

data/implementation data

about, 172

collecting, 174–180

harnessing for strategic action, 180–181

simplicity and, 172–174

team roles and expectations and, 77, 78

Decide stage. *See also* IMPACT implementation framework

about, 93–94

assessing organizational readiness, 113

conclusion, 116

decisions for, 96–99

developing the goal, 109–110

evidence-based solutions and, 110–113

gearing up for success, 94–102

growing the implementers and, 153

IMPACT implementation planning templates and, 99–100, 102

implementation teams and, 83, 102–104

key activities and objectives, 97

naming the problem/need for change (the why), 104–109

reproducibles for, 117–118

Spread and Sustain stage and, 191

de-implementation, 134–135. *See also* implementation strategies

Devil Is in the Details: System Solutions for Equity, Excellence, and Student Well-Being, The (Fullan and Gallagher), 68

documentary evidence, 195

Donohoo, J., 33, 34, 155

DuFour, R., 63

DuFour, R., 63

E

Eaker, R., 63

Education Endowment Foundation, 190

evidence for sustainment, 193, 194, 195

evidence-based solutions/practices (EBPs)

assessing organizational readiness for change and, 113

cost of non-implementation, 1

deliberately developmental implementation of, 7

identifying, 95, 110–113, 133

identifying the active ingredients and, 124–125

IMPACT implementation planning templates and, 99–100

naming the problem/need for change (the why) and, 104, 105

Expert Recommendations for Implementing Change. *See also* change

about, 128–129

infrastructures and schedules, 131

professional learning plans, 129–131

staff communication plans, 131–133

F

feedback

communication and, 80, 132, 133

feedback carousel, 169–170

implementation data and, 174, 179, 180

implementation literacy and, 25

infrastructures and schedules and, 131

professional learning and, 32, 51

self-report measures and, 141

what? so what? now what? protocol and, 171

fidelity/implementation fidelity. *See also* monitoring the implementation

fidelity assessments, 145–147

fidelity checklists, 137–138

fidelity monitoring, 172, 174–175

harnessing data for strategic action and, 180

implementation teams and, 34

fishbone diagram, 106

Fist to Five consensus-building tool, 77–78

Fixsen, D., 22, 35, 104

formula for success, 19–20

four A's protocol, 168–169

Fullan, M., 68, 84

G

Gallagher, M., 68, 84

Gardner, M., 31

Glows and Grows protocol, 205–206

goals

collective efficacy and, 34, 52

developing the goal, 95, 109–110

IMPACT implementation planning templates and, 99

meaningful leadership and, 30

Golden Circle, 106–107

Gomez, L., 105

Grant, A., 17

growing the implementers, 3–5, 153–155. *See also* implement stage

Grunow, A., 105

guiding coalitions, 63–64. *See also* implementation teams

H

Hall, B., 64

Hattie, J., 33

Heath, D., 22

Higgins, M., 83

Hite, S., 155

horizontal and vertical team configurations, 72–73. *See also* implementation teams

Horne, B., 152

human- and learning-centered design elements

about, 27, 29

assessments and adjustments and, 32–33

collective efficacy and, 33–34

IMPACT implementation framework and, 7–8, 26–27

implementation teams and, 34–35

inclusion and, 29–30

meaningful leadership and, 30–31

professional learning and, 31–32

why together is better, 160–161

Hyler, M., 31

I

immunity to change, 41–42

Immunity to Change: How to Overcome It and Unlock the Potential in Yourself and Your Organization (Kegan and Lahey), 41–42

IMPACT implementation framework. *See also specific elements or stages of the IMPACT implementation framework*

about, 7–8

human- and learning-centered design elements in the, 27, 29–35

IMPACT implementation strategies for change, 48–50

IMPACT implementation team communication map, 79

stages of, 27, 28, 92, 95

supporting people through change and, 51–52

understanding, 25–27

IMPACT implementation planning template

about, 99–100, 102

fidelity assessments and, 147

harnessing data for strategic action and, 181

identifying the active ingredients and, 124

implementation strategies and, 134

problem identification and, 104, 106

reproducibles for, 117, 148, 185, 208

sample of, 101

Implement stage. *See also* IMPACT implementation framework

about, 151–153

building supportive structures, 155, 158–159

conclusion, 181, 184

cultivating a learning culture and using improvement cycles, 160–172

data, gathering implementation data, 172–180

data, harnessing for strategic action, 180–181

decisions for, 156–158

growing the implementers, 153–155

key activities and objectives, 154

reproducibles for, 185–186

sample implementation action plan for use after learning walks, 182–183

sample implementation monitoring tool, 176–180

Spread and Sustain stage and, 187

implementation

celebrating and rewarding implementation success, 204–206

deliberately developmental implementation and, 6–7

discussion tools for strategic implementation, 24

monitoring. *See* monitoring the implementation

navigating to sustainment. *See* navigating the implementation to sustainment

as a science. *See* implementation science

implementation checklists, 127

implementation means change for all. *See* change

implementation science
about, 17, 21
caring about, 21–22
conclusion, 35
defining, 23
getting strategic about implementation, 23–25
human- and learning-centered design and, 27, 29–35
IMPACT implementation framework, understanding, 25–27
reproducibles for, 36–39
vignette for, 17–21

implementation strategies
about, 126–127
de-implementation, 134–135
Expert Recommendations for Implementing Change and, 128–133
IMPACT implementation planning templates and, 100
IMPACT implementation strategies for change, 48–50
process of identifying, 133–134
use of term, 47

implementation teams. *See also* IMPACT implementation framework
about, 59, 63
assembling your implementation team, 102–104
building teams and configurations, 68, 70–80
characteristics and behaviors, identifying, 67–68, 69
conclusion, 84
Decide stage and, 94
defining, 65–67
diversity in, 70–71
empowering, 5–6
guiding coalitions and, 63–64
human- and learning-centered design elements and, 34–35
Implement stage and, 154
implementation data and, 172, 174
implementation team meeting agendas, 165, 166–167
leadership teams and, 50–51
Plan and Prepare stage and, 121
versus PLCs, 85
recognizing uniqueness of, 83–84
reproducibles for, 86–90
sample implementation team communication plan, 81–82
Spread and Sustain stage and, 192, 193
supporting people through change and, 51
vignette for, 59–63

improvement cycles. *See* cultivating a learning culture and using improvement cycles

inclusion. *See also* IMPACT implementation framework
human- and learning-centered design elements and, 29–30
Implement stage and, 154
Plan and Prepare stage and, 121
Spread and Sustain stage and, 191, 192
supporting people through change and, 51

infrastructures and schedules, 131. *See also* Expert Recommendations for Implementing Change

introduction
about implementation literacy, 1–2
calling for deliberately developmental implementation, 6–7
growing the implementers, 3–5
IMPACT implementation framework, using, 7–8
implementation teams, taking a strategic approach to empowering, 5–6
mapping out your learning journey in this book, 8–13
shifting the culture, 2–3

K

Katz, S., 33, 34
Kegan, R., 6, 31, 41–42
knowing-doing gap, 4–5, 21

L

Lahey, L., 6, 31, 41–42
leadership teams, 50–51. *See also* implementation teams; meaningful leadership
learning journey maps
example of, 11–13
reproducibles for, 39, 58, 90, 118, 149, 186, 209
learning walks
characteristics of learning walks chart, 179
fidelity monitoring and, 188
implementation data and, 178–181
sample implementation action plan for use after learning walks, 182–183
sample implementation monitoring tool, 176–178
vignette for, 43

LeMahieu, P., 105
Lippitt-Knoster Model for Managing Complex Change, 52–53
Lombardi, V., 73
Lyon, A., 190

M

Many, T., 63
Mattos, M., 63
meaningful leadership. *See also* IMPACT implementation framework
human- and learning-centered design elements and, 30–31
Implement stage and, 154
leadership teams and, 50–51
Plan and Prepare stage and, 121
Spread and Sustain stage and, 191, 192
supporting people through change and, 51
models of change. *See also* change
COM-B model of behavioral change, 53–55
model for managing complex change, 52–53
monitoring the implementation. *See also* *Plan and Prepare* stage
about, 135–137
collecting implementation data and, 174–176
fidelity assessments and, 145–147
fidelity checklists and, 137–138
IMPACT implementation planning templates and, 100
for long-term success, 201–202
navigating the implementation to sustainment and, 201
observation protocols and, 138, 141
sample implementation monitoring tool, 176–180
self-report measures and, 141–144

N

National Implementation Research
 Network, 65

navigating the implementation to
 sustainment

 about, 193, 195–196

 indicators for shifting your focus to
  sustainment, 194

 monitoring and assessing for long-term
  success, 201–202

 professional learning and, 202–203

 resources for lasting innovation,
  198–199

 scaling, using strategies and
  recommendations for, 199, 201

 tools for sustaining educational
  innovations, 197–198

needs assessments, 133. *See also* assessments
 and adjustments

norms, 76–77

O

observation protocols, 138, 141. *See also*
 monitoring the implementation

organizational readiness for change.
  See also change

 assessing, 95, 113

 embracing the need for change and, 46

 K–12 implementation readiness tuning
  protocol, 114–116

P

partnerships, cultivating for spread and
 sustainment, 203–204

peer coaching, 127

Plan and Prepare stage. *See also* IMPACT
 implementation framework

 about, 119–120

building the foundation, 120–124

conclusion, 147

decisions for, 122–123

growing the implementers and, 153

identifying the active ingredients,
 124–126

implementation teams and, 83

key activities and objectives, 121

monitoring the implementation and,
 135–147

reproducibles for, 148–149

selecting implementation strategies,
 126–135

Spread and Sustain stage and, 191

Powerful Guiding Coalitions (Hall), 64

problem identification, 99, 104–107

professional learning. *See also* IMPACT
 implementation framework

 Expert Recommendations for
  Implementing Change, 129–131

 fostering ongoing professional learning,
  202–203

 growing the implementers and, 3–5

 human- and learning-centered design
  elements and, 31–32

 Implement stage and, 154

 Plan and Prepare stage and, 121

 protocols to acquire skills together and
  enhance collaboration and, 163

 sample professional learning plan,
  130–131

 Spread and Sustain stage and, 191–192

 supporting people through change
  and, 51

professional learning communities (PLCs),
 84, 85

*Putting Evidence to Work: A School's Guide
 to Implementation* (Collins), 21

Q

qualitative evidence, 193

*Quality Implementation: Leveraging
    Collective Efficacy to Make "What
    Works" Actually Work* (Donohoo and
    Katz), 33

quantitative evidence, 193

R

reproducibles for

    assess and align the IMPACT
        framework with your organizational
        strengths, 38

    assess individual characteristics and
        behaviors, 88–89

    Decide stage IMPACT implementation
        planning template, 117

    Decide stage learning journey map, 118

    define implementation science with
        your team, 36–37

    evaluate a change theory, 57

    Implement stage IMPACT
        implementation planning
        template, 185

    Implement stage learning journey
        map, 186

    "Implementation Is a Science" learning
        journey map, 39

    "Implementation Means Change for
        All" learning journey map, 58

    map essential team behaviors and
        characteristics, 87

    Plan and Prepare stage IMPACT
        implementation planning
        template, 148

    Plan and Prepare stage learning journey
        map, 149

    reflecting on building effective
        implementation teams, 86

    Spread and Sustain learning journey
        map, 209

    Spread and Sustain stage IMPACT
        implementation planning
        template, 208

    "You Can't Do This Alone" learning
        journey map, 90

resource allocation for sustainability,
    198–199, 200

S

scaling, strategies and recommendations
    for, 199, 201

self-report measures, 141–144. *See also*
    monitoring the implementation

Sharples, J., 65

skill up to scale up, 126, 161

skills, protocols to acquire skills together
    and enhance collaboration, 162–164

SMART goals, 109–110. *See also* goals

solutionitis, 105

Spread and Sustain stage. *See also* IMPACT
    implementation framework

    about, 187–188

    celebrating and rewarding
        implementation success and,
        204–206

    conclusion, 206–207

    cultivating partnerships for spread and
        sustainment, 203–204

    decisions for, 197

    indicators for shifting your focus to
        sustainment, 194

    key activities and objectives, 192

    navigating the implementation to
        sustainment, 193–203

    reproducibles for, 208–209

    starting at the beginning, 190–193

    sustaining success, 188–190

    ten questions for understanding needs
        during the sustainability stage, 203

strategic implementation, discussion tool for, 24

strategies and recommendations for scaling, 199, 201

supportive structures for the *Implement* stage, 155, 158–159

sustaining success. *See* navigating the implementation to sustainment

SWOT analysis, 106, 107

systems failures, 165

systems-level implementation teams, 71. *See also* implementation teams

T

teams

    building. *See* building teams and configurations

    guiding coalitions, 63–64

    implementation teams. *See* implementation teams

    leadership teams, 50–51

Think Again: The Power of Knowing What You Don't Know (Grant), 17

three Es, 67

time

    infrastructures and schedules, 131

    time for implementation teamwork, 74–76

U

Upstream: The Quest to Solve Problems Before They Happen (Heath), 22

V

Van Dyke, M., 22, 104

visual evidence, 195

W

Weiner, J., 83

"What Does It Really Cost When We Don't Pay Attention to Implementation" (Williams), 1

what? so what? now what? protocol, 171–172

why, the

    gearing up for success, 94

    naming the problem/need for change (the why), 104–109

    process for developing, 109

Williams, G., 1

Wiseman, L., 30

Y

you can't do this alone. *See* implementation teams

Young, L., 83

Leading the Launch
Kim Wallace

How do schools and districts make true progress? One step at a time. *Leading the Launch* offers a ten-stage initiative implementation process proven to help you lead the charge for change with ingenuity, flexibility, responsiveness, and passion.
BKG030

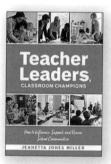

Teacher Leaders, Classroom Champions
Jeanetta Jones Miller

Gain a clear path to activate school improvement from within your classroom. This book shares a vision of teacher leadership not as teachers who lead other teachers but as those who take responsibility in supporting other teachers, students, and families in a variety of ways.
BKG110

Leveraging the Impact of Culture and Climate
Steve Gruenert and Todd Whitaker

Together, culture and climate can make or break school improvement efforts. This results-focused resource will help you learn to leverage the power of both to achieve a collaborative culture that promotes high levels of learning for all.
BKG040

Deep Change Leadership
Douglas Reeves

As 21st century educators grapple with unprecedented challenges, schools and districts require a model of change leadership that responds to shifting environmental realities. In *Deep Change Leadership*, author Douglas Reeves offers up a pragmatic model that embraces engagement, inquiry, and focused action.
BKF935